Pat Metheny

PAT METHENY
Stories beyond Words

BOB GLUCK

The University of Chicago Press
Chicago and London

The University of Chicago Press, Chicago 60637
The University of Chicago Press, Ltd., London
© 2024 by The University of Chicago
All rights reserved. No part of this book may be used or reproduced in any manner whatsoever without written permission, except in the case of brief quotations in critical articles and reviews. For more information, contact the University of Chicago Press, 1427 E. 60th St., Chicago, IL 60637.
Published 2024
Printed in the United States of America

33 32 31 30 29 28 27 26 25 24   1 2 3 4 5

ISBN-13: 978-0-226-82527-4 (cloth)
ISBN-13: 978-0-226-83445-0 (paper)
ISBN-13: 978-0-226-83444-3 (e-book)
DOI: https://doi.org/10.7208/chicago/9780226834443.001.0001

Library of Congress Cataloging-in-Publication Data

Names: Gluck, Bob, author.
Title: Pat Metheny : stories beyond words / Bob Gluck.
Description: Chicago ; London : The University of Chicago Press, 2024. | Includes bibliographical references and index.
Identifiers: LCCN 2023054097 | ISBN 9780226825274 (cloth) | ISBN 9780226834450 (paperback) | ISBN 9780226834443 (ebook)
Subjects: LCSH: Metheny, Pat—Criticism and interpretation. | Metheny, Pat—Analysis, appreciation. | Pat Metheny Group. | Jazz—History and criticism. | Jazz-rock (Music)—History and criticism.
Classification: LCC ML419.M477 G58 2024 | DDC 781.65—dc23/eng/20231128
LC record available at https://lccn.loc.gov/2023054097

♾ This paper meets the requirements of ANSI/NISO Z39.48-1992 (Permanence of Paper).

In memory of the Solomon sisters, my mother Aileen Gluck and aunt Myra Schubin, children of Essie and Al Solomon, grandchildren of Yitzhak Abba and Yenta Lipschitz Kaplan and Myron and Sarah Schuman Solomon. May their memories be a blessing.

I write this dedication a few hours after the death of Wayne Shorter, whose musical ideas have an important place within this manuscript. Just as I have found it difficult to conceive of the musical world I inhabit without the influence of Ornette Coleman and Charlie Haden, I feel the same way after Wayne Shorter's death. His imagination and innovations have immensely enriched our musical culture.

Personally, my own sense of musical identity has been shaped not only by Coleman, Haden, and Shorter but also by a cluster of dear friends who passed away during the period of the COVID-19 pandemic, particularly Richard Teitelbaum, Joel Chadabe, David Darling, and Wallace Roney.

CONTENTS

Preface *ix*

Introduction *1*

CHAPTER 1 Neither This nor That *5*

CHAPTER 2 Stories We Listen To *14*

CHAPTER 3 New Ideas about Musical Form *31*

CHAPTER 4 Motif and Improvisation *47*

CHAPTER 5 Developing That Sound: Guitars and Sonic Space *62*

CHAPTER 6 Pat Metheny Group as an Expression of an Unfolding Idea *72*

CHAPTER 7 Drummers and Wordless Vocals *94*

CHAPTER 8 *The Way Up* and Reflections on the Pat Metheny Group *113*

CHAPTER 9 Listening Interpretively: "America Undefined" and "Is This America? (katrina 2005)" *122*

Appendix 1: Remarkable Sounds: Manzer Guitars, the Roland Synthesizer in Non-PMG Settings, and Sonic Density *133*
Appendix 2: *The Way Up*: A Closer Look at an Extended Form *144*
Notes *151*
Bibliography *177*
Discography *187*
Index *191*

PREFACE

My mother often appreciated my music, even aspects she neither understood nor necessarily enjoyed. But she'd grow exasperated with me when she sought a word or two by which she could identify that music. My aunt didn't want to have this conversation at all whenever my mom brought it up in her presence. It was my aunt's strong preference to sit quietly with me at the piano, playing four-hand duets, as we often did.

Mom: What do you call it?
Bob: What do you mean?
Mom: What kind of music is it?
Bob: I don't know, it's just my music.
Mom: But when people ask me what it is, what should I tell them?
Bob: Tell them it's my music.
Mom: Come on, is it jazz? You sent me some reviews that said that it was jazz.
Bob: I guess.
Mom: But you went to school to study electronic music, didn't you? Don't you play electronic music?
Bob: That's a medium. But isn't it the piano that I've played my whole life?
Mom: So, is it like Debussy, whom you've always loved? Or Bach? But isn't this jazz?
Bob: I have always loved playing music by each of these composers, and I also love music by a lot of composers whose recordings are in the "jazz" bin at the store.

Mom: Well, I asked the man who gives jazz talks at my senior community to invite you to play a concert. He wants to know what kind of jazz do you play.

Bob: I really don't think your neighbors will like what I play. They want to sing along to old show tunes. I mostly play my own music, and people aren't going to sing along. They won't like it.

Mom: You can play some of their tunes and some of your own. Why don't you just do this for me? Just no electronics. And try to tone down some of that wild stuff.

Bob: I can't really predict how I'll play. After all, I'm an improviser.

Mom: Just try to keep it simple and not all over the place.

Bob: OK, I'll play a couple old tunes, but I can't predict how I'll play them, and I'll play some tunes they may recognize as jazz tunes.

Mom: You mean like Chick Corea or Herbie Hancock? You always liked them. OK.

Bob: You know that they each grew up playing Mozart.

Mom: Good, I can say Chick Corea and Herbie Hancock? But what kind of jazz should I tell him you play?

I did indeed play the concert, and it included some Chick Corea and Herbie Hancock. I'm glad I did because a year later, my mother died. I played a good concert. The people liked it. My mom felt proud. The man who gives the talks and introduced me didn't really know what to say beyond "Very nice. Not what my audience likes, but you have great technique. I'm not sure it's *real* jazz, but that's OK. We don't often have musically talented children visit."

This wasn't the first conversation I'd had with my mom or my late father over many years that was along the lines of "Very nice, but what is it?" I tried to engage them in exchanges about my feelings regarding the nature of musical "genres" in relationship to marketing, cultural roots and traditions, performance practices, technologies, and the expressive voice, but these chats never went very far. This disappointed me since my father was a visual artist with a very distinct and eclectic style that drew upon various traditions. He repurposed the skills gleaned from a career in graphic art and design. My mom was an American history teacher with a complex grasp of politics and historiography. I never blamed them for the road jam in our discussions about music because these conversations mirrored a lacuna at the heart of dialog about music across our culture(s). It so often seems to come down to binary attitudes about, as my mom aptly put it, "a word that describes it in terms I can easily repeat." It's either this style or genre or that one, this medium or that medium.

Interestingly enough, when my parents attended two shows in 2012 by my quartet when we were playing music from Herbie Hancock's Mwandishi band—performed with a mixture of acoustic instruments and all sorts of electronics—they seemed rather thrilled. I had recently published *You'll Know When You Get There: Herbie Hancock and the Mwandishi Band*, which was dedicated to the memory of my late uncle Milt Schubin, my mom's brother-in-law. After the concert, the conversation turned, for a change, to "Was that jazz?" and if so, "What kind of jazz?" There was never any resolution on the topic because there was none to be had. The irony is that for years I taught courses on a university level that were labeled "jazz," yet I've never found it useful or interesting to talk about ways people categorize music. Further, I've never provided students with a definition of the word in the course title, and they rarely asked. What fascinates me as a musician is on a far more granular level—the musical event taking place in any instant and how it unfolds from one second to the next. And to the students, it was, well, just music.

A few months before my dad died in 2013, he and I attended a concert by Pat Metheny's Unity Band. Dad loved it. It was quite electric *and* acoustic, and electronic *and* percussive, *and* lyrical. It was through-composed and improvised. My dad never asked me "What is it?" He just enjoyed the show. So much so that he didn't know what to say beyond "I loved that." As far as I was concerned, although my father lacked the language to explain what he liked about it, the music spoke for itself. It bridged multiple musical worlds, coming together as a unified musical experience in a way that my dad could absorb. Most important for him, it was often lyrical, and he could hum the melodies.

For my dad, words of explanation about genre were never again necessary. It seemed fitting that my father and I finally had a musical experience we shared and could simply smile about together. Sometime later, I realized that my father's response was an apt rejoinder to the interviewers, writers, and critics who have dogged Pat Metheny for decades with these kinds of genre questions.

A few years later, while working on a recording project, I turned to *The Pat Metheny Song Book* in search of a change of pace from what I was composing and rehearsing. I gradually played my way through much of the volume. Often, when I'm playing music, it grows on me in a deeper way than when I listen to recorded versions. I selected about two dozen Metheny compositions, winnowed them down to fifteen, and tried them out in various settings: as a duet with bassist Christopher Dean Sullivan, and then trio, adding drummer Karl Latham. I soon sensed that a familiar pattern was unfolding, one that paralleled the experience that had led to the Mwandishi band book. Listening to the music led to playing it, and playing the music gave me deeper insight about the processes within it. Experiencing it more deeply fed my interest in exploring it further. And that led to my desire to pass along to a reading public what I had learned. Here we are, and I hope you enjoy this book.

There are many people to thank for their assistance and support. Certainly, Pat Metheny has provided a tremendous amount of his time and energy in answering innumerable questions. I am grateful for his willingness to explain and clarify, narrate, and respond, whether I presented questions or challenges. My editor at University of Chicago Press, Elizabeth Branch Dyson, has been, as always, ever insightful, patient, and encouraging. It is a delight to have worked on our third book together. I am thankful for the attentive assistance of Assistant Editor Mollie McFee, Senior Production Editor Tamara Ghattas, and Senior Designer Ryan Li at the press; as well as Pat Metheny's management, David Sholemson and the Kurland Agency. My spouse Pamela and I have embarked on our new life together following my retirement from teaching, and she's been a tremendously attentive reader. As always, she is forgiving of my inclination to become absorbed in large projects (often subtitled "this is really the final big one"), one after the next.

Many thanks to Steve Rodby, Antonio Sanchez, and Andre Cholmondeley, each of whom has devoted substantial time to share their recollections and insights about Pat Metheny and his thinking, and about their own personal histories and perspectives on numerous musical and technical issues. My appreciation to previous interviewers of Pat Metheny and of various bandmates past and present, which allowed me to focus on interpretation rather than conducting further interviews. I do wish that I had had the opportunity to interview Lyle Mays before his death in 2020, but thankfully he left a sufficient published record to draw upon.

I offer thanks to friends, relatives, and colleagues who have read and provided feedback about this manuscript: Steve Bach, David Katz, Mitch Marcus, Peter Schubin, and, again, Pamela Lerman. I also wish to appreciate the faculty and staff at SUNY Potsdam's Crane School of Music, who invited Gary Burton to run a workshop and perform with his band in 1975, providing me a first opportunity to hear the early-career Pat Metheny.

While several of my friends were substantial fans of the early ECM catalog of recordings, I didn't take notice until 1982, soon after the release of *Offramp*. My attention became heightened the following year after I attended a Pat Metheny Group performance and also heard the album *80/81*. I loosely followed the band's and Metheny's other recordings over the years, particularly his music with and by Ornette Coleman and Coleman associates. Yet, as is the case with many of my musical interests, I only began to take a closer look when something caught my eyes and ears. That something was Metheny's first solo acoustic guitar album, *One Quiet Night* (2003), which provided solace following the first in a series of health crises for my father.

Many of the recordings I discuss in this book are ones I was not even aware of prior to this writing project and now cannot believe I had missed. *Imaginary Day* (1997) and *The Way Up* (2005) fall into this category. It was hearing the recording *Unity Band* (2012) that brought me to the concert I attended with my father, after which I began to listen more closely to Metheny's work and regularly attend his concerts.

During a post-concert chat with Pat shortly before the pandemic, he gave me a collection of his charts. This opened the door to listening "at the piano, with my hands" and led me to ask myself what his music meant to me *as a musician*. The release of *From This Place* (2020) confirmed that I had made the right choice in embarking on what became a several-years-long project culminating in the book you are now reading. Having engaged throughout my musical and scholarly career with issues of complexity, interactivity, and abstraction, I never could have imagined writing a book that featured themes of simplicity and melodicism, until, that is, I began working on this book. It has been a rewarding experience for which I am ever grateful.

Introduction

My goal in writing this book is to explore the key musical ideas that have grounded Pat Metheny's approach to making music across his five-decade professional career. I approach this endeavor as a musician of Metheny's generation who has for years taught, played the repertoire of, and published books about the innovations of the generation before us. The emerging ideas of musicians born in the late 1930s and early 1940s — Herbie Hancock, Chick Corea, Wayne Shorter, and others — that came to fruition in the 1960s and 1970s profoundly transformed the music that followed.

My writing style addresses a broad audience that spans musicians, lay listeners, and academics. Some chapters will provide historical and theoretical background, yet in many ways, this book is a listeners' guide, with interconnecting tissue provided by narrative and other information. The descriptive and metaphorical treatment of music begins in the middle of chapter 2 and is scattered throughout the book. My hope is that my readers will pair viewing the notated examples and reading my commentary with listening to the music. Almost all of it can be readily found on multiple music platforms. Ideally, a combination of reading and listening will help you connect specifics with broad principles and thus facilitate clearer understanding of Pat Metheny's musical ideas. I hope you also trust your own subjective experience of the music. This book generally follows a sequential historical timeline. To maintain this structure, discussion of some key topics has been placed in the appendixes.

This is not the first book to address Pat Metheny's music. He has been a popular subject for feature writers, music critics, and interviewers. But so

2   Introduction

far, there have been few full-length books that explore his life and work in depth. Two of the works I reference in this book are Mervyn Cooke's *Pat Metheny: The ECM Years, 1975–1984* (2014), a comprehensive musical survey of Metheny's recordings on the ECM label, well supported by analysis and commentary; and Carolyn Brewer's *Beneath Missouri Skies: Pat Metheny in Kansas City, 1964–1972* (2021), which addresses Metheny's early career in the Kansas City region. I also reference additional books about Metheny,[1] and I quote and cite the extensive collection of journal articles and academic writings that have been published about his work.

I draw upon interviews I have conducted in recent years with Pat Metheny and some of his associates. In addition, I excerpt a sampling of the voluminous interview material conducted by other writers, the most substantive of which is Richard Niles's *The Pat Metheny Interviews* (2009), a transcription of his interviews that aired on BBC Television in 2007.

Pat Metheny's musical perspectives reflect core principles that emerged early in his career and have remained constant across the decades. These include ideas regarding musical form, the integration of improvisation and composition as complementary and interpenetrating expressive modalities, the importance of melody, orchestration as an integral element within both composition and improvisation, the conceptualization of music as narrative, the expansive use of guitar and other musical technologies as sonic elements, and ideas about band leadership. Above all, Metheny seeks to treat simplicity and complexity as nonbinary, complementary, and interpenetrating musical qualities. A soaring lyrical melody can rest side by side or even be juxtaposed with highly complex musical activity.

Metheny's musical vehicle of longest duration to date has been presented under the name Pat Metheny Group (PMG), but this is but one of numerous projects that Metheny views as an integral part of a single, career-long project. For him, *Unity Band*, *Unity Sessions*, and *Secret Story* are no less projects that fit under the broad umbrella of his ongoing work. In fact, *Secret Story* drew a larger audience than work with the specific PMG moniker. Pat Metheny's fascination with automata, as reflected in his ongoing *Orchestrion* robotic musical instrument ensemble; his film scores; and—with a few exceptions addressed in this book—his duets and trios deserve much more space. These too are part of the same stream of Metheny's creative work.

One indicator of the interconnections between Metheny's various projects may be found in his annual tour bookings, which repeatedly return to the same venues no matter what he is playing or with whom. These concerts often present new work alongside representative selections from his compositional repertoire. PMG could easily have been named the Pat Metheny Quartet (or Quintet), and his *80/81*, *Unity*, or "An Evening with Pat Metheny" bands (the latter recorded *From This Place*, 2020) could each have been titled Pat Metheny Group. Future Metheny bands could certainly resume usage of the PMG moniker and reflect a related (or even different) set of musical values.

It is hard, though, to identify a parallel phenomenon outside of rock music to the classic formation of the Pat Metheny Group during its first three decades. Its concerts grew into a unique kind of "happening," as PMG keyboardist Lyle Mays referred to it.[2] Certainly, Keith Jarrett and Charles Lloyd (whose band brought Jarrett to broad attention) have had large, devoted followings, and they too helped pave a path for rock audiences to listen to music labeled as jazz.

What has made the classic formation of PMG distinct is its three-decade continuity, the sheer scale of its productions, and the breadth of its instrumental and sonic palette. Some of the key musical performance practices of the classic PMG are discussed in chapter 6 by bassist Steve Rodby, particularly what Rodby refers to as "that style," a mélange of melody and rhythmic feel that can at times draw upon popular music, played with the looseness, flexibility, and interaction of jazz musicians. Again, the classic formation of PMG represents but one expression, now more than a decade in the past, of Metheny's vast and continuing creative output.

It is my hope that this book assists listeners familiar with Pat Metheny's work to experience the music with greater depth and encourages music lovers unfamiliar with his music to engage with this fascinating body of work. I hope this book spawns further study and additional books, and an openness to ideas and expressive forms that push against perceived boundaries and divisions, a consideration that there is a vast creative world not governed by expectations that music be confined in preconceived containers of genre and style. Inherited musical traditions certainly provide ideas, materials, models of excellence, and inspiration, but they need not constrain the imaginative possibilities of searching individuals and groups.

CHAPTER 1

Neither This nor That

> You know, I've never been a good "one-sentence" person. It can be easier when somebody can just go, well, so and so is "that."
> PAT METHENY, 2017[1]

For many years, the cathedral of recorded music in Lower Manhattan during the 1980s and '90s was Tower Records. Upon entering the store, one writer recalls:

> The ground floor usually consisted of the pop and rock sections; the mezzanine area would be where the cassettes or boxed sets were shelved; the upper level was devoted to classical, jazz, country, world, and blues; and the basement level consisted [of] the CD/cassette singles section.[2]

Within the store, one easily spotted large signs that identified various musical categories and subcategories in which one might find recordings. The goal was to help people navigate the store, but this principle also curated how a particular musician or their work might be categorized. It facilitated conversations with employees, who might ask people invariably wandering around the store: "What kind of music do you like?" The way my mother posed her flavor of this question to me, her musician son, was: "It's very nice, but what kind of music is it?"

6   Chapter One

A provocative answer might be found in the title of the video release of the Miles Davis performance at the 1970 Isle of Wight festival, *Call It Anything*. For Davis, broadly heralded as a jazz pioneer, the boast that he aspired to form the greatest rock band in the world might seem like a puzzling claim. Clearly, this was an era of musical boundary crossing, "fusions," and hyphens. This was the period of Miles Davis's *Bitches Brew* (1970); the ascent of the more pop- and soul-flavored Creed Taylor CTI recordings;[3] the power trio Tony Williams Lifetime; harmonically and rhythmically complex British "progressive" rock bands King Crimson, Yes, and Genesis; and exploratory boundary-crossing electric albums by Miles Davis alumni, among them Herbie Hancock and Chick Corea, and Joe Zawinul and Wayne Shorter's band Weather Report. It was also the era of Gary Burton's electric guitar bands, which would, from 1974 to 1977, include Pat Metheny.

Pat Metheny, winner of Grammy awards in multiple categories including jazz, pop instrumental, rock instrumental, new age, and country instrumental, has been annually recognized in the media as "best jazz guitarist of the year." Certainly, when he was a budding twenty-year-old jazz musician playing with a premiere jazz band led by Gary Burton, he was well positioned to assume this designation. Yet when asked to claim this mantle, over the years, Metheny generally demurred; he commented in 2017, "I've always felt nonaligned. Even now I don't necessarily feel I'm this or I'm that, or I'm in this group or this category."[4]

Metheny uses the term "nonaligned" interchangeably with "unaligned,"[5] the latter simply connoting nonpartisanship. Metheny's goal is to sidestep silos labeled "rock," "jazz," "country," "pop," "classical," "instrumental," or hyphenated combinations that emerged in the 1960s era of jazz-rock, folk-rock hybrid marketing. In a 1998 interview, Metheny urged a holistic view of musical identity, pushing back against the idea of a label reflecting a sliced, diced, and reassembled self: "I resist the characterization of being [musically] schizophrenic or multipronged. I don't see it that way. To me, it is one thing. Yes, there are different dialects and different vocabularies, but more and more, I resist the whole idea of idiom."[6] Metheny refrains from being labeled a "jazz" musician, arguing that "it's becoming an idiom."

Musical Dialects and Vocabularies; Metheny's Embrace of and Individuation from Wes Montgomery

Yet it was the "dialects" and "vocabularies" of jazz, the conceptual ideas and skill sets of bebop and post-bop jazz musicians that Metheny honed during his teens and early twenties. The Metheny family, living in the suburbs of Kansas City, Missouri, had for generations been stage-band aficionados.[7] But when Pat's older brother Mike, a trumpeter, brought home Miles Davis's *"Four" & More* (1966), the twelve-year-old Pat soon became a fan of the great jazz melodicists—not only Davis but also saxophonists Lester Young, Coleman Hawkins, and Ben Webster. He discovered the recordings of saxophonists Charlie Parker and Sonny Rollins,[8] trumpeters Freddie Hubbard and Clifford Brown,[9] and guitarist Wes Montgomery and saxophonist Ornette Coleman.[10] Metheny was also taken by Brazilian popular music, which was growing in influence on American jazz musicians: "Around that time was also when the first Brazilian wave was coming across the States in the form of Astrud Gilberto singing 'Girl from Ipanema' and all those great Antônio Carlos Jobim songs, which became part of the American music vocabulary. That had a big effect on me."[11]

While he was a young teenager, Metheny further developed his skills as a jazz musician by attending the 1968 National Stage Band Camp, where he studied with guitarist Attila Zoller, who would later guide him through the New York City jazz scene. Until that point, Metheny's musical focus had been on the French horn, but his attention had shifted to electric guitar. That year, Metheny worked his way through fake books in informal jam sessions, where he learned the standard show-tune jazz repertoire and skillful navigation of its cyclical chord changes. He began to perform regularly around Kansas City at the conclusion of each day's school activities, and he cultivated mentors, including drummer Tommy Ruskin.

Metheny initially sought to emulate the musical language and technique of his guitarist role model, Wes Montgomery, whom he had the opportunity to see perform and meet in person at the 1968 Kansas City Jazz Festival.[12] Not long after meeting Montgomery, Metheny experienced a growing self-awareness that shifted his musical direction and sense of self: "When I was 14 or 15, I realized that what I was doing was really disrespectful because that wasn't me, that was him. I grew up in Lee's Summit, Mo. I didn't grow up in New York City.[13] I'm white; I'm not black. I'm from a little town where you couldn't help but hear country music, and I loved it. I always wanted to address those things with certain notes, qualities of chords, kinds of voice leading."[14]

Metheny made the decision not to turn his back on what he was learning from Montgomery but to commit to identifying and cultivating his own authentic musical voice. Thus began a self-reflective exploration of Metheny's personal musical direction and self-positioning in relationship to jazz traditions. Unlike Duke Ellington,[15] Charles Mingus, and Ornette Coleman, who

8   Chapter One

found the term to be limiting, Metheny was not among those who resisted "jazz" as an identifier.

Aside from his reflections about his relationship to Montgomery's music and persona, Metheny was, and remains disinclined to address his relationship to jazz in terms of race or culture. For many, including this author, identification with jazz as a descriptor or genre is bound up in its intersection with African American historical roots,[16] collective experience,[17] and culturally informed performance practices.[18] Jazz has long borne a diverse set of contextual meanings and been a locus of contention in light of the historical power imbalance between Black and white America,[19] leading some to view it as an expression of the struggle for freedom[20] and others to declare it "America's classical music."[21] As George Lewis observes, "for many, the very mention of the word *jazz* brings race to the table."[22]

That Pat Metheny prefers not to engage in the musicological and cultural debates and polemics[23] regarding jazz and race says little about the depth of his intimate care for the lineage of, and his numerous connections with, Black musicians, or the breadth of his fluency with the musical languages of African American bop pioneers.[24] By speaking about "dialects" and "vocabulary" in his 1998 interview quoted earlier, Metheny's own dialect draws upon culturally diverse sources. One can affirm and celebrate the beauty and integrity of African American performance practices yet "speak" a different musical "dialect"—or two or more. His early recognition that he was not Wes Montgomery indicated an awareness that it was the sum of Metheny's personal influences and authentic life experience that would shape his musical self.

Metheny's eclecticism may have been ahead of its time, but there is now a tremendous amount of music whose roots include a broad range of bebop dialects. Consider the eclecticism of Robert Glasper, Mary Halvorson, Snarky Puppy, and Esperanza Spalding, each perceived as a jazz musician while crisscrossing musical influences and perceived musical boundaries.[25]

Mentorship and Relationship with Jazz as Genre or Process

Metheny began to build a reputation as a developing young jazz player at age fifteen, in 1969, the year of his first engagements at Kansas City clubs. By the following year, he was playing nightly with cornetist Gary Sivils's trio at a Ramada Inn cocktail lounge in nearby Independence, Missouri.[26] The repertoire mixed popular music with Montgomery repertoire and standards. Before Metheny departed for college at the University of Miami (whose dean, Bill Lee, had traveled to hear Metheny play with Gary Sivils and recruit him), where his brief time as a student quickly transitioned into a position on the guitar faculty, he played three performances at the 1972 Kansas City Jazz Festival[27] and participated in a big-band gig with renowned trumpeter Clark Terry. Key musicians a generation older than Metheny were seeking musical spaces that engaged jazz but were untethered to it as a genre, as Kevin Fellezs comments:

> These "ain't jazz, ain't rock" musicians [Tony Williams, John McLaughlin, Joni Mitchell, and Herbie Hancock] troubled genres by *staying between them*, creating an informal, even feral, set of musical practices and aesthetics. By doing so, they articulated a way of being both inside and outside of genre categories, disturbing assumptions about musical traditions. . . . The "ain't jazz, ain't rock" music of these young musicians was not so much a hybrid as an "in between" categorization that could conceivably be an "is jazz, is rock" as much as an "ain't jazz, ain't rock" set of musical practices and aesthetics. Importantly, their music *remained between* genres—indeed, the kind of music they created has yet to coalesce into a genre of its own.[28]

If genre is a useful mode of speaking about music, "in between" offers a potential entry point to the work of Pat Metheny by the mid-1970s. Playing in the Gary Burton band—he first met Burton at the 1973 Wichita Jazz Festival, where they spoke and, at Burton's invitation, Metheny sat in with him[29]— meant engaging in a setting that consciously blurred musical boundaries. While Burton always identified as a jazz musician, as we shall soon see, he actively drew upon musical ideas from rock and pop. This was an exciting period when the older generation of Herbie Hancock, John McLaughlin, Chick Corea, and Gary Burton were at inflection points, seeking to define where this historical period, in which the idea of "genre" was being sapped of meaning, might lead.[30]

Metheny's early composition "April Joy," written before he headed to college, was already difficult to categorize in genre terms. His first album, *Bright Size Life* (1976), recorded while he was a member of Burton's band, further articulated the very personal musical profile he had been shaping with his own trio performing in Miami and Boston. The recording, which included bassist Jaco Pastorius and fellow Burton band member drummer Bob Moses, pointed in a direction that would lead him to become, arguably, the most prominent example of "ain't jazz, ain't rock" in his generation. This position, once considered controversial, has now become commonplace among younger musicians, who today resist boundaries with greater fervor than in the past.

10   Chapter One

While eschewing categorization with jazz (or rock, or . . .) Metheny references the term "jazz" as an *approach* to making music: "To me, if it's anything, jazz is a verb. It's more like a process than it is a thing."[31] His bands often draw upon a model of composition that is structured to incorporate improvisational navigation across a musical form and that reflects a strong familiarity with the vocabulary developed by bebop and post-bop innovators.[32]

Developing a Personal Vision with Jazz as Platform and Process Rather Than Genre

The source of Metheny's continuity within the history of jazz, however, hasn't meant developing a new form of bop but, as he articulated in a 1995 radio interview, "bringing a personal view of music, filtered through whatever aesthetic that I've managed to develop as a jazz musician."[33] Metheny embraces the "process" that emerged within the "platform" that jazz developed—solos embedded within compositional forms, often retaining the sense of groove that is core to many jazz traditions, albeit with a straight eighth note rather than the more conventional triplet "swing" feel that had been prominent in much of American jazz. This process "has emerged to allow us to report on the moments in our lives that have the most meaning."[34]

Pat Metheny's first three albums (*Bright Size Life* and *Watercolors*, released under his own name, followed by the self-titled debut of Pat Metheny Group), recorded between 1975 and 1978, during and immediately following his tenure with the Gary Burton band, document Metheny's intent to present his personal vision. It should be clear that his musical palette was strikingly different from existing models within jazz. The harmonies are novel, often using simpler chords, combined in ways different from the vocabulary and structures of bop traditions.

Sonically, the instruments, particularly Metheny's guitars, charted a new path. By the release of *Watercolors*, the sound of his electric guitar and the addition of a strummed acoustic guitar had introduced a tool kit of highly distinctive, original sounds. Metheny's attention to textural devices, sonic spaciousness, and a broad dynamic range were unusual within jazz, rock, or country music. The highly resonant electric bass sounds of Jaco Pastorius, Eberhard Weber, and Mark Egan had little precedent. Danny Gottlieb's and Bob Moses's drumming emphasized the higher frequencies by focusing on the cymbals, with, Metheny notes, "Tony Williams and Roy Haynes,[35] rather than rock or funk drummers, as models,"[36] and the rhythmic patterns of instrumental lines were, as already noted, organized in straight eighth notes.[37] The music was fresh, new, and eclectic, displaying a diversity of moods, textures, forms, and aesthetics, transcending conventional categories.

The title track of Pat Metheny's first recording, *Bright Size Life* (1976) blends angularity, symmetry, and rhythmic vitality, while "Sirabhorn" and "Unity Village" are lyrical, "Midwestern Nights Dream" spacious, and "Unquity Road" rhythmically driving. The folk expressiveness of "Omaha Celebration" contrasts with the abandon of Metheny's treatment of the first Ornette Coleman compositions he heard, "Round Trip" and "Broadway Blues" (on Coleman's *New York Is Now* [1968]).

On *Watercolors* (1977), the lyricism and intuitive harmonic movement of the title track rests comfortably alongside the floating textures of "Icefire," the folksiness of "Lakes," and the lyrical pop catchiness of "River Quay." But also on this album is the Ornette Coleman–informed "Florida Greeting Song," the surprising appearance of acoustic guitar on "Legend of the Fountain," and the multidimensional sonic qualities of "Sea Song."

Pat Metheny Group (1978) introduces repeated modular rhythmic motifs, which enliven "Phase Dance" and the anthemic "Jaco" (which would be continued in the off-kilter rhythmic patterns on "Fallen Star" from *New Chautauqua* [1979] and the opening section of "(Cross the) Heartland" on *American Garage* [1980]). "San Lorenzo" heralds many multisectional works to come (including the thirteen-minute closing piece of *American Garage*, "The Epic"). "April Joy" features a circular form. Rhythmically, the music on *Pat Metheny Group* embraces that particular straight-eighth-note "feel" discussed earlier.

Vibrant acoustic guitar strumming comes to the fore in the title track of *New Chautauqua* (1979); the folk-song-like "Country Poem" displays the acoustic guitar in a different light, with its spare eloquence and overlay of sonically liquid layered electric guitars. A patient rhythmic motion lifts the lyrical, multilayered "Hermitage," matched well by the gentle rhythmic patterns and single-line electric guitar sonorities of "Daybreak."

In contrast, *American Garage* (1980) features a steady beat and melodic pop-song quality on "(Cross the) Heartland," the singable melody of "Airstream" projected by electric guitar joined by a voice-like synthesizer, and the rock/pop homage "The Search." Despite moments of assertive rock-and-roll rhythms and riffs on *American Garage*, its unexpected harmonic turns, the use of the title track as an improvisational vehicle, and its transpositions in "The Search" resist simple categorization.

Metheny's music found a footing among young people, many of them white, whose musical affinities were idiosyncratic. These audiences were comfortable attending venues suited to rock bands during a period when clubs offered a more eclectic fare than one might expect; the broad dynamic range (at times quite loud) of the Pat Metheny Group was a familiar experience. Some of these fans also attended jazz festivals where the program included some bands familiar to them, and they were open to music that had a distinct, hybrid identity.

The unfolding of a more expansive and increasingly eclectic PMG musical profile begins with *Offramp* (1982) and *First Circle* (1983), marking changes in the ways Metheny composed and performed, with an increased use of electronics, sequences, Latin rhythms, voices, and other elements. The music was growing in musical complexity while maintaining, if not enhancing, its songlike qualities. The dramatic liveliness of the music, the breadth of its group sound—the rise and fall of its emotional contours and broad dynamic range—the drama of its rhythms, and the lyricism of its melodies all served to excite and engage audiences. Just before making these albums, Metheny had recorded the less through-composed, more improvisation-focused *80/81* with a band that included Ornette Coleman associates Charlie Haden and Dewey Redman, highlighting the expanse of Metheny's projects that were already in play during a period when much of the jazz media attention was focused on PMG.

As Stuart Greenbaum observes, what is most important is that Pat Metheny, like other composers who look to multiple sources for inspiration, "create[s] music whose worth will outweigh the stylistic influences upon it."[38] For Metheny himself, the idea of genre had become "superfluous":

> I basically love music and see it—like humanity itself—as one big thing. I feel very happy that I have the capacity to get goose bumps listening to just about anyone playing just about anything if they are doing it at their very best. . . . That quality can be found in the most unlikely places.[39]

A self-definition as musically "unaligned" came to extend to a long-term fascination with the music of cultures outside the United States. These include Indonesian gamelan in "Imaginary Day" (1997); hints of rhythms and vocal melodies of Latin America scattered throughout the repertoire, documented on the live album *The Road to You* (1993); and the panoply of cultural influences on the long-form work *Secret Story* (1992), which at times appears to be a collection of separate compositions. In these and other recordings, Metheny's culturally exploratory interests seem to be the fruits of his search for compelling musical material to add to his palette. They reflect Metheny's borderless perspective that human beings share a reservoir of musical information within which a multiplicity of people can both contribute to and draw from.[40] Metheny observes that musicians now listen and are informed across national borders:

> The truth is, most of the pop music in the world now, whether it's from Thailand or wherever, is as influenced by Western pop music as by anything in its own culture. Everybody's got variations on that four-four backbeat but it's still rock and roll to me, whether it's being sung in Thai or French or what. Because of the communications revolution it's really natural now for all of us to be influenced by each other.[41]

Pat Metheny's view of musical creativity began in childhood when he bathed himself in a vast reservoir of intriguing sounds and possibilities. While surrounded by regional country-and-western music and by his family's favored marching-band music, Metheny discovered the electric guitar sounds of the Beatles; the lyricism of the Brazilian songwriter Antônio Carlos Jobim; the polyphony of Johann Sebastian Bach; Miles Davis; and newly emerging trends within jazz, seemingly all at once. His emerging musical worldview might have been formulated as "Why not listen to Ornette Coleman *and* country-and-western songs *and* the Beatles *and* Sonny Rollins? Why choose or value one above another?

CHAPTER 2

Stories We Listen To

I believe that the spiritual significance of music is an intelligence and consciousness that we are all given by our life. Babies in the womb respond to music and as our ears are emptied of the water at birth, sounds/music begin their profound influence on our life. Music is the highest spiritual entity that I know about in my life. Music transforms our daily life moment by moment. We walk, run, dance, sing, chant, whistle, hum, groove to music our entire life. We are moved to tears by music and of course it is the key element in all rituals of the human experience. We are born into musical sound, and we pass to the next dimension with music as our friend and guide.

DAVID DARLING[1]

Human beings are storytellers. Maybe that's what we are in our essence. We respond to nearly any stimulus with the beginnings of a story about what we are sensing or feeling, and a version of what it means. We see a bird and we wonder what kind of bird, where it is from, where it is going. We remember other times we have seen birds, where we were, and what unfolded that day.

Pat Metheny often refers to music as "telling a story": "When I improvise, it's a matter of telling a story, and when you go to see a good movie, or see a painting you like, or hear somebody talk to you, there are certain qualities that make it interesting."[2] For Metheny, "story" is a metaphor for the dynamic unfolding of a musical work rather than a plotline.

A young child can pick up a piece of string or other inanimate object and treat it as a character whose story must be told. Grown-ups may not be conscious of it, but we, too, craft narratives about objects we encounter, naming, providing context, and often projecting an imagined identity upon whatever it may be. We hear a voice and, without being aware of it, we begin to tell ourselves a story about whose voice it might be.

Associations form in our minds and we are internally off and running, linking memories of people, places, and activities and speculating about what these may mean to us. At the mere hint of a potential storyline, an unquenchable desire arises within us to know how our story is going to unfold and how the saga will conclude.

A story well told captures our imagination and creates within us a desire to follow it from beginning to end. When we hear or read a story or see it unfold on-screen, we yearn to find an overarching logic, a sense of inevitability from beginning to end. We want to intuit a sense of completion. A story well told, not unlike the stories that intrigued us as children, brings a sense of fullness and meaning to our lives. So too can a sound or a scrap of melody become an opening to a musical narrative that is waiting to unfold. Moments of surprise capture our attention. We notice when music takes an unexpected turn, and we find ourselves curious about the outcome of each significant element of it, whether or not an actual storyline is intended.

Musicians can organize sounds that take us to places in our imaginations that we cannot fathom, evocatively sparking memories, associations, and fragments of storylines. Music may not be able to convey literal stories, since music is not language, but we can experience metaphorical highs and lows, as if characters were experiencing conflicts or traveling to unfamiliar places, that even momentarily trigger within us a mental image. Or a melodic line may hold our attention, move us in a particular way, and "ask" us to stay with it to follow where it leads. Music can spark our anticipation of the start of *something*, a sense of suspended animation and waiting, and the experience of relief in its completion.

While there are important differences between composing and improvising, each of these can provide a platform for "storytelling." This is the ability to spark a listener to perceive a narrative line or evoke thoughts, memories, or images. Musical events that capture our attention can elicit a sense of fascination and carry us from one musical place to another. At times this travel is from a beginning to a conclusion, evoking an imagined journey. The idea of music as metaphor, and the differences between improvisation and composition as they relate to storytelling, are topics I will say more about later.

Music and Subjectivity, a Contrast to Language

It is not a simple task for a musician to draw us in and carry us along in this manner, since music defies so much of what language promises. Language can provide a direct connection between a word or a phrase and a specific reference. Rules of syntax guide how we can build a sentence and convey meaning. In contrast, the musician faces what Metheny terms "the intrinsic abstraction of how a set of consecutive or shuffled musical ideas can add up to a coherent whole."[3] Musical coherence is an illusion that musicians magically bring forth, taking sounds or melodic fragments, or a sequence of chords or some other mode of organization, and render them interesting enough that listeners can find the music sufficiently compelling to engage their imaginations. But it is precisely this lack of literal associational power that grants music the ability to spark our emotions, as Metheny notes:

> One of the many things I love about music is that it is always just out of sight, just out of reach. You get glimpses of it here and there, now and then—but it is ultimately always out of reach, because as you become a better musician, the universe of what is possible keeps expanding outward, faster and faster, it seems. I often talk about how words seem like unwieldy blocks that you can move around but are not really intrinsically malleable, while music remains loose and free in its inherent abstraction.[4]

One can find analogies to the inherent subjective quality of musical listening. Metheny suggests one of these:

> Four people traveling in a car at the same time could be looking out the window in four different directions and have four wildly different descriptions of the trip even though they literally were in the same vehicle at the same time. And that same trip might be taken again, same route, over and over again, at different times of the year, using different forms of transport even.[5]

Each individual listener can experience the same music multiple times but, as with a kaleidoscope, find something different in it each time. Listening to a musical work with a large amount of detail can be like exploring a physical object that draws our sustained interest. Metheny says:

> [Like a sculpture] . . . you can do a 360-degree walk around it and you can find stuff from a melodic standpoint that you wouldn't hear the first time.

You can find structural things that you wouldn't hear the first time . . . stuff that we almost bury in the mixes that will emerge after the thirteenth time that you hear them.[6]

The Storytelling Metaphor among Jazz Musicians

Pat Metheny is certainly not the first to use a storytelling metaphor for musicianship. This mode of conceptualizing making music is deeply embedded within jazz history and more generally throughout African American musical traditions. It has long been common parlance among jazz musicians. Pianist Randy Weston describes himself in this way: "I'm really a storyteller through music."[7]

Analogies to conversational and other forms of interaction, narrative, and expression of historical memory are at the core of many African American musical practices, as articulated by Samuel Floyd, Ingrid Monson, and others.[8] Using the term "Afrological" to refer to musical values "historically emergent"[9] within African American traditions, George Lewis notes: "One important aspect of Afrological improvisation is the notion of the importance of personal narrative, of 'telling your own story.' . . . part of telling your own story is developing your own 'sound.'"[10] "Story" can imply deeper cultural resonances and collective histories; Esperanza Spalding correlates the navigation of harmonic structures with the constant historical "grappling with the dynamic shifts of oppression," transmuted expressively into "a through line of beauty and coherency."[11]

Paul Berliner articulates the idea among improvisers within jazz traditions as "saying something." In doing so, he references the music making of many who are rooted in African American aesthetics. His focus on crafting a musical line that embodies a coherent inward logic, unfolding from start to finish, is well suited to Pat Metheny. One example Berliner gives is that of pianist Kenny Barron, who articulates his narrative concept of soloing in this way:

You start off just playing very simply and, as much as possible, with lyrical ideas. And as the intensity builds, if it does, your ideas can become a little more complicated. They can become longer. The way I look at it is that you're going to start down so that you have somewhere to go. It can build to different points in different parts of the solo. It's hills and valleys.[12]

Barron argues for a nuanced approach that draws upon the idiom of bebop to conceive of a solo as terraced, its ebb and flow akin to the hills and valleys

18   Chapter Two

of a mountainous landscape. He applies a topographic metaphor to suggest contrasts between calm and intensity, simplicity and complexity, minimalism and expansiveness. Barron connects a visual metaphor, as if looking at a landscape painting, with the experience of a vigorous journey, like a hike that ascends a scenic path, then gradually dips to a plain, only to repeatedly rise and descend.[13]

Pat Metheny credits his Kansas City mentors with introducing him to this concept,

> particularly the drummer Tommy Ruskin and cornetist Gary Sivils. Tommy used that specific phrase as a personal goal, and something that he recognized in whatever my very early playing seemed to indicate to him. . . . He then demonstrated it every time he played.[14]

> Gary is one of those guys who, no matter what is happening around him, always "tells a story," and he does it with an almost narrative flow. In fact, this "storytelling" quality is something that I think all the great KC improvisers have had in common.[15]

Economy of means within a "storytelling" approach is a goal that Metheny learned from Ruskin, Sivils, and Gary Burton. This is an attribute that Metheny believes enhances one's ability to perceive an improvisation as a story, as he has pointed out on multiple occasions:

> It goes beyond the quantity. It is the atmosphere that you create on a narrative level that separates musicians that are improvisers who can manifest images as opposed to just notes, they can make a sound have an almost literal meaning. It can be done a lot of different ways.[16]

> You don't wanna hear the guy say the same thing over and over and over again as he's telling you a story. You want him to say it once in the most vivid possible way and then you get the message, and you can imagine what it is he's talking about.[17]

Even with concision in mind, Metheny finds extended musical forms well suited to exploring this metaphor:

> [For] me, thinking in longer ideas is much easier than thinking in shorter ideas. On a structural level, having to come up with little things [one] right

after another is one of the hardest things to do. . . . It would be very difficult to talk about a different subject one sentence at a time 40 subjects in a row. It's much easier to keep talking about one thing until you've exhausted what you have to say about it, and will take you to the next thing.[18]

Let's now take a leap of faith and assume that you can embark on a journey while listening to a work by Pat Metheny recorded by the PMG, the song "Imaginary Day" (1997).

Listening with Curiosity to "Imaginary Day"

Pat Metheny's compositions varied from brief, succinct musical statements to extended works. By 2005, a single work, *The Way Up*, would fill an entire album. In 1997, several of the compositions that comprise the album *Imaginary Day* are symphonic in scope. One of these, the title track, "Imaginary Day," is intriguing for its conceptual unity across a span of ten minutes, and for its integration of diverse sections—"subplots" might be a useful metaphor here—each of which could stand on its own.

The descriptive treatment of "Imaginary Day" that follows is not a storyline. Rather, it is a narration of the unfolding musical events, a guide to help you listen more closely. Consider this methodology: Listen to the music first without this guide and then again with it. Periodically pause and repeat sections. Notice your own reactions and pay attention to what you imagine. See what each section of the composition communicates to you and how this changes as you listen to the contrasting sections. How do you respond to the whole? What aspects of the music speak to you? What stories do you find yourself telling?

The dramatic opening of "Imaginary Day" might seem to lay down a gauntlet. The second of two heavily accented sounds reverberates, setting the stage for Metheny's guitar to respond with a brief pentatonic improvisation. This pattern will repeat: a call and response between the guitar and the dense web of crashing cymbals, piano, birdcalls, non-Western flutes, and Hindustani *tambura* sounds.

The sonic qualities of this particular guitar caught this listener by surprise. I continue to wonder at it after multiple rounds of listening. Each note begins percussively but rings with a slight buzzing timbre. Might this be a Dobro, the steel-string guitar fronted by a metal resonator played in country music, bluegrass, the blues, and Hawaiian music? The buzzing of the strings is of a different quality than any of these, so the nature of this guitar suggests a story of its own.

20   Chapter Two

This mysterious-sounding instrument is in fact a fretless nylon-string guitar, one of several unusual guitars custom-built for Pat Metheny by Canadian luthier Linda Manzer. Its unique qualities derive from its hybrid design. Metheny points to some of its special qualities:

> Fretless guitar is kind of hard thing to achieve. Quite often it kind of winds up sounding like a banjo. A quick attack and very little sustain. Because of the higher pitches requiring thinner string gauges, you don't normally get the kind of sustain we all dream about getting as a fretless bass with its heavier-gauge strings can get to pretty consistently. It was Linda's idea to try it with wound nylon strings.[19]

The wavering of each pitch produces a sound that differs from Western intonation. The flexibility of the nylon strings lends well to note bending, but its pitch instability is, in fact, also built into its design:

> In the end, the fretless thing has a connection to instruments that have been developed in countries where a relationship to tempered pitches are less important. With nylon, or gut strings, the immediate connection for me was with the North African oud, usually eleven strings on a shorter fretless neck.[20]

The improvised melodic line also catches my attention. Its tonality and Metheny's pitch bending suggest a blues inflection, yet the guitar's unpredictable, slight wavering in pitch, even when the notes aren't being bent, adds another level of ambiguity. Which culture does this music inhabit?

The harmonic setting remains within a Western structure, yet the guitar's unusual sound qualities and pitch instability lead me to wonder where in the world this melody and its sound belong. There's a story being told within the jolting opening sound mass and the guitar's response. Knowing the identity of the guitar does little to suspend my fascination with it. New questions continue to arise from the multiple meanings the sounds suggest.

A minute and a half into the performance, the first melodic theme begins. An E pedal tone (a bass note that doesn't change) anchors this catchy melody. The harmonies suggest the blues (the fifth-degree tone B wavers between B♮ and B♭). Yet, the tonality also hints at North African, Central Asian, and Middle Eastern modes. The melody takes a more Western harmonic flavor when the E pedal leads us to a brief resting place in A major. The melody concludes with a winding pentatonic passage that returns to the E pedal.

The shift from harmonic ambiguity to harmonic clarity provides this melody with a distinct, compelling character. If you listen closely to each of the layers, ignoring the others, there's the harmony itself, which could be a familiar song form: Em–A–F^{maj7}–G–A–C^{maj7}–E. But ignoring the harmonies, there's the guitar improvisation alone, with its own story to tell. And wrapped around the improvisational lines are the jarring percussive events.

The second section of "Imaginary Day" enters distinctly different musical territory. My first reaction was to think of it as an Irish flute melody, moving stepwise in a march-like rhythm. But in program notes to the recording, Metheny points to a very different influence. In a studio discussion, Metheny and Lyle Mays considered how the nylon-string guitar and its blues inflections could be part of a larger transcultural pastiche. Metheny recounts:

> We were recalling our recent concert tour to Indonesia and a gamelan concert we attended there. It was an ensemble of 25 Indonesian musicians playing on metal instruments, and it was one of the tightest, most well-organized ensemble sounds we had ever heard. I suppose we thought we could draw some influence from that, in that our focus on ensemble playing has also been a priority over the years, and there were things about what they were doing that paralleled our thing even though we draw from different musical vocabularies. So that was the starting place for that tune; us wanting to combine the natural bluesiness of what the fretless guitar offers with something inspired by that Indonesian ensemble sound.[21]

Listening again to this section, one can hear the gamelan influence, particularly in its regimented rhythm, but also in the multiple layers of overlapping material. Neither Indonesian nor Irish, this melody is a theme that contrasts with the first melody, and each concludes with the same phrase. Despite this similarity, the contrast between sections calls the listener to listen closely and wonder about what connects them. What is the music telling us, and where are we headed?

The composition then returns to the first part of the melody and repeats the dramatic accented figures that shook us at the very beginning. Quite unexpectedly, the jolting figures open a door to another surprising development. A slowly unfolding anthemic, lyrical melody articulated on Mays's synthesizers arises. We want to hear it for all it may convey, but it is relatively brief. Don't worry, we will hear it again later in an expanded form. For now, this ephemeral moment provides a bridge to two improvisational segments, each with its own distinct character.

From our present vantage point, we can now hear the contrasting emotional and musical qualities of each of the three now-concluded sections in our memories, transforming a series of otherwise unrelated themes into a conceptual unity. With the movement from one theme to the other and back, only to now steer in a completely new direction, "Imaginary Day" facilitates within us a journey from one "imaginary" place to yet others. The experience is akin to a removing the layers of nested Russian dolls. When each layer is removed, something new appears, and we can dwell on the novelty or consider every layer that preceded it.

The two improvisational settings that follow provide Metheny and his bandmates with space to insert their own ephemeral musical ideas within each performance. A touring band finds itself playing the same repertoire repeatedly on a nightly basis. The composed materials and the structure of the improvisational sections must be durable, capable of sustaining interest for audiences, but even more critically, for the musicians themselves, again and again.

Each improvisational section of "Imaginary Day" has its own character, one markedly different in structure from the next. Since Pat Metheny began to compose, one of his prime musical goals has been to craft forms that elicit expressive improvisations with a clear sense of direction.

The first solo is played by Lyle Mays; this is a rare instance when Mays solos on synthesizers rather than on the piano. There are two sections, one leading into the next. The task of the soloist is to traverse each in a way that presents a unified conception. Mays achieves this by transitioning smoothly from one segment in the musical form to the next, de-emphasizing changes in the patterns and feel. The form of the keyboard solo section draws upon a principle Pat Metheny began to favor while playing with the Gary Burton band: to craft cycles of slowly changing harmonies within which periods of stasis are interspersed.

Often, Metheny structures solo sections using passages built on stepwise bass movement, juxtaposed with simple, relatively static chords. As a result, the harmonic flavor shifts gradually and subtly (this combination is discussed further in chapter 4). While "Imaginary Day" is less concerned with stepwise motion than other Metheny compositions, the structure of the solo sections, particularly for Lyle Mays's keyboard solo, distinctly unfolds over extended periods of time. This allows the solo to develop over a long arc, providing narrative-like direction. As a result, the structure itself helps the soloist carry the listener from the beginning of a section through various twists and turns, ending in a perceivably logical conclusion. This perception of "direction" is at the heart of this instance of "telling a story."

After an extended introduction, drummer Paul Wertico establishes a rapid pulse. The speed of that continuous pulse contrasts with the slowly changing harmonies grounded at first on G♯. Soon, more quickly changing chords come to a sense of stasis on B♭. Mays opens his solo interjecting fleeting bird and flute motifs. From there, he shapes flowing lines that alternate between keyboards, creating call and response between the different sonorities. Mays's solo next soars across eight bars of rhythmically percussive chord jabs that are grounded by a steady pedal tone on A. It builds a dramatic arc, relentlessly pressing ahead as the bass departs from the A pedal and transitions into passages shaped by an active bass line that ascends and descends, leaping in fifths. The harmony changes more rapidly, traversing across A♭–E–B♭–B♮.

After a pause in the harmony, the drums steadily mark time while the birds and flutes jab and flutter, and Mays begins the third section of his solo. Here, the chordal form repeats, transposed to a new key, starting on D, but ending in a steady groove in B♭. When this form repeats, Mays builds momentum to expand his solo. He moves into higher registers, as the rhythm churns and the bass settles into an extended B♭ groove.

The sudden return of the shock waves that opened "Imaginary Day" opens the door to Pat Metheny's guitar solo. The form is an adaptation of a slow G-minor blues (specifically, a vi chord replaces the V chord). Metheny's playing, over a spare, syncopated bass, is an impassioned blues performance. The mood shifts into more upbeat territory, centered on a C (mixolydian) mode, extending across another slowly evolving series of chord changes. The harmonic movement concludes on an E pedal, upon which Metheny's repeated phrases call out, akin to an emotional plea.

The tone color of Metheny's guitar sounds exactly as we would expect in a soaring blues that is played on a solid-body Fender Stratocaster or other classic electric blues instrument. But this guitar is nothing of the sort. The well-designed electric pickup and electronics of the Linda Manzer fretless nylon-string acoustic we heard earlier is, in fact, now producing this rich, distinctly electric sound.

Metheny's solo continues across a repetition of the harmonic form, but ultimately, his expressively repeated calls build the tension to a fever pitch. This brings us home to the opening of the first half of the "Imaginary Day" melody, this time transposed to G. This time, the melody soars, self-assured and satisfying, as if an old friend has returned.

The melody continues triumphantly until the dramatic sonic booms of the opening again return, this time leading to an emotionally charged coda. The lyrical anthem that preceded the solo sections is now extended with a searing melody. The multimovement "Imaginary Day" closes with roaring gongs and barely audible echoes of a B♭ drone.

At ten minutes' duration, this is a substantial work, traversing many moods, musical "feels," perceptions of the pace of motion, and expressive musical ideas presented by the soloists. The music can sustain repeated listening, each time offering something new.

By presenting the opening melody first in a harmonically ambiguous manner, the work rewards the listener when the melody confidently returns following the guitar solo. Repetition of the brief anthemic melody that preceded the keyboard solo, now greatly expanded into a soaring, lengthier statement after the guitar solo, provides a grand finale for "Imaginary Day."

Melody as a Focal Point of Continuity and Interest

The grandeur of the resounding melodies within this work points to one of Pat Metheny's strengths as a composer. His gift at crafting simple but elegant melodies is a key to the staying power of his work. "Imaginary Day" is a case in point, offering the listener something firm to hold onto through the many contrasting sections of a complex work. The melodic grandeur of this work was a continuation of a lifelong passion that had begun in childhood. In 1980, Metheny told an interviewer:

> I remember singing melodies since I was about two or three years old. I was always real melodic. I remember singing "Red Sails in the Sunset" for about two years, till everybody was ready to kill me. I liked those kinds of soupy melodies.[22]

The song in question was from the 1930s,[23] popularized by Bing Crosby, Louis Armstrong, and, later, Nat King Cole. Metheny's interest in melody helps explain why Wes Montgomery, a guitarist with a gift for melody, became such an important model for him. Metheny's inclusion of wordless vocalists, beginning in the 1980s, particularly when Pedro Aznar joined Pat Metheny Group, served to heighten the vocal qualities of his music.

Melody alone, however, cannot sustain an extended work like "Imaginary Day." A blend of rich and varied instrumental colors and attentive management of changing overall densities and dynamic levels are among the musical elements that add nuance to melody, harmony, and rhythm, thus holding the interest of listeners across a lengthy work, realizing Metheny's conception of musician as "storyteller." Presenting the fruits of this project in a manner compelling to a listening audience is not a task with any guaranteed success, he says:

> What gets challenging in these kinds of discussions is the intrinsic abstraction of how a set of consecutive or shuffled musical ideas can add up to a coherent whole. And, no less importantly, the listener's requirements on the receiving end to be able and willing to make that leap of abstraction.[24]

Storytelling with and without Referential Associations

There is a paradox in describing music as storytelling. Unless there are lyrics, musical sounds, however they are organized, are inherently abstract. Music is intangible and amorphous. What one person imagines as conveying a story about love gained or lost, another may experience as the vicissitudes of life, or hinting at a not yet discovered place. Music described as narrative can more easily obscure than inform.

There are in fact musical works based on the assumption that music has the potential to literally reference nonmusical sensations and images. The Japanese shakuhachi flute is said to evoke the sound of wind blowing through a decaying bamboo grove.[25] Some nineteenth-century European and American tone poems and programmatic works are thought to tell literal stories. In Richard Strauss's *An Alpine Symphony*, rapidly descending motifs draw upon a "vocabulary" of associations that have been understood to suggest a waterfall; in Beethoven's Sixth Symphony, the *Pastoral*, rumbling and swaying musical gestures in the cello and double bass sections are said to evoke a babbling brook and distant thunder; and in Aaron Copland's *Rodeo* and *Billy the Kid*, "open" harmonies are said to suggest the open spaces of the American West.

There is nothing inherent in music that suggests any of these associations; rather, connections of meaning accrue through the repetition of shared cultural "vocabularies" of associations that connect music with that which is nonmusical. People unfamiliar with the associations will not recognize them. As Vladimir Jankelevitch suggests, music resists fixed associations, yet can suggest "innumerable possibilities of interpretation":

> Music creates a unique state of mind, a state of mind that is ambivalent and always indefinable. Music is, then, inexpressive not because [it] expresses nothing but because it does not express this or that privileged landscape,

26   Chapter Two

this or that setting to the exclusion of all others; music is inexpressive in that
it implies innumerable possibilities of interpretation, because it allows us to
choose between them.[26]

Ironically, it may be music's inherent intangibility that opens the potential for every listener to discover, again and again, deep personal, subjective
metaphors and stories within music. When Pat Metheny employs the word
"storytelling" to speak about music making, he is using the idea of narrative as
a metaphor, a term that means "understanding and experiencing one kind of
thing in terms of another."[27]

Metaphor and Music

While metaphor is generally defined as "a figure of speech"[28] and music is not
language, musicians and musical scholars constantly make use of metaphors
to conceptualize their work. Melodies are said to "rise" and "fall,"[29] and we
speak of musical intensity that builds to a degree that requires resolution[30] as
"tension and release."

As George Lakoff and Mark Johnson, the authors of the seminal book
Metaphors We Live By, teach, metaphors draw upon our bodily experiences:
we reach upward to grasp a book on a high shelf and we bend down close to
the ground to tie our shoes and we experience physical tension in our muscles
when we stretch.[31] We draw upon the ways we perceive somatic experiences
to address emotional states, elation as "heightened" and sadness as "low"
moods. We talk about anxiety in terms of "tension."[32] Metaphors identified by
Lakoff and Johnson connected to tension and release also include "blockage,"
"enablement," and "restraint/removal." Other metaphors are applied by musicians to a wide range of aspects of musical organization: the term "cycles" invokes repeated patterns, harmonic and rhythmic; cyclical units of beats define
meter. The metaphor of "part" versus "whole" is applied to the relationship
between sections within a musical work and its entirety.

We of course make use of metaphors to translate our perceptions into
literary narrative structures. Characters in a novel are said to journey "far"
from home, as if they are stretching out their arms to reach an object. But
the same metaphor suits our description of harmonic relationships, which
we say "move away" or "drift" from, and then return to, a consonant center. A
sequence of notes increasing in pitch is said to "ascend," even though in reality
"higher" pitches on a guitar simply vibrate with greater frequency per second.

Metheny's storytelling analogy implicitly draws upon a collection of associated metaphors identified by Lakoff and Johnson. A "path" draws upon the idea of a physical path to suggest the route one travels from one metaphorical "place," a beginning point in a narrative or a state of mind, to another. In musical improvisation and composition, a "path" can be a way to speak of a musical idea unfolding through time.

Storytelling is a useful metaphor for music making because music, like stories, unfolds dynamically over time across a narrative arc, a series of events that we perceive as following a discernible logic. Music is analogous to other expressive forms because it can be experienced in a way that embodies the strivings of human hopes and dreams, sorrows and concerns, and, of course, it engages our bodies and spirits. As Pat Metheny describes it, "the narrative flow of storytelling may be the closest thing we can point to outside of the syntax of music itself to explain it in similar terms." By "syntax" Metheny refers to the various conventions we apply to how musical ideas can be organized.

Metheny's listeners, like you and me, have the power to translate what we each hear into our own personal perceptions, images, stories, and experiences. By injecting our sense of meaning we make the music our own and thus meaningful to us. Let Pat Metheny craft his narrative arc, "telling a story" through the music, and in turn, the task of the listener is to listen attentively, follow the music's unfolding, and find their own story within it.

Musician as "Reporter"

Metheny's explication of his approach to music making employs a useful metaphor—to serve as a "reporter," that is, a translator and transmitter of what the musician can discern about the present moment.

Pat Metheny first encountered the concept of musician as "reporter" while playing in Gary Burton's band. Metheny recalls that Burton addressed "the immediate nature of improvising as having the capacity to 'report' on the feeling of a moment in way that is unique to our community."[33] This idea predates both Burton and Metheny. Duke Ellington wrote in an appendix to his 1973 autobiography, "I think the artist's true position is that of an observer. Personal emotion could spoil his *piece de resistance*."[34]

For Ellington, the goal was to witness and dispassionately report what one discerns. In the mid-1960s, saxophonist Archie Shepp described the jazz musician as a politico-cultural reporter: "Culturally, America is a backward country, Americans are backward. But jazz is American reality. Total reality.

28   Chapter Two

The jazz musician is like a reporter, an aesthetic journalist, an aesthetic journalist of America."[35]

Pat Metheny doesn't specify the precise nature of what he seeks to report,
but you'll find musical examples in this book that suggest possibilities. I think
that he would urge you to listen for what you yourself take away from your
listening experience. Certainly, the nature and focus of "reporting" is subject
to change along with the changing nature of society and of music as a medium.
Just as the "way people talked, the way they danced, the politics of a certain
time and place" change, so too does musical expression:

> For that matter, if I were to try to re-record *Bright Size Life* right now, if such
> a thing were possible, I couldn't even simulate what the full "report" on the
> conditions were that were particular to that moment in time in 1975 allowed
> the three of us to talk about.[36]

A half century after that first recording, Metheny's perception of musician as
reporter continues to motivate him: "With now the benefit of a lot of years
myself, that [conception] seems more accurate than ever. There is something
about the immediacy of improvising that is kind of supercharged" to suit the
immediacy of awareness during a rapidly changing time.[37]

Music as a Mission

A mission-based interpretation of the musical arts may seem confusing because of Metheny's application of terminology associated with language to a
medium that defies linguistic interpretation:

> Everything that happens around you affects you as a musician. However, it
> may not happen in an overt way. For myself, I often think of the whole thing
> of being an improvising musician as being kind of like a reporter—you
> *talk* about the things that are going on inside and around you. But I think
> each person's response to the events of their time are very personal and
> unique. . . . There are ways of discussing things in the syntax of sound that
> just cannot be expressed any other way.[38]

> When I sit down to write something, or work on something in a "produc-
> tion" kind of a way, the best that I can hope for is that it might open the gate
> in some way to place where the timeliness of the "report" at hand can reveal
> itself.[39]

Note the modifiers Metheny applies in his use of the words "reporter," "report," "talk," and "discuss." Metheny modifies the word "reporter" with "kind of like," and he places quotation marks around the word "report." In brief, he is speaking metaphorically, not literally, reaching to reconcile the impulse to communicate with the inability of music to literally convey ideas. I have already noted Metheny's use of the metaphor of "telling a story."

I believe that Pat Metheny simply wants his listeners to understand that he approaches music with a sense of mission, not as a technician. He aims to organize and project coherent musical ideas that arise out of his sensitivity to the world around and within. He fully understands that his experience cannot be interpreted by listeners in a literal manner, if at all, and he recognizes that a musician "reporter" is not a journalist.

What musicians seek to convey is different in kind than what writers and speakers explain using language. Yet what moves each of these people to broadcast beyond themselves something that matters to them, each within their respective medium, may arise from the same impulse. Metheny seeks not to assign concrete, verbally *definable* meanings to music, but simply to suggest that music can convey something that each listener can perceive or interpret in their own unique way. He treats a musical phrase or melody, improvised or composed, *as if* it were a message in the sense that there is a beginning and an end, with twists and turns along the way. The craft of musicianship is the ability to guide the listener from start to finish, providing the sense that a coherent whole has unfolded. In Metheny's terminology, a "story" has been told or a "report" has been offered.

Inquiring Listening: Melodic Shape and Direction and Suggestive, Metaphorical Journey

Ballads predominate on Metheny's duet album with Charlie Haden, *Beyond the Missouri Sky (Short Stories)* (1994), and his solo acoustic guitar albums *One Quiet Night* (2003) and *What's It All About* (2011). Ballads may be found throughout Pat Metheny's repertoire and recordings.[40] The early ballads "The Bat"[41] (first recorded on *80/81* [1980]) and "Farmer's Trust"[42] (*Travels* [1984]) are the examples I've chosen for brief discussion.[43]

Each piece begins with an upward-sweeping melodic gesture, the opening notes articulating different spellings of a simple G triad. The shape of these gestures immediately grabs our attention and builds our anticipation. The independence yet interdependence of melody and harmony in what follows suggests, at once, an evocative song and something akin to a Bach chorale.

30   Chapter Two

"The Bat" is the simpler of the two pieces. Its melody begins with a brief repeated phrase. The second iteration has a slight but poignant variation, continuing longer, opening a portal to another musical statement.[44] If this opening section posed a question, its closing phrase would be a response. The periodic resting points are one of the nods at a Bach chorale. And then we begin again, rising upward in another ascending sweep, but this time, a longer narrative is abetted by successive three-note descending gestures,[45] leading us toward a logical conclusion.

The opening section of "Farmer's Trust" is longer, eight full bars. After its initial upward ascent, the melody gradually tapers downward. A second section then begins with another figure rising upward, this time spelling out a different triad (C instead of G). In due course, the melody leaps upward, landing on an A♭-major triad, which provides dramatic emphasis, before slowly descending. Just when we think the melody has concluded, we are guided into a third section, this time in a minor key. The melody gradually ascends before ending, resolving on the C chord, the same tonality where the second section began. After the entire cycle repeats, a coda reassuringly provides closure by reminding us again of the final bars.

Each of these ballads takes us on a brief journey through points of harmonic tension and resolution. A sense of drama is heightened by leaps to the next higher register. Each section suggests a slightly different mood, which we can intuit or interpret in our own personal and subjective ways. Brief passages can stand alone, seeking a musical response; or they may open a door to lead us further onward, before pausing or concluding.

These are tender ballads that hold our attention from beginning to end. The sense of flow and continuity helps the listener experience an internal logic. Each piece tugs on our emotions, evoking something unique and personal at each listening.

One of Pat Metheny's gifts is the ability to present ideas in an approachable and accessible manner. The two ballads are examples of work that conveys emotion directly and simply. Deeper levels of nuance become apparent upon repeated hearing.

CHAPTER 3

New Ideas about Musical Form

> Initially, I came to composing as a way of expanding my reach as an improviser. It was a way to set up environments for myself to hopefully get to the kinds of playing that I was hearing and that had been eluding me while playing standards or blues forms or the music of other composers.
>
> PAT METHENY[1]

The repertoire of jazz in the bebop era heavily drew upon Broadway show tunes of the 1930s. This choice reflected the usefulness of a strand of popular music of its time for the improvisational interests of small-ensemble jazz musicians. While for some this repertoire continues to provide a fruitful catalog of material, it offered an alternative lesson for others, one that has driven innovations over the subsequent decades: the idea that jazz musicians can look to the contemporary popular music of their own time, in every era, rather than to the past. Some jazz musicians of the 1950s and 1960s looked for musical ideas within rhythm and blues, and soul. Others, many of them white, looked to rock and roll.

Paul McCartney, a marquee songwriter and bassist of the British Invasion of 1960s rock, represented an unexpected compositional model for a stream of jazz musicians, including Gary Burton and Pat Metheny. McCartney remembers an inflection point in 1966 when the Beatles evolved from a teencraze pop band to a group of mature, original songwriters: "As things went on, we started to just write for ourselves, and figured that the fans would listen to our extension of what we wanted to write. So, we got into more sort of slightly different things."[2]

Modeling their vocal style on the tight harmonies of the Everly Brothers and adding a rock beat, the Beatles began to create what McCartney refers to as "funky folk":[3] their music changed from an early rock-and-roll derivative into a kind of fusion: "You do one style and juxtapose it with another."[4]

Stepwise Bass Lines

Starting in the mid-1960s, some of the best-known Beatles songs drew upon a distinctive, yet not entirely new idea, combining simple triads, familiar to folk and rock, with bass lines that move stepwise up or down. First came Paul McCartney's "Yesterday" in 1965 (released in North America in 1966)[5] and "Penny Lane" in 1966, followed in 1968 by George Harrison's "While My Guitar Gently Weeps" and John Lennon's "Dear Prudence," and finally in 1969, Harrison's "Here Comes the Sun."[6]

For McCartney, the origin of one of his key musical ideas, that the bottom and top notes of a chord might move in contrary motion—that is, in opposite directions—dates to the very start of his life as a songwriter. He recalls:

> My first one [song] was when I was like fourteen. It was just a little guitar thing. . . . I liked the idea that the bass line [G–B–C] would go up. Then I wanted this [G–F–E, the top notes of the chord] to come down. So, you get that little thing. That [contrary motion] was the big thing for me. . . . It is interesting [that] the first thing I should write has got a little contrapuntal thing going on.[7]

David Remnick speculates that McCartney may have picked up some of this idea from musical members of his family, particularly his father, "who had led Jim Mac's Jazz Band—and from his 'aunties' singing at holiday parties at home."[8]

The idea that would most stick with McCartney, reappearing a decade later in Beatles songs of the late 1960s, was stepwise bass movement. It was a common device of Baroque-era basso-continuo writing, for instance within Henry Purcell's aria "When I Am Laid in Earth" from his opera *Dido and Aeneas* (1680); and Bach's B-minor Mass, in the setting of the word "crucifixus" in the Credo movement. It surfaced again in twentieth-century popular songs as early as 1930, in Hoagy Carmichael and Stuart Gorrell's "Georgia on My

New Ideas about Musical Form   33

Figure 1 Descending bass lines from the Beatles and Keith Jarrett

Mind" (which would become a Ray Charles theme song in 1955). It would also play a structural role in several 1960s soul and Motown songs.[9]

McCartney's "Yesterday" and "Penny Lane" were followed by other songs of late-1960s rock bands that drew upon similar devices.[10] A unique feature of many of these songs is passages in which sequences of triads are, at least sometimes, juxtaposed with stepwise bass lines. This adds a sense of motion and emotional depth to diatonic harmonies.

The same year Paul McCartney composed "Penny Lane" and "Yesterday" became available in the United States, jazz vibraphonist Gary Burton began to puzzle over what new direction his own music might take. Burton and bassist Steve Swallow had left the Stan Getz Quartet, with whom they had played from 1964 to 1966. Tired of playing music modeled upon the jazz repertoire of bebop, to which Getz had returned following a run of successful Brazilian-inflected recordings, Burton and Swallow together faced their own inflection point. They turned to ideas found within the music of the Beatles and other rock groups in a manner that would subsequently influence Pat Metheny's compositional conceptions.

Burton and Swallow were certainly not alone in sensing a fork in the road. By 1966, Ornette Coleman, John Coltrane, and Cecil Taylor, among other innovative musicians, had long since moved past the cyclical chord progressions that were now frustrating musicians of Gary Burton's younger genera-

34 Chapter Three

tion. Coltrane had recently released three of his more far-reaching albums, *Ascension, Meditations,* and *Live at the Village Vanguard Again.* Taylor's *Unit Structures,* Coleman's *The Empty Foxhole* and *Chappaqua Suite,* and Roscoe Mitchell's *Sound*—the first recording by a member of the Chicago-based Association for the Advancement of Creative Musicians—were also released in 1966.

The influence of Coltrane and Coleman was also represented by an aesthetic middle ground. While 1966 was a quiet year for the Miles Davis Quintet, the end of the year netted recording sessions for Davis's band that displayed a balance between collective, intuitive co-creation with self-directed individual improvisation, following upon the previous year's *ESP.* The band's three significant albums in 1967[11] showed that harmonic ambiguity could be compatible with melodic accessibility, appealing to a broader audience.

Similarly populist in its appeal were Charles Lloyd's *Forest Flower* and *Dream Weaver,* the first two albums by Lloyd's new quartet that featured Keith Jarrett, Jack DeJohnette, and Cecil McBee. That band's international following spanned rock and jazz audiences and venues. Tracing yet another path was organist Larry Young, whose intensity and openness of solos on *Unity* in 1966 looked forward toward his role in the Tony Williams Lifetime three years later. One can find parallels here to the transition from Herbie Hancock's sextet in 1968–70 to its subsequent Mwandishi formation.[12] Some 1966 jazz albums reflected a continuation of historical forms from recent decades, including the hard-bop direction of Cannonball Adderley's *Mercy, Mercy, Mercy: Live at the Club* and Art Blakey and the Jazz Messengers' *Indestructible.*

Burton described his aesthetic quandary and proposed solutions in a 2019 interview with Rick Beato:

> My original concept—and I sat around with Steve Swallow, hours and hours of discussion and debate . . . was to use a variety of different kinds of music, classical, jazz, rock, country. . . . I felt jazz was in a straitjacket. We were all playing the same 150 standards, over and over again, in slightly different tempos and different arrangement. It was in syncopated time, and all the harmonies were based on Broadway show-tune compositions. It was beginning to feel repetitive to me. And I said, let's see what it's like to play with harmonies that don't do this ii–V–I kind of normal chord sequences we were so used to.[13]

After the breakup of the Getz band, Burton participated in a jam session where he met guitarist Larry Coryell, who "was in a rock band at the time. But he'd started out as a jazz player. He'd have this weird combination; two licks would be jazz licks, and then he'd do some kind of rock lick, back and forth."[14] A new recording by Coryell's band Free Spirits[15] documented this eclectic direction.[16] For many jazz musicians, Coryell's musical integration was controversial, as Peter Keepnews observes:

> Most established jazz musicians regarded rock with suspicion if not hostility when Mr. Coryell arrived in New York from Washington State in 1965. But a younger cohort, steeped in the Beatles as well as bebop, was beginning to explore an approach that bridged the stylistic gap. Mr. Coryell, who had grown up listening to a wide range of music, became one of the leaders of that cohort.[17]

Three years after Gary Burton's incorporation of an electric guitarist into his band, the level of contention had increased within the broader jazz world. The programming of rock bands, particularly Led Zeppelin, at the 1969 Newport Jazz Festival occasioned Ira Gitler to write in *DownBeat*, "George Wein started out as a jazz person but now seems to have become a festival producer rather than a jazz producer. . . . He claims that an exclusively jazz festival cannot [find] success unless financially subsidized."[18]

It wasn't the inclusion of music not termed "jazz" per se that was at issue, but more a concern about rock music and its audiences. Gitler condemned the programming of Sly and the Family Stone (although the group might be better described as a funk band), while Dan Morgenstern, writing in the same *DownBeat* issue, lauded funk star James Brown's performance:

> The next afternoon, in brilliant sunshine, an orderly, enthusiastic crowd of some 8,000 enjoyed the James Brown show. This was the most professional presentation of the festival. . . . To bring James Brown to Newport was a bright idea. . . . But the rock experiment was a resounding failure. George Wein should have had enough faith in his audience (an audience he himself has built) to leave the currently fashionable type to the many "pop" and rock festivals throughout the country, held in areas that have either free access or proper security.[19]

Burton entered the fray slightly earlier, at the pivotal point in 1966 when rock bands like the Beatles were entering the commercial mainstream. The timing might have been unintentionally beneficial for Gary Burton, who initially selected a repertoire composed by musicians like Coryell, bassist Steve

36   Chapter Three

Swallow, and himself that reflected some features these composers observed in rock music. He notes:

> The famous [statement that] there are only three chords in a rock song was somewhat true. But mostly there were unexpected combinations. I would listen to a Beatles song and thought I would never go to that chord. At first it almost sounded wrong to me. By the time I'd heard it a little bit, and I wondered "Who thought that up?" and I realized they didn't come from show music. They were making it up themselves by ear, so that's what we started doing. We started to write songs using these newer kinds of harmonies.[20]

Burton's repertoire of the early to mid-1970s added works reflecting related ideas—triads and stepwise bass lines rather than the more complex chords of the bebop repertoire—by a raft of composers, including Keith Jarrett, Chick Corea (prior to his more vamp-oriented Return to Forever band), and Carla Bley. Mike Gibbs was also a major contributing composer. Soon, a young guitarist, Pat Metheny, would join the band and add contribute compositions[21] to the Burton repertoire.

In 1974, Metheny moved to Boston, where Burton had offered him a teaching job at the Berklee School of Music.[22] Many of Metheny's students were older than he was at just nineteen. Among them was Mike Stern, who would play with Miles Davis less than a decade later. As Metheny recalls, "Teaching [at Berklee] was always interesting and challenging for me and the level of the students that I had was quite high."[23]

In Boston, Metheny began to play the local jazz scene, sometimes joined by Miami cohorts Jaco Pastorius and Danny Gottlieb, as well as Bob Moses. He also co-led a quartet with vibraphonist Dave Samuels. Sensing Metheny's promise, Burton welcomed Metheny into his band, joining Mick Goodrick as a second electric guitarist. Metheny played a Guild Starfire[24] twelve-string electric to contrast with Goodrick's six-string sound. Burton's band appealed to Metheny as "a group that was trying to push the limits of jazz and that was really of interest to me." It was also essentially the only one to treat the guitar as more than peripheral.[25] Beginning in 1967, Burton's bands most often included an electric guitarist.[26] After Metheny joined, the band recorded Ring[27] in 1974, followed by Dreams So Real: Music of Carla Bley[28] in 1975, and finally Passengers[29] in 1977.

In addition to his teaching and tours with Gary Burton, Metheny was active composing and continuing to perform around Boston:

New Ideas about Musical Form   37

A lot of the music that became *Bright Size Life* was written during that period, not just for the trio [with Pastorius and Gottlieb] but also for various ensembles and lesson plans. . . . Mick Goodrick and I used to do a lot of duet gigs and sometimes trio gigs with Steve Swallow too (who was also teaching at Berklee then). I also played quite a bit with some other great musicians who were living around town at that time like Dave Samuels and Gary Chaffee. I also did things in New York with people like Paul Bley and did the odd week at the Jazz Workshop when I could as a sideman with people like Hubert Laws. All of that plus teaching a full load kept me pretty busy.[30]

Metheny recalls the three years he spent with Burton's band as a tremendously developmental "trial by fire":[31]

Gary was and continues to be a very effective band leader who was able to articulate in very specifically terms what he wanted and what I was unable to deliver at that point, and what I needed to work on so I could deliver . . . [for instance,] to develop a solo on a narrative level over time . . . telling long narrative stories. . . . But it was hard. Gary was one of the toughest leaders possible. . . . I was very lucky to have someone at that level be willing to spend time with me.[32]

Burton, an expert in the art of applying music theory into soloing practice, became a mentor to Metheny as a player and future bandleader. Metheny recalls this period as

massively important period for me . . . even though I had played with some great players and been in other high-level situations, this was a whole other thing, this was international level, world class improvising musicians. . . . It was during that time that my sound and approach to the guitar, "my thing," came about.[33]

Pat Metheny was now at the point of increased clarity about his musical goals. Translating these new ideas into practice meant forming a band based upon a new model, and this became Metheny's new mission:

At that time, let's say when I was really starting to write my own stuff and having my first band with Jaco [1974], I was into the idea of playing with a lot of dynamics within phrases, having a looser kind of rhythm section

38 Chapter Three

approach as opposed to backbeats and that sort of thing. And the idea of having a narrative, expositional approach to improvising.[34]

Mervyn Cooke's *Pat Metheny: The ECM Years, 1975–1984*[35] provides useful detail and commentary about Metheny's compositions of this period, including several included on Gary Burton's *Passengers* (1977), Burton's third recording with Metheny.[36] As Metheny concludes about that time: "There was a sense of a possibility then that was very unique."[37]

What Burton and subsequently Metheny sought also differed from the methodology of Burton's generational peers starting in 1969. These included Metheny's elders John McLaughlin, Tony Williams, and Miles Davis and his electric band, as represented by *Bitches Brew* (1970) and *On the Corner* (1972), and, beginning in 1973, Chick Corea and Herbie Hancock during his Headhunters period.[38] These bands at their height produced music of great drama, pairing rapid, high-volume guitars processed with distortion—particularly in the hands of McLaughlin—with high-intensity drumming by the likes of Tony Williams and Billy Cobham. Emblematic is Mahavishnu Orchestra's *The Inner Mounting Flame* (1971).[39]

These ensembles showed that improvisatory music in the context of contemporaneous funk and the driving rhythms of rock and rhythm and blues could also provide a vehicle for musicians to construct solos with arcs across extended durations. Two of the bands provided useful models for Metheny's later development: the constant invention of Herbie Hancock's Mwandishi Sextet (which Metheny saw perform twice in Kansas City when he was a teenager) and the rich orchestration of Joe Zawinul and Wayne Shorter's Weather Report.[40] But this was not a model that interested Metheny:

> There were a lot of vamps [repeated minimal chordal or rhythmic patterns] happening in the world back in those days. I never liked that a one- or a two-chord vamp could stand as a destination for improvising when there usually were plenty of other more interesting ways to get to a place where the material could evolve in ways that went beyond the usual "playing on the form" thing that was the standard in most settings. *Midwestern Nights Dream* is an early example of that.[41]

Many of the Corea, Jarrett, and Metheny compositions included in Burton's repertoire combined sequences of triads (and/or seventh chords) in some sections, and elsewhere, sequences of ii–V–I and other more complex chord changes. Carla Bley's tunes are more difficult to categorize but often

New Ideas about Musical Form   39

follow a simpler harmonic model.[42] These were unusual devices for jazz musicians. As Pat Metheny has pointed out, "many jazz guys don't know how to play on very simple triads, without using upper extensions and tension notes."[43] The balance of the Burton band's repertoire was composed by long-time Gary Burton associate Michael Gibbs.

Slash Chords

A Metheny composition from before his time with Gary Burton, "April Joy," provides a hint that Metheny was already on a track that would be further sparked by the Burton repertoire. "April Joy" was composed while Metheny was a senior in high school, for a 1972 Kansas City Jazz Festival gig with the Pete Eye Trio. He had agreed to perform with the locally high-profile but musically conservative Eye on the condition that he could also front his own band at the festival:

> My reasons for writing that tune were that I could tell Pete to stick with the common tones of D, E, and A across the tune for the comping, and I knew that I could play with him at least on that one tune in a more personal way. It was the first indication that I might be able to get to the thing that was starting to emerge in that zone that I was hearing; somewhere in between Wayne Shorter and Dolly Parton.... The first rehearsal ... was like this door swung open where even under the kind of limited sets of options that came with Pete's thing, there was a glimmer of infinity there.... I would still point to that KC Jazz Festival gig as the pivotal moment, well before the Gary Burton thing or anything that followed.[44]

The surprising, hyphenated reference to Shorter and Parton implies that Metheny sought to balance expressive tunefulness and emotional directness with Shorter's harmonies. Shorter's approach offered wide latitude for an inventive melodic improviser within a jazz language.

Among the musical devices employed by Shorter are slash chords, a configuration that provides tension and emotional ambiguity, pairing a sense of solidity and sureness with instability, a yearning for harmonic resolution. These can include (1) chords that in bebop traditions might be spelled as eleventh chords,[45] but instead, the upper notes aligned with the root in the bass are configured as a major triad or seventh chord, and the chord notated as if the root were a whole step higher than the triad—for example, C/D or E♭/F; (2) an inversion of a dominant seventh chord with the seventh placed at the bottom, and thus the

40   Chapter Three

bass note a whole step lower than the chord root—for example, C/B♭; and (3) a pedal tone in the bass juxtaposed with a series of chords in which one or two notes change over the course of a sequence, subtly shifting the harmonies.

In Shorter's composition "Paraphernalia,"[46] recorded by the Miles Davis Quintet in 1967, a D pedal tone holds fast during the entirety of the opening section, upon which small handful of slash chords add intrigue. Yet in the second section, during the final nine bars—exemplifying the third type of slash chord listed above—a steadily moving series of (mostly) slash chords rests upon a sequence of two pedal points, B♭ and D♭ (or its enharmonic spelling of C♯),[47] before returning to the beginning of the work on the opening D pedal. Here are the chords of the final nine measures:

B♭ pedal: B♭m^{11}–G^6/B♭–G♭$^{maj7(♯11)}$/B♭
D♭ pedal: C/D♭–B/C♯–Gm/C♯–C♯m^7–B♭^{6}/C♯

These slash chord juxtapositions serve two seemingly conflicting goals: the pedal tones suggest a feeling of stasis, while the subtly and steadily changing chords juxtaposed upon them suggest rapid motion, pressing the composition to its conclusion where it cycles back to the beginning. Shorter's technique—as it is interpreted by Herbie Hancock on piano—resists the gravitational pull of the tonic, as would occur in conventional harmony—and thus our perception of the harmonic context of each bass note continually changes. This creates tension that is only resolved with a return to the starting D pedal[48] in this circular form. Each successive instrumentalist responds in a personal way to how they perceive the rate of harmonic change, affording a distinct flavor to each solo. The improvisational pathway is quite malleable.

It is in "April Joy"[49] that Pat Metheny's work begins to use slash chord formations. This piece is a simple composition in two sections, with melodies that draw upon a pentatonic scale and harmony consisting of minimal chord structures. It is an early example of a Metheny tune that facilitated "a personal way" to improvise. His recorded solo will be discussed in chapter 5.

The opening section toggles harmonically between B♭^{maj7} and Am^7/D chords,[50] pausing on an A/B♭ chord, which heightens the tension, and eventually finding resolution in D major. Slash chords are used in several places, with D, B♭, and C pedal tones, and at times, the bass toggles between two adjacent notes. Thus "April Joy" combines two devices that would become important compositional organizing principles for Metheny: stepwise bass lines juxtaposed with simple chords, and passages using slash chords. Gary Burton's repertoire, with which Pat Metheny was already familiar before joining his band, aligned with these ideas, providing a bouncing board for Metheny's further musical development.

Juxtaposition of Triads with Stepwise Bass Movement

What Gary Burton, Steve Swallow, and the others drew from Beatles songs was more than ideas about chord progressions. These composers recognized that chords could be juxtaposed with the steady, stepwise movement in the bass also found in that repertoire. Harmonic movement could, consequently, be perceived as a subtle shift in shading rather than as dramatic chord-to-chord changes with the sense of inevitability presented by ii–V–I progressions.

Stepwise movement in the bass *wasn't* foreign to jazz, although its combination with triads and seventh chords was something new. Pianist Bill Evans employed chromatically descending bass lines, first in his 1958 recording of Sonny Rollins's "Oleo" on *Everybody Digs Bill Evans*[51] and again in "Blue in Green," which appears on the Miles Davis album *Kind of Blue* (1959). Of great interest to jazz players was Dizzy Gillespie's "Con Alma" (1954),[52] recorded in the late 1950s and 1960s by Sonny Rollins, Oscar Peterson, Cedar Walton, Wes Montgomery, Stan Getz, and numerous others. The innovation in the repertoire of the Gary Burton band was not stepwise bass lines but their juxtaposition with simple triads or seventh chords.

"Con Alma" opens with a sequence of chords with chromatically descending roots, E^{maj7}–$G\sharp^7/D\sharp$–$C\sharp m^7$–B^{13}–$B\flat^7$, leading into a cadence. A second sequence then begins a minor third lower, on D♭, followed by a more extended cycle of chords that leads back to the opening. From the perspective of diatonic harmony, and of great interest to improvisers, "Con Alma" continually changes key centers. The bass-line motion is a novel feature, while the constant ii–V–I chord changes are a preview of Coltrane's steady flow of cadences in "Giant Steps" (1959), which also includes a stepwise bass line during the presentation of the tune but not in the improvisational section.

Figure 2 "Con Alma" opening section bass line

42   Chapter Three

While Burton seems to *have been* interested in navigating complex harmonies, and these remain a strong feature within this tune, Burton and his bassist Steve Swallow had an eye toward finding an alternative organizational device within musical form, such as using stepwise bass lines juxtaposed with simple triads and seventh chords.

The first composition within Burton's repertoire to decisively build upon these new ideas is Steve Swallow's "Falling Grace,"[53] from Burton's 1967 trio album *The Time Machine*.[54] On one hand, the composition *could* be viewed as a chain of variants and fragments of ii–V–I progressions. But if you focus on the sequences of stepwise bass lines, Swallow's core idea comes to light. The first sequence, between bars 5 and 8, chromatically descends in the bass[55] from A♭ to G to F♯ to F♮ to E♮. The second, between bars 15 and 18, ascends from C♮ to C♯ to D♮ to E♭. Each brief chord sequence is followed with a pair of ii–V–I chord progressions, a cadence.

The final two chords of the first of two endings of "Falling Grace" reveal the circular nature of its form; the B♭^{maj7}–E♭^{maj7} chord pair leads back either to the A♭^{maj7} opening chord for repetitions of the tune or to the end of the composition, A♭^{maj7} resolving to D♭^{maj7}.[56] This circularity, the lack of resolution until the end of the form, and the stepwise bass lines are characteristics shared with "Blue in Green."[57] Steve Swallow points out that this was quite intentional:

> Miles Davis' "Blue in Green," which appeared on his album "Kind of Blue" was important to me when I was beginning to write. I admired how it circled around; it's so succinct, only ten bars long. It was on my mind when I was writing "Falling Grace," which is one of my most frequently played compositions and also one of the earliest (the second). I was living in George Russell's apartment, and it was written on his piano. Each of the sections of "Falling Grace" is unbalanced and asymmetrical. There is ambiguity at all the junction points, the double bar lines smudged so as to keep it flowing around. When you first play on forms of this sort it's kind of dizzying. If you lose your place, it's hard to jump back on. But once you've assimilated these forms, you're free from the sense of returning to the same place every twenty-five seconds. It keeps itself new.[58]

Pat Metheny describes Swallow's "Falling Grace" as having (compositionally) "really defined what I was looking for."[59] He found the new harmonic conception championed by Gary Burton's band to be of great personal interest. Aspects of it—the simpler chords—were culturally familiar from his musical upbringing in a small Missouri town, where he remembers, "The guys [guitarists] at the barbershop in my hometown, my neighbor with his hootenannies, all those guys were playing triads. I always felt like, why can't that be part of the language? The guitar is great at those kinds of sounds."[60] He concluded, while playing in the Burton band, that "some really strongly triadic based songs was something that I wanted to really address."[61] He later expounded:

> I liked the idea of having things that were independent of the form itself that maybe only happened one time (the tag to "Missouri Uncompromised"), and forms that were challenging beyond the normal kinds of tunes—"Unquity Road" which has some unlikely resolutions and an odd 4/4 bar in the middle of the blowing that really has to be dealt with.[62]

Other compositions within Gary Burton's repertoire in which sections are grounded in stepwise bass lines include Keith Jarrett's "Coral" and "Fortune Smiles" (Figure 1, p. 33) and Chick Corea's "Crystal Silence" and "Desert Air." Two of Metheny's early compositions included in Burton's repertoire that follow this pattern include "Midwestern Night's Dream" and "Sirabhorn" (in its second section, the bass line descends A–G–F♯–F♮). Both of these compositions appear on Metheny's first album, *Bright Size Life* (1976). Neither was recorded by Gary Burton's band.[63]

Stepwise bass lines continued to provide Pat Metheny, throughout his subsequent career, with an effective strategy to achieve compositional goal of maintaining a long arc during the melody and solos, particularly in ballads. Extended stepwise bass lines—initially ascending and then descending—are a major feature of "Always and Forever" and "Antonia" (each from *Secret Story*, 1992). Most often, these sequences resolve in a cadence.[64] As Metheny

Figure 3 Excerpts of bass lines in "Antonia" and "The Bat"

Figure 4 Directionality of Metheny's melodic contours and bass line in his solo to "Always and Forever"

constructs his acoustic guitar solo on the recorded version of "Always and Forever," he attends to two structural aspects of the composition's form: the harmonic cycle and the direction of the stepwise bass lines.

Rather than focusing on an analysis of how Metheny's lines in "Always and Forever" address the harmonies in a very direct way (something that will be apparent to musician listeners), I want to discuss the bass-line movement, remembering that such movement represents an important aspect of Pat Metheny's core compositional concepts. I'll then briefly look at the motifs as they unfold. (We will return to this solo in chapter 4 from the perspective of Metheny's use of motifs.)

In response to the first ascending bass line in "Always and Forever," Metheny's melodic line initially descends, in contrary motion to the bass, but then levels off before rapidly ascending. When the bass line descends, the pitches in Metheny's melody remain relatively level, zigzagging before ultimately slightly descending. Following the notated passage, there is a second, briefer descending bass line. Here, Metheny's improvised melody again remains relatively level in pitch, ascending only at the end.

When the initial bass pattern repeats, Metheny addresses the initial ascending bass line by crafting a melody that for a time ascends but then rapidly descends, only to ascend again and level off. Next, when the bass line descends, Metheny's line moves in the same direction and then zigzags, ascending slightly before again remaining level.

What is most striking about this solo is its melodic beauty and elegant construction, so you may fairly ask "What is the significance of bass line movement?" The direction of Metheny's melodic line, particularly at subtle points of sustaining and releasing tension, is at least in part a function of parallel or contrary motion.

At the beginning of the initial ascending bass line, it is Metheny's descending motion, pressing against the rising bass line, that gives energy to his first phrase. The conclusion of this melody, which parallels the direction of the bass line, resolves the tension. As the bass line descends, Metheny's melody remains relatively level, providing a pause in the tension/resolution dynamics. During the repetition of the first bass descent-ascent cycle, Metheny begins by paralleling the bass motion, with one brief exception, a swift descent. But next, as the bass line descends, Metheny's zigzag motion leads to an ascending melodic line. The contrary motion helps build tension, which is resolved in a cadence.

Metheny's coordination of harmony, melodic direction, and—to be discussed in chapter 4—motivic shape and organization, all with an ear toward rhythm and attuned to shaping each individual solo, provide a useful guide to how to listen closely to Metheny's solos. I believe that this is a more useful approach to Metheny as soloist than the consideration of muscle memory,

Figure 5 Descending bass lines in five Metheny compositions

musical habits, or "finger positions and navigational routes" that are noted by some scholars (also discussed in the next chapter); an internalized somatic vocabulary might have some degree of reliance when an improvisation is moving at a lightning-fast clip.

Metheny's compositions have continued over the years to make use of stepwise bass lines, slash chords, and juxtapositions of triads (or seventh chords) with stepwise bass lines. This combination represents a distinct compositional strategy, one that has provided, in Metheny's own words, "a way of expanding my reach as an improviser."[65]

CHAPTER 4

Motif and Improvisation

Gary Burton and Steve Swallow's new ideas about musical form, juxtaposing simple triadic harmonies, stepwise bass lines, and melody, represented a distinctly original compositional path. In the context of the Burton band, Pat Metheny began to extensively compose, actively experimenting with music that served his interest as an improvising guitarist. He recalls:

> Initially, I came to composing as a way of expanding my reach as an improviser. It was a way to set up environments for myself to hopefully get to the kinds of playing that I was hearing and that had been eluding me while playing standards or blues forms or the music of other composers.[1]

In particular, stepwise bass lines were valuable to Metheny because they allowed him to structure his solo playing around motivic material, which he could combine and vary as he shaped solos. It is this motivic idea that helped shape his development as a soloist, and the concept remains important in his more recent work.

Metheny was, of course, not the first to use motifs as an organizational principle. John Coltrane mined brief motifs to craft extensive improvisations,[2] and motivic development was a central idea for Beethoven, for example, in his development of the famous opening motif movement of his Fifth Symphony. A significant model for Metheny was Wes Montgomery's solo on "If You Could See Me Now" from Montgomery's live recording with the Wynton Kelly Trio, *Smokin' at the Half Note* (1965).[3]

Wes Montgomery

Metheny describes Montgomery's solo as having

> defined so many things for me. Rhythm section playing, melodic playing, Wes's solo on "If You Could See Now" is the greatest guitar solo I have ever heard. That's the one. It is like Coleman Hawkins' solo on "Body and Soul" or some of the other great solos to me. That solo is the ideal, perfect improvised statement that any guitarist has ever made.[4]

The most unmistakable aspects of this Montgomery solo are the five distinctive motifs that appear and return. Most of them are fundamentally melodic (rather than rhythmic or textural). These melodic motifs and variants gain emotional poignancy through repetition at different points in the chord progression, with an effect parallel to changing the color of a room, or the lighting in a movie set with the same object in view.

I will describe a sampling of the motifs in the early section of the solo. I refer to each of these melodic fragments as a "motif" because they continually reappear in some form throughout the solo. The distinctiveness of such motifs and their subsequent reappearance and variation is characteristic of Montgomery's melodic invention.

As I hear it, the ascending figure (Motif A) that opens the solo at 2:57 of "If You Could See Me Now" is so striking that it is akin to the dramatic first appearance on stage of a major character in a show. This first phrase is followed immediately by an ornate variation of that theme, this time in triplets. We soon meet a second character, in the form of another memorable melody (Motif B, at 3:14). One feature that distinguishes Motif B from Motif A is its landing on an accented beat, the downbeat emphasized by its grace note introduction. This melodic statement is presented with authority, and it injects

Figure 6 Motifs in Wes Montgomery solo on "If You Could See Me Now"

new rhythmic energy to the solo. Motif A briefly reasserts itself as a bridge to new variants of Motif B, when these appear, at 3:21.

Montgomery next invokes the language of the blues by alternating between flatted and non-flatted versions of the same note within a passage. This passage opens with a syncopated, inverted variant of Motif A (Motif C, at 3:36). The ambiguity between whether this section is in a major or minor key is a source of emotional depth. The question is resolved by a satisfying harmonic resolution on A♭ major at the end of the next passage, at 3:42. This is Motif D, a down-up figure-eight-shaped phrase. Looking ahead, a similar figuration will occur two measures before the conclusion of the solo. Chromatically weaving lines spin off from the various motifs.

This leads to the most striking melodic statement of Montgomery's solo, at 4:06. This motif (Motif E), a series of slowly and steadily repeated Gs, is a mark of the paradoxical simplicity of Montgomery's musical ideas. The repeated notes, placed within the environment of a series of rapid-note figures, provide a remarkable emotional depth to this passage. The high point arrives as the passage concludes with a leap up to F. Even if stated in isolation, the phrase would be interesting, although it might lack the emotive power the context provides.

During the latter portion of the solo, Montgomery shifts from single notes to octaves. Here, he draws upon a previously introduced triplet theme, but now, articulated in octaves, the solo builds in intensity that continues for the duration of the solo.

In this solo, Wes Montgomery displays his gift for melodic invention by constantly introducing new ideas that subsequently morph into new shapes. Each time, the listener can experience, all at once, a combination of familiarity and freshness. By continually injecting versions of similar melodic phrases at different points in the chord progression, Montgomery draws out new harmonic implications. He also provides connective tissue between his melodic ideas by interweaving each thematic statement with rapidly moving phrases. Overall, Montgomery creates a richly woven fabric, drawing upon a limited store of motivic material. He builds, sustains, and releases tension by invoking the blues in his tonality and by shifting from single notes to octaves. These devices captivate the attention of the listener not only in the moment but also from one passage to the next and from the beginning of the solo to its conclusion.

Ornette Coleman

Another important model for Pat Metheny as motivic improviser is Ornette Coleman. Coleman's continuously unfolding free-ranging solos and compositions, often built upon brief motifs, has been described by Paul Bley as "an A to Z form . . . in which repetition was anathema."[5] Metheny's set lists have often included music by Coleman, organized in open forms in the model of—and in 1985, *with*—Coleman.

The iconic ballad "Lonely Woman"[6] provides a brief useful example of Ornette Coleman's approach. The composition consists of a series of six-to-eight-note phrases, many of them the length of a breath. Each phrase responds to the one before it. Following two statements of the melody, Coleman's solo opens with a phrase flowing directly from the composed theme. Soon, he expands upon this opening phrase, embedding it within a longer sequence of notes, a two-note preface, and a half-step upturn conclusion.

Coleman briefly pauses, something he does constantly within this solo. It is as if he were making a verbal declaration, pausing, and then moving on to his next statement. He then presents a variant of the second phrase of "Lonely Woman." Pausing yet again, Coleman begins anew on a slightly higher pitch, lengthening the notes to shape a phrase longer than its predecessors. Phrase by phrase, Coleman reflects upon and then extends or varies the previous phrase. He turns the intervals from his motif upside down and inside out, milking what melodic invention he can find within it. Having done so, he pauses and moves on to the next phrase. Gradually but steadily, Coleman edges further away from his starting point in the composition, on to new motivic material. Ekkehard Jost calls this kind of construction a "chain of motivic associations."[7]

Metheny substituted Coleman's ephemeral approach to musical material—brief motifs and continuous melodic invention—with a different goal: to build from a small collection of motifs and variants a single organic whole across a long arc. Metheny's musical motto of "tell a story" is reflective of this approach. As we saw in chapter 2, this is a metaphor familiar to jazz musicians. Well suited to this endeavor are forms that continuously unfold, delaying full resolution, over extended periods of time. This is because they contain fewer built-in structural points of resolution, such as cadences, than standard bebop song forms.

Pat Metheny, Developing an Approach as an Improviser

Pat Metheny began to employ a tool kit of devices for improvisational motivic development that were well suited to stepwise bass-line movement. Among these are variation, inversion, expansion/contraction, and using one motif to complete a phrase begun with another motif. Metheny found that tension could be built through the interplay of melody and a stepwise ascending or descending bass line. Juxtapositions between that bass line and simple chords could create subtle shifts in harmonic flavor and emotion. With the "gravitation pull" of the cadence weakened, freer melodic options opened. The arc of a stepwise bass line could support a solo that had a particularly extended narrative arc. (I discussed stepwise bass lines in chapter 3.)

I seek here to discuss Pat Metheny's improvisations from the perspective of motivic organization in part to provide a useful tool to guide more attentive listening. Where there is simple melody, little assistance is required, but when the music grows in complexity or a narrative arc is lengthy, tracking motifs as they repeat in myriad variations helps to identify a source of continuity. With multiple listenings, this aspect of the "glue" that sustains the forward movement of musical line can emerge with greater clarity. With this clarity, one can sit back and listen actively but with less attention to the details as the solo lines unfold.

Metheny's solo on Steve Swallow's "Falling Grace" during a 1976 concert with Gary Burton provides an early example of his motivic improvisations.[8] It is important to consider Metheny's early motivic construction in the context of this landmark composition. The solo is built using two main motifs plus variants of those motifs. Motif A is a five-note descending line. Metheny transposes it and flips it upside down so that it ascends. At times, he extends

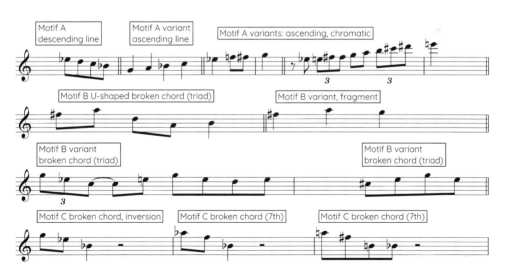

Figure 7 Guide to motifs within Metheny's solo on "Falling Grace"

Figure 8 Excerpt from Metheny's solo in "Falling Grace," highlighting his use of motifs

the resulting phrase by continuing it further upward. Other variants are more chromatic or reflect alterations of its pace. Small fragments drawn from the melodic line could be assembled into a new phrase.

Motif B is tuneful, its notes drawn from a major chord with the fifth in the root: F♯ up to A, down to D and then A, and finally resolving a step upward to B. There are variants of Motif B, constructed from major and minor triads, also played note by note. Each of the two motifs is subject to repetition and often transposed up or down a half step. The two motifs and their variants are assembled into one coherent, continuous narrative line, with pauses between passages. The improvised line tracks the harmonic changes while engaging with the descending bass line in a kind of counterpoint.

This solo, two years into Pat Metheny's tenure with Burton, and around the same time he was engaged in his own first recording, already displays many of the hallmarks of the mature Metheny's approach to improvisation. The solo displays clarity of design, a balance between his organization of motifs and thoughtful attention to the harmonic form. The combination of the two serves his artistic conception. Metheny's motifs are selected for their potential to function as flexible material to build imaginative melodic lines, and with them, to construct a unifying narrative arc that unfolds from beginning to end.

Pat Metheny's experience of constant touring during the mid-1970s, with Gary Burton and others, spurred his development of concrete ideas about improvisation. The "Falling Grace" solo documents his exploration of how motivic construction could provide improvisational cohesion and direction. What emerged were clear ideas about how the structure of compositions could foster an environment within which those improvisation skills could blossom.

The recorded version of "April Joy" on *Pat Metheny Group* (1978), Metheny's early composition discussed in chapter 2, begins with a quiet electric guitar introduction. After the melodic theme is stated, Metheny's solo section tracks the form of the second section: pentatonic, tuneful, and closely related to the melody.[9]

Metheny constructs his solo from the three motifs: a stepwise triplet figure (Motif A), notes drawn from simple triads (Motif B), and a U-shaped four-note scalar figure (Motif C), played sometimes in eighth notes and other times in sixteenths. Metheny finds substantial improvisational freedom in the limited points of tension, with resolution delayed until the end of each section. Except for the final three measures of the first round of the solo, the motifs are rarely adjusted to the minimal harmonic structure, where the alignment coincides with the closing cadence, building and resolving tension (and joining two asymmetrical and chromatic arpeggios). The balance of the solo

Chapter Four

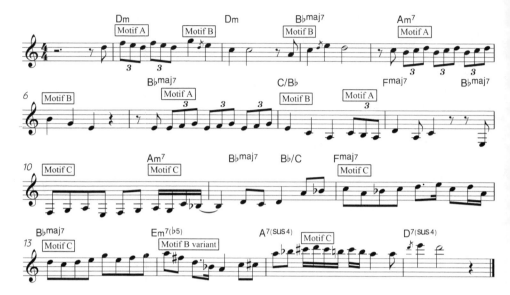

Figure 9 Opening segment of Metheny's solo on "April Joy," from *Pat Metheny Group* (1978)

continues to draw upon a pentatonic scale and incorporates rapidly repeated descending broken chords—a figure that had become and would remain part of Metheny's vocabulary.

A third example of Pat Metheny's many motif-informed improvisations can be found on a trio performance of "The Bat"[10] recorded in 2000. The composition was first recorded in a moving rendition, during a highly productive period, on *80/81* (1980),[11] and it reappears in brief form as "The Bat, Part II" on the premiere album of the revamped Pat Metheny Group, *Offramp* (1982).

The melody, simple and elegant, is akin to a D-major chorale. The form is built upon stepwise descending bass lines. This composition, over many years, has proved to be a strong vehicle for improvisation. The chromaticism of the stepwise bass line and the harmonic movement built upon it, leading to a ii–V–I chord cadence, provides substantial solo space for Metheny to navigate.

Metheny's solo in the live recorded version on *Trio → Live*[12] begins during the final two bars of the form of the composition, effectively utilized as a jumping-off point. Metheny immediately introduces the first of the main motifs. He constructs his solo with this minimal material, pregnant with possibilities, but with little or no quotation from the composed melody.[13]

Here, Metheny focuses more on interweaving motifs than tracking the chords, although he addresses the chord changes. Often, a function of the

Figure 10 Metheny's use of three motifs in his solo on "The Bat" from *Trio/Live*

harmonies during the solo is to provide an evolving harmonic context for the motifs. With these tools, Metheny builds a solo of emotional depth. Serpentine chromatic lines interconnect the motifs.

The first motif is introduced at the beginning of the solo. This motif, as it appears across the solo, is often four to seven notes long, generally starting with an ascending three-note scale fragment. Motif A returns, sometimes inverted, or in variant or fragmentary form, as notated in Figure 10, in bars 2, 3, 4, 6, 9, 13, 26, 31, and 47.[14] In this listener's subjective experience, the motif conveys hopefulness and possibility.

The second motif is more complex. It often includes a melodic leap, sometimes across registers, followed by a descending half step. Often, this motif floats over ii–V–I cadences. When it does, the half steps land on a target note emphasizing the resolution of the harmony. This heightens the emotional charge of the passage.[15] The most affecting portions of the solo occur during the melodic leaps within Motif B—for instance, in bar 2, with the leaps from E♭ down to D, and F♯ down to A♮[16]—and in their stepwise resolution—for instance in bars 6–7, where the melody resolves downward after an upward leap. Motif C consists of repeated notes.

For one, brief final example, let's return to "Always and Forever," discussed in chapter 3, with respect to the relationship between bass movement and directionality of the solo line. Here we turn to Metheny's motivic approach to the same solo. Once again, Metheny constructs a solo drawing upon a small collection of the three motifs noted in Figure 11 and Figure 12 as they appear during the opening segment of the solo. Each one is treated freely and with variation in speed and direction.

A close listening or reading of the transcription shows the constant presence of each of these motifs. They do not define the nature of the solo, nor are they developed in a linear fashion, but they provide its basic musical materials and thus serve as a source of continuity.

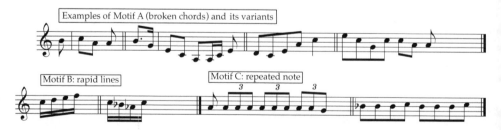

Figure 11 Guide to the motifs within Metheny's solo on "Always and Forever"

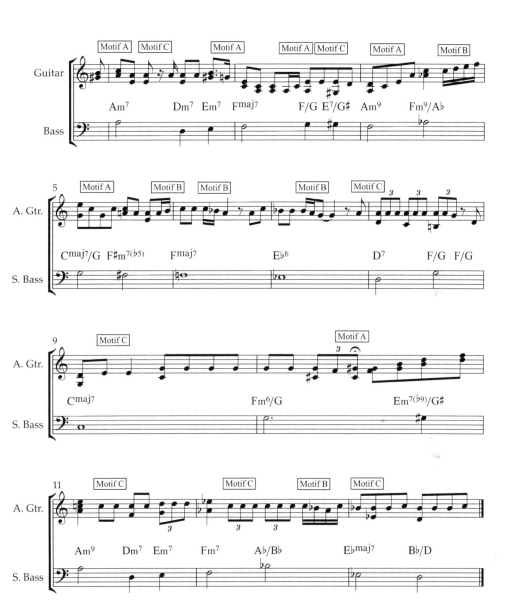

Figure 12 Opening section of Metheny's solo on "Always and Forever" highlighting core motifs

58   Chapter Four

This sampling of Metheny guitar solos, spanning "April Joy" (1978), "Always and Forever" (1992), and "The Bat" (2000), demonstrates the centrality of motivic structures in his work. An additional example, "America Undefined" (2020) will be discussed in chapter 9. Motivic improvisation has consistently offered Metheny a source of continuity and structure for his creative improvisational imagination, and it has held a substantive place in his improvisational work for decades. We'll build on this discussion in the context of forms built upon stepwise bass lines, triads, and slash chords in appendix 2 (*"The Way Up"*).

Gunther Schuller Analysis of Sonny Rollins as Counterexample

Prompted by an influential 1958 essay by Gunther Schuller,[17] concepts of motivic improvisation became associated with tenor saxophonist Sonny Rollins. Schuller bemoaned a practice among jazz of musicians of "running the changes," that is, playing up and down scales and arpeggios associated with the chord cycles.[18] The corrective to what Schuller called a "relative failure" of these "less inspired" solos was Sonny Rollins's 1956 solo on "Blue 7,"[19] which Schuller describes as the systematic development of a single main theme displaying "a unifying force," "cohesiveness and direction." I view Ornette Coleman, John Coltrane, and Wes Montgomery as more important reference points for Pat Metheny, yet Schuller's analysis and the debate it occasioned requires mention because it has been a focal point for scholarly discussion about improvisation built using motifs.

Schuller's analysis has been heavily criticized by subsequent scholars. Robert Walser describes it as "partial and forced,"[20] its exclusive focus on formal structure ignoring the cultural context of the music and its historical setting.[21] For Ingrid Monson, Schuller portrayed jazz improvisers as "less inspired" if their musical values did not match the criteria set by a European analytical perspective.[22] Benjamin Givan criticizes Schuller's reliance upon his analysis of a misread single example.[23] Ted Gioia tempers his disagreement with Schuller by contextualizing it in light of Rollins's less systematic contemporaries.[24]

Pat Metheny's motivic approach would be no more likely to meet Schuller's criteria for being "inspired" than that of any other improviser. Why should it? Metheny employs motifs in an intuitive, nonsystematic manner, drawing upon two or three phrases as material to organically shape a solo. The goal is not developmental exposition of those motifs in a manner akin to Beethoven or some of the *composed* portions of *The Way Up*. Rather, the logic of Metheny's solos may be found in an unfolding narrative arc that relies on building and releasing tension, sustaining melodic interest. Structure may be found in Metheny's flexible relationship to the stepwise bass lines and chordal forms that he prefers compositionally. Ultimately, if one were to attempt to assess Metheny's solos, the most useful criteria would not be analytic but would measure whether a solo is perceived as compelling by listeners and how well it adds value to the overall composition. Pat Metheny as an improviser is an expressive musician, not a structural engineer, and this is key to his success.

As a young player, Metheny was in fact fascinated by the intensity and depth of Rollins's sound and approach. Were there any young jazz musicians coming of age in the late 1960s who were not similarly inspired by Sonny Rollins? For Pat Metheny, Rollins was compelling because of his personal sound, his expressivity, and his improvisational gifts. Metheny's performances with Rollins in 1983 and 1986[25] point to his continued interest in the saxophonist. But after all is said and done, the scholarly discussion of Gunther Schuller's mythic Sonny Rollins challenges an exclusively structural analysis of jazz performance while offering little to inform a consideration of Pat Metheny.

Improvisation and Composition as Interrelated Activities

However intently Metheny may develop his motifs as he shapes a solo, he has always striven for improvisational spontaneity. Yet as he points out, fully spontaneous invention is an idealized concept. No improviser, particularly one who plays the same tunes night after night, can generate hundreds of solos that are completely unique. A vital improviser must develop what Metheny refers to as a "personal language," a musical vocabulary to draw upon:

> There are not, and never have been, improvising musicians who can completely reinvent their entire language, or even vocabulary, every time they play, no more than any one of us can change our voices, our choice of words, or our accent every day we are out in the world. The best and only approach is to understand this, know your bandwidth, try to do your best in every way, and then be yourself. From the musician's standpoint, it is literally impossible to make up a new way of being yourself every time you play. . . . [It is ultimately] a matter of language in the service of bringing a particular creative response to an idea or a setting into being. It is the creative impulse itself that attracts me—much more than any arbitrary sense of what makes one set of possibilities different from any other.[26]

60   Chapter Four

Complete spontaneity and fully composed work are binary positions, while improvising musicians engage across the spectrum that lies between those poles no matter what musical world they inhabit. Improvising engages a collaborative effort of human mental, emotional, physical, auditory, and other faculties. Playing a musical instrument is a distinctly physical activity. The "sound" of an imaginative improviser will in part reflect the muscle movements that have become embedded within that player's performance practice, and in turn instrument design and muscle memory play roles in the development of that "sound." Some scholars have tracked Metheny's finger navigation patterns in search of patterns, characteristic navigational routes.[27] Parallel questions have been explored regarding pianist Bill Evans.[28]

The three Metheny examples I've provided reflect a general principle of motific usage. Surely some of those motifs, across multiple solos, share features in common, but this does not mean that Metheny prepares a store of motivic material from which to select and apply to a solo on a particular composition. A partnership, not a polarity, exists between Metheny's spontaneous musical thought and the embodied practices that enable its actuation, as it does for other musicians. Pat Metheny's melodic sensibility and his overarching narrative arcs are more central to his improvisational approach than the structural details of his treatment of motifs. Characteristic types of melodic phrases and ornamentation are certainly present; to some degree they are an aspect of his musical identity.

It's important to observe that Metheny does not idealize the concept of improvising; ultimately the distinction between composition and improvising is not of great consequence to him. These are simply two modes of making music: "Ideally the kinds of things that I love as a listener and a music lover are what I aspire to represent, regardless of how they come to be," he says.[29] Within a historical jazz context, this is true for many musicians who ever meld, to varying degrees, composition and improvisation. While the big-band era privileged composition, providing brief time sequences for individual solos, improvisation often assumed center stage in the bebop era and its descendants, including the work of open ("free jazz"), collective improvisational proponents.

The hybridization of composition and improvisation has been an interest key to Pat Metheny's work. Recall that his early impetus for composing was to provide vehicles for his approach to improvisation. Some of his larger works include extensive composed segments or are primarily composed but integrate improvisational sections. These begin with the Metheny-Mays collaboration *As Falls Wichita, So Falls Wichita Falls* (1981)[30] and continue through

First Circle (1983), the concept albums *Secret Story* (1992) and *Zero Tolerance for Silence* (1994), several long-form pieces on *Imaginary Day* (1997), the full album *The Way Up* (1995), and most recently "America Undefined" (2020) and *Road to the Sun* (2021). And then there are Metheny's film score compositions. Is Pat Metheny a composer or an improviser? I think the question lacks significance because he is clearly both, and he enjoys and has been effective at each modality.

Pat Metheny has commented that composition and improvisation are in fact "related activities that happen at wildly different temperatures." Their difference is that "improvising on stage night after night with great musicians is about as hot an environment as there is in music, while sitting in a room alone pondering the merits of a B♭ over an A♭ for a week can represent an almost glacial pace of musical decision making."[31] Neither is an activity privileged over the other. Each has its time and place, often separated by a mere instant.

CHAPTER 5

Developing That Sound

Guitars and Sonic Space

It was a wash of electric guitar sound that first captured my attention. The setting was a 1983 Pat Metheny Group performance in Philadelphia at the Mann Music Center, an outdoor concert space. My first thought was that the acoustics of the open-air space seemed unusually lively. And they surely were, with the sound of the drums and bass ricocheting around the center. But as I settled in and paid closer attention to the sound of the guitar, I realized that what I heard was unique and different in kind from the rest of the mix. Metheny's electric guitar had a crystalline, slightly unstable quality. Most unusual was the movement of the sound around the stage and around the music center.

The sound of electric guitar in jazz settings had long been constrained by the nature of guitar design. Sonic variation within any individual guitar was limited to adjustments of the volume and tone knobs, and a player's string-picking technique.

By the 1960s, rock guitarists were taking a far more expansive sonic approach through their use of distortion boxes, wah-wah pedals, and other electric devices. What Metheny admired most about Jimi Hendrix, who came to national attention in 1966, was less his technical innovations than the emotional depth and expressivity he elicited from the instrument as he uniquely conceived it. What Metheny heard in his work was the same thing he appreciated among innovative, genre-defying saxophonists:

> To me, Jimi was a lot like Albert Ayler or Dewey Redman or Pharoah Sanders—a genuine storyteller that could use raw emotion in extended doses, for extended lengths, with a core that was always natural and real.

Like Wes [Montgomery], he is another musician who sounds better and better in retrospect—everything he played was so true.[1]

It was in the context of rock that Pat Metheny first experienced an electric guitar. Metheny was among the millions of young people in 1964 who tuned into the Ed Sullivan Show to see the Beatles. Their arrival in the United States was a signal moment, bringing a new sound and a cultural phenomenon. For those raised on television and home record players, this was a mass event of unprecedented proportion, initiating the "British Invasion" of rock music in America. Amid the screaming fans who could barely hear the Beatles' singing voices, the *sound* of two electric guitars was unmistakable. On one side of bassist Paul McCartney stood George Harrison, holding his Gretsch Country Gent. On the other side was John Lennon with his Rickenbacker 325.[2]

The two guitars presented a study in contrast, the Rickenbacker with its flat, two-color light-and-dark body (flat, to create the impression it was a solid body), three pickups, and grittier look,[3] and the glistening black sheen and small open hole of the clearly hollow Gretsch. Together the two guitarists—and their guitars—projected an explosion of electric sight and sound previously unknown to a broad American public.

It isn't that electric guitars were new to American music; the instruments date back to the 1930s. Blues, gospel, and R&B guitarists Sister Rosetta Thorpe, T-Bone Walker, and Muddy Waters, as well as early rock and rollers Bill Haley and Little Richard, played electric. These musicians were best known to Black audiences. Charlie Christian, Django Reinhardt, and a handful of other jazz musicians had also played electric guitar. For fans of country musician Chet Atkins, Harrison's Gretsch electric guitar was a familiar sight. And looking further back than Atkins, saxophonist and writer Allen Lowe identifies Muryel Zeke Campbell, a member of country-and-western swing band the Light Crust Doughboys in the 1930s and '40s, as an electric guitarist whose work defies a simple distinction between country music and jazz guitar.[4]

Two electric guitars plus an electric bass on the sound stage of the Ed Sullivan Show was something very new and startling.[5] What young boy would *not* want to play electric guitar? Metheny recalls the electric guitar, his new choice of instrument, as "kind of the instrument of our generation," in part "pre-pubescent angst" and rebellion.[6] In that mid-1960s historic moment of cultural change, the electric guitar represented "literally the moment that the world shifted from black and white into color TV, photographs . . . a major shift, a major chasm in the universe in the moment—and I was attracted to

64   Chapter Five

it."[7] From that moment, Metheny says, even "before I ever owned a guitar, I was so captivated by the instrument that I would draw pictures of them."[8]

The first guitar that Metheny touched was a neighbor's dad's Gretsch 6230, also known as the "Chet Atkins." "To my young mind," he recalls, "this electric guitar was just coolest thing on earth."[9] Metheny successfully cajoled his parents to allow him to buy a guitar:

> I begged and begged my mom and dad to let me buy one with the money I had earned from my *Lee's Summit Journal* paper route and a garage sale that we had had where I had sold all my stuff—and finally they gave in . . . [and] the guitar became my passion. I would practice literally as many hours as I could stay awake.[10]

Metheny purchased a used Gibson ES-140 that he found in an ad in the *Kansas City Star*.[11] It was a hollow-body electric guitar, designed with a cutaway. Now that he owned a guitar, the next step was to learn some songs. His first was the theme from *Peter Gunn*, followed by "The Girl from Ipanema."[12]

After a brief interval, Metheny replaced the 140[13] with a Gibson ES-175N, a guitar with "a sound of its own . . . my pride and joy." It was a model that had been played by Joe Pass, Herb Ellis, and Kenny Burrell and was of particular importance to the teenage Pat Metheny, being one of the guitars that Wes Montgomery played. Metheny's ES-175N remained his main electric for two decades until, eventually, it became too fragile to travel. Beginning in the 1990s, Metheny turned to a prototype of a new guitar made by Ibanez in consultation with him: the PM signature model.[14]

Once Metheny's musical interests had turned toward jazz, Wes Montgomery became an important model. He admired Montgomery's lyricism and the warmth of his sound. This was shaped by Montgomery's unconventional use of his thumb rather than a pick to initiate a note. We discussed Montgomery's solo on "If You Could See Me Now," on the Wynton Kelly Trio's *Smokin' at the Half Note* (1965),[15] in chapter 4. This was the solo Metheny called "the ideal, perfect improvised statement that any guitarist has ever made."[16] Another Metheny favorite is Montgomery's "Down Here on the Ground" (1968),[17] which, while more commercial in flavor, includes

> some of the most profound playing that Wes ever did, exactly because it was so simple. The way he plays the melody on the song "Down Here on the Ground" is about the closest thing that I have heard that any guitar player

Developing That Sound   65

has ever done to achieve the kind of melodic playing that Miles (Davis) did . . . he could play simple and make it sound so beautiful and so deep.[18]

The simplicity and directness of Montgomery's playing was, in Metheny's estimation, highly unusual in its depth and concision. Like Miles Davis, Montgomery was not simply lyrical but also able to communicate a depth of human feeling with unusual directness, something even less common for guitarists. Montgomery's trademark moves, like his use of octaves, are often spoken about, but Metheny believes that

> too little is said about the details of his phrasing or the amazing vocal quality that he could invoke at will. Not to mention the amazing quality of melodic development that seems to inhabit virtually every solo he ever played. That sense of finalizing ideas is so embedded in his art as to be almost unnoticeable as that rarest of gifts, which even the best players possess in small doses.[19]

Pat Metheny came to admire Django Reinhardt as well, particularly his sound and the melodic quality of his improvised melodies.[20] Metheny was also fond of Kenny Burrell's sound and rhythmic conception. Burrell's recording *Blues — The Common Ground* became one of Metheny's favorite guitar albums. Jim Hall (who much later recorded *Jim Hall and Pat Metheny* [1999] as a duo album with Metheny) provided a model of a jazz electric guitarist who employed a broad dynamic range, from barely audible to loud. Hall achieved this, in the words of Metheny,

> by picking softer and letting the amp do part of the job. Jim says by using the amp he could play softer and my interpretation of that is that he doesn't have to pick as hard to get the sound out of the instrument, and then when he does pick hard, it's bigger . . . [thus] he has that much further to go. So, you increase the apparent difference from the softest note to the loudest note.[21]

This technique, Metheny explains, "opened up five or six degrees of dynamics on both sides by picking softer. He could then make certain things jump out a little bit more."[22]

Yet throughout this history, the idea that a jazz guitarist's sound could be crafted to create a sound so different in kind from those of other guitarists to constitute the *sound* of a Coltrane or a Hendrix had barely entered the con-

66 Chapter Five

versation. An electric guitar in jazz generally remained just that, an *electric* guitar, with the signal from its pickups routed through an amplifier, and use of the instrument was not very common. Before the early 1970s, the number of sonically pioneering guitarists in jazz remained limited to Sonny Sharrock, Pete Cosey,[23] and John McLaughlin, with one of the few experimental labs being Gary Burton's band. Among their important recordings with guitarists strongly influenced by rock guitar innovations were *Duster* (1967), with Larry Coryell, and *Country Roads and Other Places* (1968), with Jerry Hahn. The latter was Steve Swallow's first recording on electric rather than acoustic bass. Following Hahn came Sam Brown,[24] Mick Goodrick,[25] and then Pat Metheny.

When Pat Metheny joined the Burton band in 1974, the eloquent electric guitarist Mick Goodrick was a member of the ensemble. To provide sonic contrast, Metheny played twelve-string electric, an instrument virtually unknown in a jazz setting. Metheny's solo space expanded on *Dreams So Real* (1975) and *Passengers* (1977). Nearly a year before *Passengers*, Metheny's first solo record, *Bright Size Life* (1976), provided hints of Metheny's glassine electric sound. The guitar sound projects beautifully, with a singing sustain. *Bright Size Life* and Gary Burton's *Dreams So Real* were recorded a day apart, in December 1975.

Metheny's generational peers at the time were early in their careers; some who come to mind include John Scofield, John Abercrombie, Mike Stern (Metheny's student at Berklee), Stanley Jordan, Emily Remler (an occasional Metheny student), and Alan Holdsworth. Metheny noted in a 1976 interview, "I feel that the guitar has yet to really make its way into the jazz scene of today."[26]

For listeners of Pat Metheny's early recordings, the first hint that a new "sound" was emerging is to some degree audible within the reverberant quality of "Sea Song," the final track on Metheny's second album, *Watercolors* (1977).[27] You can hear it rather subtly at the instant when the guitar moves forward in the mix and a delay effect multiplies its sonic depth and breadth, around two and a half minutes in. This provides a small taste of the far more multidimensional, shimmering sound fully realized on Metheny's next recording, *Pat Metheny Group* (1978).[28] The new approach would subsequently continue throughout Metheny's concert appearances and albums for years to come.

Metheny's admiration for Wes Montgomery, Jim Hall, Jimi Hendrix, and, later, Eddie Van Halen came in part because these musicians transcended what he calls "the 'guitar-ness' of it,"[29] the sound of a guitarist being overdetermined by the physical design of the instrument. But as Metheny's playing was growing in breadth and depth, he came to realize that the very physical and sonic features of the guitar could limit one's expressiveness. One adjustment he made was how he initiated the vibration of the guitar strings through his picking style: "I hardly pick at all. Most of what I do is in my left hand.... You also can't get the dynamic possibilities when you're picking every note that you can when you have all kinds of articulations."[30]

Metheny's conception of articulation was also colored by his early experience of playing the trumpet: "Trumpet was kind of the sound that probably defined my early relationship to music of all kinds and remains probably my touchstone in terms of sound."[31] He explains further:

> I think in terms of how I would tongue a phrase in the back of my mind all the time. Back then as well as today, many jazz guitar players often sound stiff and wrong in terms of articulation.... I have worked very hard to simulate the kind of articulation that rings true as a horn player.[32]

Projecting Sound through Space

The essential limiting feature of playing jazz on electric guitar is the conventional thinking that the instrument should project its sound from single source, a speaker. The sound thus lacks dimensionality, even if that same signal is transmitting through multiple speakers. Metheny sought a more dynamic sonic profile akin to that of a tenor saxophone, an instrument that projects sound in every direction from its bell. A guitar speaker is inherently unidirectional and spatially static. This was a dilemma Metheny felt a strong need to address.

Jazz musicians highly value a musician's "sound," what Ben Ratliff, in his book about John Coltrane, calls "a full and sensible embodiment of his [a musician's] artistic personality, such that it can be heard, at best, in a single note."[33] Certainly, Pat Metheny's sound is one that is immediately identifiable. Many factors contribute to the uniqueness of his sound, among them touch and sound production, particular ways he navigates fretboards, choices of tunings, nuances of expressivity. The list could go on further. Yet a parallel question could be posed regarding notable classical pianists: what distinguishes the sound of a Chopin étude played by Mauricio Pollini from the same piece performed by Vladimir Horowitz? Pianists and guitarists can speak about technical details of performance practices and sensibilities, preferences for instruments and their relationships with those sonic vehicles. But the reality

68   Chapter Five

is far more intangible and something one needs to listen to and experience to understand. One partial technical answer may be found in the choices Metheny made early in his career regarding how he projected the sound of his electric guitar in space.

Metheny describes the approach he developed in the late 1970s as shaped by what he refers to as "modulated delay."[34] This is quite different from what has become known as a "chorus effect," which is often housed in a guitarist's stomp box and is designed to increase the complexity of a single instrument's sound, resulting in a richer multiplicity of sound within a single speaker.[35] In an era of digital chorus effect and delay boxes,[36] Metheny was searching for a way to craft a sound that provided a sense of actual movement in space, while remaining focused. Unlike a cloudlike sound mass that would lose its identity as it diffused, Metheny's new sound was achieved by sending his guitar signal to three speakers at once: one delayed by 14 milliseconds, another across the stage delayed by 26 milliseconds, and a third with no delay. The result is a complex, constantly but subtly changing guitar sound, happening "in the air" rather than in the speakers, which seems to be coming from everywhere. Metheny refers to this as an "ambient aspect"[37] in which "everything is always kind of discrete and then it mixes together in the air to make this bigger sound that has life to it."[38] This is the guitar sound I heard at the Pat Metheny Group concert that opened this chapter.

Drummer Antonio Sanchez, who has worked on many of Pat Metheny's projects over the past two decades, describes his experience of Metheny's conception and stage layout in this way:

> I remember once on one of those tours, I think I counted 8 or 10 monitors surrounding Pat. It was just like a vortex. I remember what he told me, one time, that one of the things that he didn't like about the guitar is to hear himself through a box. When you play a piano, you hear the piano. If you play the saxophone, you hear the saxophone. A tenor saxophone has a big sound, and it fills the room pretty well. When you play drums, you hear the drums. But with a guitar, if you play through an amp, then you hear it through the amp. So, he wanted to be to be surrounded by the guitar sound. That's why he would have so many monitors.[39]

Even with this elaborate approach to projecting his distinct sound, Metheny came to recognize that this sound was not simply a product of technologies but, in fact, of how he played the guitar. He was playing informal jam

Developing That Sound   69

sessions in Eastern Europe during the 1990s, without his complex setup. "I played one night on a Polish guitar and a Czech amp. Someone taped it and gave me the tape the next day. I was shocked to hear that I sounded JUST LIKE ME!!!!"[40] What he recognized was "that it's more about conception and touch and spirit and soul etc., than whether my hardware was in place."[41] His multidirectional sound profile nonetheless remains important to him.

Metheny's sound is also the sum of a sonic palette broader than electric guitars. Acoustic guitars were integral to the sound profile of *Watercolors* (1977), *Pat Metheny Group* (1978), and *New Chautauqua* (1979) and have remained so ever since. With rare exceptions—for instance, Ralph Towner—the acoustic provides a sonic element not often associated with jazz. Metheny's use of acoustic guitars is arguably one of the ways he differentiates himself from any specific genre category.

Pat Metheny treats the acoustic guitar as distinct from the electric—sonically, technically, and in its immediacy, intimacy, and emotional directness:

> The depth of the acoustic guitar is so much greater than the electric guitar in many ways. You can somehow get so much more information from the acoustic guitar because the sound is going through the mikes rather than a pickup. You get this much (big gesture) rather than that much (small gesture). The bandwidth is somehow just greater than it can ever be from a simple magnetic pickup.[42]

Metheny aims for the least technological mediation possible between acoustic guitar and sound system, as he described in 2001: connecting two outputs, a pickup, and a microphone directly into the PA.[43] There is little mediation between touch; picking; finger and hand motion on the strings, fingerboard, and guitar neck; and the sound projected by the guitar. Metheny explains, "I never try to play the same things on it that I would play on an electric—you need a different touch and mindset. What you do with your hand and how you touch the instrument has much more impact on what the audience feels."[44]

Pat Metheny has played an array of acoustic guitars over the years. In 1985, he described his array as including an "Ovation six string, classical with a pickup on it, and a Fender acoustic twelve string . . . that I could tune to an open chord,"[45] one of three twelve-string guitars he owned.[46] The collection continued to grow; by the mid-1990s it included a sound palette of "about 20 that I use regularly."[47] During his early ECM period, Metheny experimented

70   Chapter Five

with alternate guitar tunings. In 1980, he described his acoustic guitars as "all strung up weird ways." On "San Lorenzo," from *Pat Metheny Group* (1978), he said:

> It's basically all E strings tuned to an E♭ pentatonic scale in fifths. I'm not into open tunings so much as I'm into redefining the high to low configuration.[48] Sometimes I'll have the highest string in the middle or the lowest string on top to come up with different things. On some tunings you have to order this special string from England that's an .006. Human hair is .005 [laughs]! . . . in "San Lorenzo" [I] hit harmonics across the 12th and 7th frets. But the tuning makes it sound mysterious.[49]

Metheny felt an affinity with Joni Mitchell's career-long interest in guitar tunings, reflecting his description of Mitchell as not "really think[ing] of notes or chords, she just really likes sounds."[50]

One of the tunings with which Metheny has been associated is what he refers to as "half-Nashville" tuning, which emulates the sound of a twelve-string guitar on a six-string by retuning the bottom four strings up an octave. That raises them into the same register as the upper strings, or even higher, thus clustering the pitches more closely together. The lower-wound strings are replaced with strings of a much lighter gauge. We can hear this sound[51] on "Phase Dance," on *Pat Metheny Group* (1989).

A novel performance practice on acoustic that Pat Metheny incorporated within his sonic/textural profile is strumming. Acoustic guitars were ubiquitous in Metheny's hometown of Lee's Summit, Missouri, "hanging from barbershop walls and when there were no customers, they'd pick them up and all play."[52] In that setting, strumming was, of course, a popular technique. Metheny embraced it beginning with *The New Chautauqua* (1979), and later on *80/81* (1980). Strumming can be heard on his duet album with bassist Charlie Haden, *Beyond the Missouri Sky* (1997), a recording Metheny speaks of as a conscious attempt "to evoke the literal sounds that I remember growing up with in Missouri."[53]Strumming is associated with country and folk guitarists like Bill Monroe and Woody Guthrie, but rarely with jazz, where a single horn-like line and solid, once-picked chords prevail. In early jazz, strummed banjos played a harmonic/rhythmic role that would later be assumed by the piano. Charlie Christian, who came to fame in the 1930s and '40s, exemplifies the concept of the electric guitar as a melody instrument akin to a saxophone. Chords, when he played them, were articulated with rapid attack, more akin to piano than to the banjo, adding the gritty sound of picked strings. In contrast, Metheny came to embrace strumming as something natural to the guitar, "[one] of the things that the instrument is really good at."[54] For Metheny, strumming "crept into my jazz playing . . . having grown up out there," but his interest was really sonic. When he embraced strumming, "a new way of thinking and playing opened up."[55] He says, "Today, that kind of playing has blended into the vernacular, but for then, that was a fairly bold move."[56]

CHAPTER 6

Pat Metheny Group as an Expression of an Unfolding Idea

My thing is in line with the long tradition of leadership in our general community of a guy who is the leader who starts their own band. Within that definition, there is a subgroup of folks who not only come up with a conception of what their band is going to sound like but, through their work as composer, define the sound of the band and who they choose to be in it to get to the best result. The Duke model comes to mind first as the clearest role model for me in that regard.

PAT METHENY[1]

I look for cats who can express some kind of personal meaning to what they play . . . a deep *understanding* of music and what it really is— defined by not just the mechanics of it but a conception of it built on their own personal beliefs and experiences and point of view. And across years of thinking about it, I think that *good notes* informed by a *conception* that is based on something personal and real have a way of sticking around in ways that go beyond what anyone around at the time they are created often notice.

PAT METHENY[2]

Becoming the Leader of a Small Band with a Big Sound

By citing Edward Kennedy "Duke" Ellington as a model, Pat Metheny identifies with the hybridity of Ellington's role: a figure who defines a band's sonic conception by composing, arranging, selecting personnel, and defining his place within it as an instrumentalist. The comparison may not be obvious because these two musicians are so different culturally, racially, and generationally, and in their places in the American imagination. Unlike Ellington, Pat Metheny never had to navigate the complexities of race in America, including the narrow path Ellington etched between acceptability, respectability, racial pride, and serving as a role model within the self-consciousness of Black America.[3]

Pat Metheny became a mature bandleader in his early twenties. He was simultaneously self-guided and mentored by Gary Burton, and he sought, like Ellington, to bridge the aesthetics of popular music and art music. Metheny's music required a far bigger sound than four musicians could produce, but the multilayered sound of electric and polyphonic electronic instruments made it sonically possible and economically feasible. Keyboardists Josef Zawinul, Stevie Wonder, Keith Emerson, and others had already demonstrated that musically skilled and physically nimble players with keen ears for sound blending could produce a substantial multilayered sound. Portability of instruments was essential for endless van travel with, initially, a limited income draw.

Despite a historical bias within the jazz world in favor of all-acoustic ensembles, the idea of a compact electric and electronic sound was normalized by Gary Burton, rock ensembles, and the electric bands of Miles Davis, Herbie Hancock, Weather Report, and Chick Corea. Metheny describes how he built upon their shared technological interests, while simultaneously differentiating himself from their musical approaches:

> During the period [of] pre-official bandleader, my dream/conception of what I wanted to get to with a band was that I wanted to try to get to a place like what Weather Report had suggested in terms of scope and color and texture—but not in a "rock" kind of way. I was really interested in form, and particularly mining the issue of how dynamics and color in a small-group setting with electric instruments applied to advanced harmonic contexts had not been explored hardly at all.

Metheny, who, like Ellington, is simultaneously a bandleader and instrumentalist, understands that the

> main job in virtually everything I have been up to over these years is bandleader [not guitarist]. I really try to find guys who are the best people for my

zone of interest at that time. And since I have always written almost all the music, I'm going to get these great musicians to play, I have a particular sense of the result I hope to get with them . . .[4]

A multifaceted skill set is required to constantly tour a band made up of very musically distinct members performing highly orchestrated and richly textured music under the guidance of a strong bandleader—who is also the featured soloist and composer. Every band member needs to feel fairly and equally represented, although both Ellington and Metheny recognized the centrality of a reliable, trustworthy, and creative drummer. Metheny's novel challenge was mixing and matching, blending, and contrasting acoustic and electric/electronic sounds. Metheny made the transition from band member to bandleader after a briefer period of apprenticeship than many (for Herbie Hancock, it was a year with Donald Byrd and then five with Miles Davis; Wayne Shorter worked with Maynard Ferguson, Art Blakey, and then Miles Davis over several years before co-founding Weather Report). He also didn't have the multiple albums under his own name that had helped propel Hancock's and Shorter's solo careers.

Assembling Personnel

Drums

Metheny's "first and most important decision was 'Who is going to play drums?' From that, everything else followed. . . . I always have understood that the actual leader on every bandstand, everywhere, is the drummer." He easily decided on Danny Gottlieb, an old friend with whom he had played since his time in Miami[5] and who had been, for its final year, a member of the Gary Burton band:

> So, if anyone would be the "co-founder" of that first [Pat Metheny Group] band, it would be him. I knew his playing really well, and I knew that I could write to his strengths and that the overlap he and I had would cover most of the territory I was interested in at that point in time. . . . In addition to being an excellent drummer, and one of the few guys in 1973–1974 who had an understanding of both playing in a more traditional way (he was Joe Morello's[6] star student) as well as the more even–eighth note kinds of playing that was focus for me at that time.

Pat Metheny Group as an Expression of an Unfolding Idea   75

While Pat Metheny was eager to record his first album early in his time with Gary Burton, instead, at Burton's urging, he waited until his second year, when he released *Bright Size Life*. Fortunately, the album "had gotten a fair amount of attention and the idea of starting my own band was being talked about as something that folks seemed to think was inevitable, even Gary." Metheny had imagined the possibility of moving to joining a second major band, maybe with Stan Getz. His musical conception had gelled and found expression on *Bright Size Life*, which "still remains the cornerstone of the whole *thing*." This was an alternative to what he viewed as the dominant musical direction of the time: "various bands playing one- or two-chord vamps. Even the heaviest cats like Miles seemed to be in on that. I had absolutely no interest in doing that, no matter whose vamp it was. I am still like that."

Metheny's sonic conception for the guitar was taking shape, and it also differed from those of his older peers John McLaughlin, Larry Coryell, and others within their musical circles, who were "playing with a fuzz tone, wah-wah kind of sound, which was what was mostly expected of guitar players during that era—nothing against it—[I] just wasn't interested in that at that time."

Once he had settled the drum chair for his new band, the next steps weren't readily apparent, but most appealing at first was instrumentation less conventional than guitar, piano, bass, and drums: "I had the idea of marimba (Dave Samuels) and oboe (Paul McCandless) plus acoustic bass and drums, and even proposed that to ECM as my second recording project."

A more practical and sustainable alternative, in light of Metheny's "interest in what was happening in the world of musical instrument technology of that time, particularly the advent of polyphonic synth," led Metheny to realize that "some kind of guitar, keyboard, bass, drums thing was most realistic." The question was which keyboard player would be best up to the task.

Keyboards

Metheny's first thought was his close friend pianist/arranger/composer Gil Goldstein, or maybe one of the "'big band arranger/piano player' guys of that era, my favorite being Alan Broadbent, but also Andy LaVerne, Biff Hannon, or Allan Zavod." These were all players with the chops and imagination to use keyboards as a kind of "orchestral" instrument. Yet few if any among them were really possible to hire on Metheny's very limited budget at the time, what Gary Burton's (and soon Metheny's) manager Ted Kurland "projected to be about 250 bucks for the whole band per night."

An unexpected option then arose:

76   Chapter Six

In April of 1976, while performing in Wichita, Kansas, with Gary's band, there was a college combo competition going at the same festival. A quartet from North Texas State was set to perform, and I remembered that my friend Dan Haerle (by then a teacher at North Texas State) had told me about a piano player from Wisconsin that I should hear, and I recognized his name on the program, that being Lyle [Mays]. As they started to play, right away I noted that not only was Lyle an exceptional musician, but in a way that occasionally happens, I could immediately hear in my mind what he and I might sound like together and that he could be a real candidate for me to use at some point.

Metheny invited Mays to play a gig with him at the Zircon just outside of Boston, and "from the first note of that first tune," he felt an immediate rapport, "just the same way I always felt with Gil [Goldstein]," something that "was never a given for me with piano players." Goldstein and Mays each "played more like arrangers rather than being just good piano players," and for Metheny, that was what he had been seeking. With Metheny's first album *Bright Size Life* gaining attention and thus forming the core of his repertoire, Metheny found that Lyle

really understood how to play those tunes in a way that was very difficult (actually, almost impossible) for me to find back in those days. . . . It was really cool to find someone else who got exactly what that language was and was able to fit right into it all.

With ideas unfolding for what would become *Watercolors*, Pat Metheny's second album (1977), Metheny hired Lyle Mays to be pianist on the upcoming quartet session, which would also include Danny Gottlieb on drums and fellow Burton band member Eberhard Weber on bass. Despite Mays's lack of exposure, ECM agreed to Metheny's choice of pianist[7] for the recording in Oslo, Norway (just as they had agreed previously to the then-unknown Jaco Pastorius), timed around an upcoming Gary Burton session with overlapping personnel:

Whatever fit Lyle and I had experienced on the gig of the previous summer was mirrored in the immediate connection that all four of us were able to get to in our rehearsal for the date. You can hear on the record that it was fun to make and came off almost exactly as I had envisioned and hoped it would.

There is no single logic behind the successful navigation of a young adult's career trajectory in the jazz world. Timelines vary for the career point when young musicians land their first recording contract, front their own band, or tour in a sustained way. Musical talent, vision, and a tremendously sustained effort alone don't even launch a solo career. For Pat Metheny, like most successful musicians before him—what was also needed, as Duke Ellington pointed out, is also "luck . . . being in the right place at the right time."[8] In Metheny's case, it was helpful to draw upon connections facilitated by Gary Burton and to have the trust and support of ECM Records behind his musical vision. Pat Metheny had talent, a unique vision, and good fortune.

In May 1977, when Metheny departed from Gary Burton's band with *Watercolors* about to be released, he recalls, "I had to really make a choice between Gil and Lyle, and that was one of the hardest things I have ever had to do. It almost came to a coin toss situation for me with lots of sleepless nights." The first formation of Metheny's new band had included Gil Goldstein, Danny Gottlieb, and Mike Richmond, but Mays had clocked some time on the road with Woody Herman and, Metheny says, "I was pretty sure that he was up for doing it, which I wasn't sure about with Gil since he was doing so many other things around New York by then." Metheny then joined Mays on a tour with singer Marlena Shaw, as Mays recalls, "just to spend the whole time talking me into forming a band. That was fascinating. Nobody had ever courted me with such intensity. He convinced me that he was serious. . . . His belief in his vision was so strong."[9] Indeed, Mays became the Pat Metheny Group's keyboardist for the entirety of its classic formation.

Bass

The missing piece needed to complete the new Pat Metheny Group was a bassist, and once again personnel questions raised financial and logistical considerations:

> My estimate was that I could pay thirty-five to fifty bucks a night. That ruled out pretty much everyone. Rufus Reid was my first choice, and I knew he was at least a hundred-buck-a-night guy, plus being older than us I couldn't really see him in the van doing a thousand miles of driving between gigs. And I loved Mike Richmond too, but [he was] also older and more established and quite busy. . . . All of those "older guys" were definitely out of my price range for anything extensive like I could see appearing on the hori-

78   Chapter Six

zon. . . . Danny thought of our friend Mark Egan, who we both knew from Miami. Danny and I went up to Nyack, New York, where Mark was playing in a little club, and he sounded fine. I asked him if he might be interested, and he was. So that first edition was set.

Finally, the personnel for the early Pat Metheny Group was in place.

Musical Dynamics within the Rhythm Section

In a recent set of interviews conducted by Joseph Vella, Danny Gottlieb and Mark Egan reflect on their earliest days with the Pat Metheny Group. Gottlieb says:

> At that point, I had been playing many straight eighth note tunes and feels and would usually start with a feel on the spur of the moment as I felt it. If Lyle or Pat liked that approach, that was fine. If they had a specific feel in mind, they might say maybe play less busy, or this tune has an "Elvin" [Jones, best known for drumming with John Coltrane's band] feel, or the groove doesn't feel exactly right, can you try something else? It was very open, and I was free to try things. . . . Lyle and Pat would be vocal both if they liked something or didn't like a specific part, and then I would try something different.[10]

Recall that straight eighth notes ("straight eights") is an approach to keeping time that contrasts with the syncopated triplet feel that was dominant in big-band jazz, bebop, and hard bop.[11] Egan remembers:

> Danny and I worked together on developing the grooves and were always listening to each other and evolving the various rhythmic feels. When I started playing fretless in the group it really complemented the touch and sound of Danny's drums and cymbals as well as the overall sound of Pat and Lyle. . . . I think for both Danny and I, supporting Pat and Lyle's solos helped us evolve as a rhythm section. . . . Each solo had a building curve to it, and we were all listening and reacting to the soloist.[12]

Metheny's preferred drum sound emphasized cymbals, specifically the flat version of ride cymbals, a design that lacks a resonant bell at the center. Each drummer in the Pat Metheny Group's history has added several of these to their kits. As Paul Wertico, Gottlieb's successor, explains, flat ride cymbals "work so well in Pat's group because of their clarity and definition. They don't . . . 'muddy up' the sound, so it's possible to play very intricate patterns on them even while using a wide range of dynamics. They also allow you to play very intense and busy, while still maintaining a certain lightness."[13]

Danny Gottlieb's drum sound profile on stage also mirrored Metheny's preference for a multidimensional sound image, with the result that, as Gottlieb notes, "the audience would be immersed in the cymbal sound from left and right. . . . I tried to move the ride focus around the sonic location (separating the ride beat between the two cymbals) so it would be an interesting sound for the audience."[14]

First Steps into the World

With the Pat Metheny Group personnel settled, the next challenge was the serious effort of building an audience and growing a personal reputation as a guitar player. This entailed sustained life on the road. Lyle Mays remembers the decision to embark on the new enterprise as a gutsy undertaking:

> Neither of us exactly felt powerful or confident at the time and there was little external evidence to indicate that bold moves would be rewarded in that economic climate. But you know, that just makes Pat's decision to quit Gary Burton, recruit me, form a band, and strike out on our own even more surprising. Mortgage rates were approaching 20% by the end of the 1970's. Nobody was betting on the future, except for maybe Ronald Reagan and Pat Metheny.[15]

Metheny's estimate in 1980 was that during the early days, "we drove something like 50,000 miles in a year, and that was with us packing all our own gear, making virtually no money at all."[16] This, of course, would change, but at that time, Metheny's finances were tight:

> Between what I had saved up from my paper route as a kid and my three years with Gary Burton, I had enough to buy a van to drive around in and the new Oberheim four-voice synth that had just come out.

Electronic Keyboards

That Oberheim, along with other synthesizers, would become a key component of the PMG sound. Metheny continues:

I had been hanging out quite a bit around then with Joe Zawinul through Jaco [Pastorius], who had recently joined Weather Report, and of course the idea of synth orchestration took a big leap with the advent of polyphonic synths, with Joe being the major innovator of how to integrate those new instruments into an ensemble via Weather Report.

Following the lead of Ray Charles, who had begun playing the Wurlitzer electric piano in the 1950s, Zawinul had been an early adopter of the Wurlitzer during his tenure with Cannonball Adderley and later with Miles Davis. Like Herbie Hancock, Chick Corea, and Paul Bley, Zawinul migrated to the Fender Rhodes and, searching for a more expansive electric sound in the age of Jimi Hendrix, began treating its sound with Echoplex tape delay,[17] Ring Modulator,[18] and other devices, each of which transformed the sound in a distinct manner. One might think of the combination as a proto-synthesizer.[19] The Oberheim polyphonic synthesizer increased Zawinul's capacity to create a larger, more orchestral sound,[20] and the idea of large and timbrally varied synthesizer orchestration appealed to Pat Metheny as well.

Lyle Mays and Pat Metheny conceptualized the use of synthesizers in an unusual way, not as a solo instrument but, as Mays recalls, to expand the band's palette to include the sounds of

French horns, clarinets, string sections and all those many other exotic instruments that a young struggling band could not afford. I viewed synths as a way to express my orchestrational visions, not as a way for me to express my personal performance aspirations. . . . Another function of the synthesizer is to enrich or thicken chords supporting melodic structures.[21]

Metheny also points to his own substantive, yet underrecognized, role in the synthesizer conceptions and realizations on Pat Metheny Group recordings: "When people hear piano or synths on a [PMG] record, they think that that is Lyle." But, as Metheny recounts, he prepared the working drafts of material in advance of the recordings, which included synthesizer tracks: "I write almost exclusively on piano and I do the [multiple] demos of the tunes with piano and synth. The fundamental sound of what an upcoming project was going to be was established in those early demos." Mays would then play what Metheny developed, "and of course, it would be better," but some of Metheny's original synthesizers remained in the final mixes. "And even just for vibe reasons," Metheny acknowledges, "I didn't want to start giving myself credit as a keyboard player too; it just would have been weird."

Transitions

The Pat Metheny Group was almost constantly on the road touring when it recorded its second album, *American Garage* (1980). Metheny then made the album *80/81* (1980) and toured with another set of musicians, some associated with Ornette Coleman. He felt at an impasse regarding the direction of the Pat Metheny Group: "By 1980, I had really run out of ways to incorporate Mark Egan's very Jaco-based way of playing into things."

Metheny already knew where to turn next. "From the start, I had wanted to get this guy I had heard from Chicago into the band, Steve Rodby." The addition of Rodby as bassist marked the beginning of a new chapter that led to a fuller flowering of PMG. Rodby had watched the original band closely since its founding. He recalls, "They played a million gigs, driving a zillion miles during those first three years. They made a huge impression on the jazz world and on no one more than me. They were, simply put, my favorite band."[22]

Early Meetings

For much of twentieth-century jazz history, young musicians learned their craft through mentorship, jamming with or joining the bands of more senior musicians. Few examples existed of the present-day institutional systems of formal jazz education. One exception was the Stan Kenton Band Clinics, sponsored in the 1960s by the National Stage Band Camp. Bassist and educator Jamey Aebersold was first a student and then a faculty member within that system.

Aebersold came to recognize the need for a small-ensemble alternative "in which all students learned to improvise,"[23] and in 1971 he founded the Jamey Aebersold Summer Jazz Workshops.[24] Teaching musicians how to play effectively in groups of four or five required a pedagogy that emphasized thoughtful soloing integrally paired with dynamic and supportive engagement with musical partners.[25]

In 1972, the second year of Aebersold's workshops, Steve Rodby and Lyle Mays participated in the program and played together in a combo. When Rodby returned the following summer, nineteen-year-old Pat Metheny had joined the faculty, following a year teaching guitar at the University of Miami.

82   Chapter Six

Danny Gottlieb, whom Metheny had known and played with at Miami, attended as a camper. Rodby concludes:

> These summer weeks would change the course of my life. . . . I received incredible encouragement from so many of the teachers at the camps, not only Pat but Gary Burton, Jack Peterson, Dan Haerle, Michael Moore, Rufus Reid, Mick Goodrick, all brilliant players and defining giants of jazz education.

One highlight of the second season, says Rodby, was playing "in a combo with Pat and Danny Gottlieb, and with Bill Evans on tenor and the late great James Williams on piano." Yet one night proved propitious:

> When it was Pat's turn to perform on one of the evening faculty recitals, he decided on a trio with Danny and me. That night, in a poetic way, my career started. And though I was really a jazz beginner compared to them, I felt an immediate affinity for both Pat's tunes, and *that style* of playing, a hybrid approach that integrated diverse musical practices that would continue to be part of my musical life to this day. So, ironically, in quite a trippy sense, I'd played with the members of the future Pat Metheny Group five years before it would even be formed. . . . I met both Pat Metheny and Lyle Mays while I was still in *high school* . . . how far out is that?!

After high school, Steve Rodby attended college at Northwestern University in Evanston, Illinois, as a classical bass major. Those years living near Chicago provided a broad berth of "incredible opportunities to play with a veritable 'who's who' of the jazz greats touring at the time. I was often part of the 'house rhythm section' at the seminal Jazz Showcase." Rodby was also playing studio sessions, often pop music, on electric bass. "I was wearing a lot of different stylistic hats, older jazz and newer jazz, and pop music, all of which reflected my broad tastes in music." The mix "gave me a special opening into newer music worlds that required traditional jazz experience but drew upon it in novel ways."

While Rodby was in college, Pat Metheny remained closely on his musical radar. Whenever Metheny played in town, Rodby would attend and chat with the guitarist, and for Rodby, "when the Pat Metheny Group was formed, each new composition and arrangement on those first two records and endless tours was defining." In turn, Metheny was watching Rodby, whom he remembers as the best young bass player I had heard, playing both acoustic and electric, and being a very solid musician across the board. Steve was always interested, but he wanted to finish his degree at Northwestern and felt like he couldn't go on the road until then . . . Anything a good bass player in Chicago of that era could do, he was doing . . . [including as] a house bass player at the Jazz Showcase at night, playing with everyone . . . who played a week there with a local rhythm section.

When Metheny decided to change bass players in the PMG, Danny Gottlieb called Rodby on Metheny's behalf, netting a tryout session in New York City and then an invitation to join the band. Metheny feels now that

Steve was the perfect guy for me. And a "professional musician" with experience way beyond Lyle or Danny and even me in a lot of ways, by virtue of all of his studio gigs. . . . His coming into my life and into the band was the single most important factor in how the next few decades unfolded, to this day. . . . And maybe most important of all was his "clubhouse presence." He was an actual adult, and finally there was someone else in there who I could really count on, night after night. . . . None of it could have ever happened without him.

Rodby began rehearsals with the band in early 1981. With a lineup including percussionist/vocalist Naná Vasconcelos plus Metheny, Mays, Gottlieb, and himself, Rodby learned "the primary 'legacy' tunes" from the band's existing repertoire and explored new music under development. Later that year, two tours on, another rehearsal featured "some amazing new music, specially crafted for this new band," which appears on *Offramp*. The next year, the band recorded the live album *Travels*. "*That* band, during *that* era had such a unique, great sound," Rodby says.

While Rodby's predecessor, Mark Egan, had played exclusively electric bass, Rodby was a gifted acoustic bassist, offering an important option to suit the new and broadened repertoire. For Rodby, choosing which bass to play was never complicated. The solutions proved organic and intuitive:

Since I'd grown up playing both instruments, I had the great good fortune to have each of them inform and change the way I played the other. . . . Over the decades, more tunes would end up on acoustic, but some of that probably has to do with a sound and feel that I'd tried hard to cultivate on the acoustic bass, trying to combine the best of both worlds: the bounce

84   Chapter Six

and wood and flexibility and soul of the acoustic bass with the solidity and endurance of the electric.

Rodby's choices were also not dictated by the need for volume within a highly amplified band. Rodby says he learned how to play "*really loud* on the acoustic without issues of feedback."

Pat Metheny also makes a point of saying that from the very start, "Steve was always involved in every aspect of what made the music sound the way it sounded." This included production and also providing guidance for Lyle Mays, helping him navigate "some personal challenges" in a musically successful way. "Without him [Steve]," Metheny says, "it all just would have been impossible." Rodby has continued working with Metheny through the years, well beyond his time in the PMG, serving as co-producer. Metheny notes, "Even today, whatever I have to do to get Steve involved in whatever project I am doing, I will do anything I can to make it happen."

A Musical Mélange Viewed through the Lens of the Bassist

Like much of Pat Metheny's work, the PMG reflects a blend of through-composed material and sectional forms structured as a grounding for improvisational solos. Somewhat different in form from his duet and trio settings, most of the band's music was composed in detail, with Metheny preparing working versions in advance for the band's rehearsal and studio sessions. Performance thus required a delicate blend of accuracy while injecting feeling into composed material. The degree of interpretive flexibility varied, as Steve Rodby notes:

> In general, the bass parts for the band would fall into two very rough categories: tunes with specific, composed "lines," and tunes with a more open, broken straight-eighth feel. Many tunes incorporated both elements. While the bass line on "Last Train Home" is just what it is, the seemingly very simple bass part on "Are You Going with Me?" ends up having elements of personal expression for me. Other players might have approached it quite differently. . . .
>
> Usually there is some kind of general pattern or idea of Pat's that defines "Why is this tune different from every other tune?" Yet within that underlying concept is enormous flexibility. . . . I always had the sense while playing—except for composed "melodic bass" lines on certain tunes[26]—that I was improvising the whole time . . . responding to every unique moment in

Pat and Lyle's solos and to the drumming and drama of the moment.... To me it was still music connected to jazz traditions, playing a crucial supportive role for incredible improvised solos, interactive drumming and accompaniment, and unpredictability that was always in and of the moment, and always, every time, needing to be made fresh.

Rodby's approach captured the paradox presented by material composed with a particular "feel" or sonic conception. The goal for the bassist was to present the music in a way that sounded fresh and new, no matter how many nights in a row it had been played, no matter whether it was composed, adaptively interpreted, or improvised, or how long-standing the repertoire was. This represented a less melodic or soloistic approach than that of Rodby's predecessor, Mark Egan. Rodby continues:

> My intention was to combine the solidity—very much in a pop music sense—of what the bass can do to organize music and how it's heard and felt, with the flexibility and intuition that is called for to accompany these brilliant improvisers. This means serving the composition rather than pushing individual personality into the foreground.... Each tune has its *own style*, in a sense, its own world ... present[ing] a "style problem" to be solved, especially for the bass and drums.

Rodby observes that Pat Metheny's music called upon all three aspects of his tool kit as a bassist: the orchestral player who can accurately realize detailed composed parts, the pop musician who can provide an "in the pocket" rhythmic sensibility, and the jazz musician who is flexible and improvisationally responsive. Even within a single work, there may be segments or even moments that call for different aspects of this tool kit, as well as instances when more than one approach cohabits the same musical space. Sometimes, even "in the pocket" passages can call for spontaneity and variation. Rodby observes: "I'm probably three musicians in one: the jazz musician, the pop studio player, and the orchestral bassist with a degree from Northwestern University. The orchestral guy plays the written parts, the pop guy lays down the groove, and the jazz guy makes it improvisatory."[27]

The up-tempo "Red Sky" (*We Live Here*) offers a useful example of Rodby's many roles in the ensemble. My intention is not to draw from it a single broad generalization about Pat Metheny's compositions—certainly, its form, rhythmic and harmonic feel, and emotional tone are distinct from Metheny's ballads and many other works. Yet it is instructive to track one musical work,

86   Chapter Six

explored from the perspective of a single band member's performance within the mix. From this we can more fully appreciate Metheny's rich integration of musical worlds within a single composition.

During the recorded performance of this lively and lyrical tune, Rodby toggles between a fixed pop bass line[28] and a more flexible style of playing—one that never loses the groove but dynamically treats levels of intensity, degrees of activity, and, at times, the placement of accents. These distinctions can be subtle but impactful. Early in the tune, Rodby's bass line remains close to the composed line, right in the pocket. His playing gains energy around 1:50, when he interlocks rhythmically with Lyle Mays, before quickly returning to the opening groove. The bass grows increasingly more active while remaining within the steady beat structure, facilitating a transition into the composed melody, which includes wordless vocals, at 2:30.

When the initial groove returns at 2:50, Rodby adds a small but noticeable degree of complexity during Mays's soloistic comping. At 3:20, Pat Metheny begins his solo on Roland guitar synth. Rodby returns to the initial bass line, keeping the beat steady and simple, affording Metheny unimpeded solo space. As the tune modulates at 4:36, Rodby's bass playing becomes a little looser and then decidedly freer, without losing the groove. Around 5:10, the bass periodically interjects repeated notes, and at times, the specific accented beat within each measure varies. At 5:50, the bass again locks in the groove as the melody returns, with the voices at the front of the mix. The bass now provides a more energetic, embellished line, one that continues as Metheny returns to his Roland synthesizer solo, this time played over the melody line. As Metheny's solo continues toward a conclusion, Rodby's bass is the freest and most creative on the recording. Even beyond musical details, Rodby adds, "solving how to approach every tune—since so many can be in their own stylistic world—requires paying attention not just to its 'style' but also to its musical content and emotion."

The composition *Red Sky* navigates a range of emotional perspectives, from the opening "pop tune" vamp; to the earnest qualities of the initial melody; to the tentative, building qualities of the transition to the vocal melody, the jubilance of that section; to the free-ranging, motivic construction and the ebb, flow, and resolution of Metheny's solo, unexpected for a pop tune. Making this all work from the bassist's seat requires attention to each of these qualities, modifying and adjusting, even slightly, the stylistic emphasis and feel as the performance progresses.

Steve Rodby's chief role, as the music evolved in complexity, orchestration, and layering of voices, was to serve as its anchor, to be at the quiet (albeit sometimes loud) center of what could unfold like a whirlwind: steady, yet expressive; reliable while responsive. His playing was all in service to music that called upon three skill sets: those of the orchestrally trained player who can accurately realize written parts, the pop musician who can lay down a solid groove, and the jazz musician who can flexibly respond to soloists and help build an elastic rhythmic feel.

Digital Sequencing

During this same period, new, watershed technologies broadened the scope of Metheny's performances, particularly with the inclusion of sequencers. Lyle Mays's array of keyboard instruments during this period expanded beyond acoustic piano and the Oberheim four-voice synthesizer.[29] Mays had already introduced a much older, amplified acoustic instrument, the Autoharp (first on "Phase Dance").[30]

During the 1980s, Metheny's digital technology of choice for composing and sequencing, in the studio and on the road, was the New England Digital Synclavier.[31] Lyle Mays speaks of sequencing, more than digital synthesis, as "the most important new element" in the band's music. While Metheny and Mays had used drum machines on *As Falls Wichita, So Falls Wichita Falls* (1981), performing live with Metheny's preprogrammed Synclavier sequences on "Are You Going with Me?" was something quite new and different. For Mays this included learning "how to play with prerecorded tracks."[32] Playing to clock time was not new for Steve Rodby, however, who was experienced at recording to click tracks in studios. For Rodby,

> the new technologies were always just tools, tools being used by brilliant artists who were both technological enthusiasts and, importantly, skeptics, in the best sense. . . . Pat used them judiciously. They were never robots using us. . . . His approach was often strikingly different than that taken by many others using the same hardware and software.

Rodby adds that the integration of Metheny's sequences within the rhythmic structure resisted the rigidity of pulse that is too often found in music with machine beats. The result was neither robotic nor locked-in but well suited to music with a pulse, and with a flexible sensibility, what Rodby refers to as a "dynamics of time and pulse."[33] Since the 1980s, hardware sequencers have been supplemented or replaced by software sequencers, and Metheny has always adaptively utilized the changing technologies.

88   Chapter Six

The new technological additions of the early 1980s required a period of adjustment for Danny Gottlieb, who at first, he says, took offense when "Pat came in with a drum machine box. . . . I thought it was like Pat was saying the groove wasn't solid enough and we're going to play to this machine." When Naná Vasconcelos joined in with a shaker, Gottlieb found that "it was actually very easy to play with the drum machine, and it did keep the time solid." With the Synclavier, "the repeating synth and drum machine just became part of the text of the song ['Are You Going with Me?']."[34] Software sequences have at times remained part of Pat Metheny's live performances.

The Roland Guitar Synthesizer

A second technological innovation, a new kind of guitar, arrived around the same time, adding a new dimension to Pat Metheny's sound palette and impacting the musical dynamics of the Pat Metheny Group.

The first guitar sound Metheny plays on "Barcarole," the opening track of *Offramp* (1981), resounds like a clarion call. Each sonic utterance of his guitar begins quickly, with what musicians call a sharp attack. But these notes can be long or short, coming to an abrupt halt. Or one sustained note can suddenly be reiterated and given new life. A note can be shaped as if it were not simply bent but stretchable fabric. At times Metheny plays repeated staccato notes. And with the tap of a switch, every pitch can jump an octave into the register of a piccolo trumpet, as if this were a Bach Brandenburg concerto or the Beatles' "Penny Lane."

The new instrument, the Roland GR-300 guitar synthesizer,[35] released in 1979, was, Pat Metheny recalls, "like getting a ticket to another musical planet for me. Suddenly I could play things that I had always heard in my head that had eluded me on a conventional guitar."[36] The Roland can function as an excellent, warm-toned electric guitar. But in synthesizer mode,[37] the instrument we hear is of an utterly different kind. King Crimson guitarist Robert Fripp understood the guitar synthesizer to be opening up new possibilities, a change analogous to earlier revolutions in guitar playing:

> The opportunity is to come up with an entirely new range of sounds for the electric guitar and a new musical vocabulary to go with it. For example, when Charlie Christian put a pickup on his guitar, he wasn't playing the licks of an acoustic guitarist. There was a new music to go with this essentially new instrument. When Hendrix added wah-wah and fuzz, it wasn't

an updated Charlie Christian; it was an entirely new instrument with a new sound, a new vocabulary, and new music to go along with it.[38]

The Roland makes one sound that can be filtered to produce different timbres, but Metheny's *single* chosen timbre has long remained *his* sound. Playing his Roland synthesizer means playing *this* sound. Like the sound of a trumpet, the Roland sound has piercing clarity. This is one reason I call it a clarion call. But its granularity, particularly in its lower end, hints at a bowed viola. Thus, the sound is a kind of trumpet-viola hybrid, ringing in the higher register while soaring with warmth in its lower range. This is due in part to subtle changes in the shape of synthesizer's waveform (which is like a sawtooth), and a low-pass filter opens up as the frequency increases.[39]

In 1985, Metheny spoke of it as a "high trumpet sound" because of his perception of its timbre and the way it supports a conception of phrasing drawn from his early experience as a trumpeter. In this respect, the Roland bridges the gap between conventional electric guitar design and this approach. He explains:

> When I'm using it, I tend to not think like a guitar player, but rather like a horn player and have always done so, even in my guitar playing, in the sense that I like to have natural "breaths," which sound natural if I were playing a wind instrument. All that was immediately translated, but there were even a lot of phrasing things which might sound alright on a guitar, but on a trumpet, they would sound real stiff. You have to think in those terms.[40]

Iconic keyboard synthesizers, like Keith Emerson's Moog on "Lucky Man," lack this sonic richness, while keyboard features like pitch bend wheels or ribbon controllers lack the sensitivity of a bending guitar string. The vibration of each guitar string on the Roland is tracked independently of the others (the pickup has a separate output for each of its six strings, hence the descriptor "hexaphonic"), allowing for polyphony. The Roland GR303 uses an unusual twenty-four-pin output cable that connects the guitar to a synthesizer module resting on the floor.

Andre Cholmondeley, who provides technical support for Metheny's Roland night in and night out on tour, comments:

> Pat Metheny's use of the Roland GR-300 is incredibly consistent. . . . For forty years now, he's been using this one guitar, with that one sound and the

90   Chapter Six

octave jump. It's fascinating how the Roland has been an incredibly consistent zen-like presence. He has stuck with this really cool thing that works well, while other things—the bands, styles of music, other sounds—change around it. Along with his electric "jazz guitar," it is always a paintbrush in there and I love it. It's also a lovely sounding guitar[41] simply as an electric guitar, without the synth engaged. Sometimes, he'll pick up the Roland and, after a couple of choruses with the band, he'll start playing it as a regular electric guitar, testing it and maybe just strumming for a couple bars, until the synth solo or lines. And it's a great sounding axe. Pat has explained to me he's had one of just about every new kind of guitar; he's always been a tech-interested artist, always interested to check out what's new and ask himself "Is this a tool that could be useful?" But he added that aside from the GR-300, "none of them [guitar synths] worked for me. I tried them all."[42]

To effectively play the Roland requires a technical approach that differs from how one might play a conventional electric guitar, Metheny explains:

> You have to play very light and very clean. If you pick really hard, it tends to make a sound which isn't clear to the converter, but if it hears a pure tone, or just the note, it tracks really fast. . . . As far as technical differences go, you have to be quite a bit more accurate in terms of pitches; like you play the guitar you slide over a string and touch it really quick, because the guitar has no sustain quality unless you're holding down the string. If you're playing a sound on a guitar synthesizer which has got a long sustain, you only play one, but it sounds like five notes are ringing. If you accidentally touch another note, the computer registers that you want to play a harmonic there.[43]

Musical Examples: "Barcarole" and "Are You Going with Me?" (1981)

The first time we hear Metheny on the Roland guitar synthesizer is on the Pat Metheny Group album *Offramp* (1981). The first notes Metheny plays evoke a cry, bending slightly up and down, repeated again before the phrase is completed with quicker notes. He joins a quietly pulsing, repeated rhythmic sequence that opened this track. A rich harmonic foundation gradually emerges as we hear keyboard sounds, emulating the timbres of an ethereal string section, enter the mix, slowly traversing a sequence of chords over which Metheny etches piercing cries. The synthesizer sounds are Synclavier tracks created by Metheny in the studio, overlaid by Lyle Mays's keyboards.

The guitar hints at the unfolding process of an *alap*, the opening section of a Hindustani raga, in which the sitarist plays a note and, as if feeling out possible nuances of that note, repeats it and approaches it from above and below. Here, though, melodic phrases emerge, tracking the synthesizer harmonies, occasionally leaping upward to follow the next chord. Meanwhile, the rhythms—electronic and human—steadily continue. At one point, Naná Vasconcelos doubles Metheny's melody with three notes on his berimbau, a plucked single-string Brazilian instrument attached to a gourd resonator. Around the middle point of the piece, the chords begin to steadily ascend, and soon Metheny plays a second line while sustaining an open string. This opens the door to rapid phrases, chord clusters, and what seems, for a moment, like the start of a free-form segment, which fades out.

Having introduced the guitar synthesizer on "Barcarole," Metheny has prepared the way for its more expansive use in the composition that immediately follows. Considering the warm, upbeat mood that opens "Are You Going with Me?," one might imagine the subsequent guitar sound to be Metheny's liquid-toned electric guitar, but the music has entered new sonic territory.

The rhythmic Synclavier sequences that continue throughout "Are You Going with Me?" are two-measure units. Each one predictably begins on the downbeat; a slight delay in the accented beat, which gives it a syncopated feel, resolves before the repeat of the unit. The slightly off-kilter rhythm of the sequence contributes to perception that the beat is flexible rather than robotic. As the sequences transpose across a series of chord changes, the main theme is heard on synthesizer. Mays's solo follows, played using a harmonica timbre, continuing the upbeat mood.

The first-time listener may be caught off guard by the sudden shift from Mays's lilting "harmonica" to the sonic intensity of Metheny's guitar synthesizer. Metheny's solo builds slowly, treating each phrase as a breath, followed by a pause. He makes dramatic use of the chord changes to build and release tension. As the harmonic cycles begin to ascend stepwise through a series of transpositions, the tension steadily heightens. The solo reaches a dramatic peak as Metheny plays rapid scalar phrases, but it expands even further during a final coda that seems to freeze time and then explodes as if it were the close of a late work by John Coltrane.

Mervyn Cooke offers a useful detailed transcription and analysis comparing two recorded versions of Metheny's solo in "Are You Going with Me?," the first on *Offramp* and the second a live performance on *Travels* (1983).[44] The two share commonalities: staccato repeated notes, gradual expansion of simple gestures, the lightning-fast runs (while most are ascending, one on

92 Chapter Six

Travels descends, providing dramatic contrast). The comparison points to how Metheny can, on a nightly basis, vary a related set of musical materials to craft very different solos.

These solos, plus two others on *Offramp*—on the opening track "Barcarole" and "Song for Bilbao"—demonstrate why the Roland synthesizer proved to be such a useful musical vehicle for Pat Metheny. It provides dramatic contrast with his electric and acoustic guitars, sonically and in the phrases he shapes, Metheny's articulations at times sharing the trumpet qualities he speaks of. The Roland has remained a staple of Metheny's hundreds of performances ever since.

Musical Example: "Offramp" (1981)

When I discussed the guitar synthesizer on the album *Offramp*, I skipped over the more abstract title track. "Offramp" displays sustained angularity and a suggestion of atonality. I say "suggestion" because, as is often the case, Metheny's work is grounded in bass pedal points and implied harmonies. A parallel example can be heard in sections of great density and intensity in "The Calling" (*Rejoicing*, 1983), discussed in appendix 1.

The composed theme of "Offramp" is made up of three motifs. Extended guitar synthesizer and bass improvisations are interspersed between returns of the theme. The first motif is serpentine in shape, but it moves so rapidly that the details are barely noticeable except for a closing octave leap. It sets a pattern repeated during the next two motifs, continuing with repetitions of its opening phrase, ending on a sustained note.

The second motif contrasts with the first. The opening notes of its first phrase organically lead into a brief, repeating figure. This is transposed into other adjoining keys and, like the first motif, it ends on a sustained note. Notice the arc trajectory contained within this single segment. The third motif provides an emphatic "answer" to the "question" that seems to be posed by the first two. It rapidly rises and falls and ends in an ascending leap.

A C pedal tone grounds the opening of the composition. It is transposed, stepwise and chromatically, leading to a G pedal. There it remains until it resolves on the C pedal as the theme concludes. While the composition's phrases are angular, the pedal tones and call-and-response patterns call to mind a (distant?) cousin of a blues form.

After the composed section, Metheny begins his improvisation with a lyrical melodic phrase, which he repeats and transposes. Between phrases, he pauses and continues with rapid angular runs. Then, a double-stop counterpoint segment appears, another element that will find echoes in "The Calling." After a repeat of the composed theme, a magical collage-like tinkling of bells leads to an extended bass solo, and the bass solo becomes transformed into a duet. This provides a bridge to Metheny's fleeting, solemn synthesizer passage. Metheny suddenly shifts to the opening theme, but before one final repetition, he treats the listener to a "race to the finish" dual-line synthesizer passage.

Throughout, Danny Gottlieb nods to traditions of drumming that follow and propel the energy levels of the soloist. Sometimes he engages in parallel play with the soloist. This approach can be found in the work of Rashied Ali playing with John Coltrane during his late period, Sunny Murray with Cecil Taylor, and Denardo Coleman on Ornette Coleman's *Crisis*.

The Roland synthesizer provides Metheny with an instrument well suited to his lyricism and expressivity, nuance of articulation, and alternation of percussive attack and long sustain. At times, his playing is reminiscent of Ornette Coleman's plaintive cries and downward pitch slides. Also, like Coleman's saxophone, the Roland synthesizer can cut through other layers of instruments, particularly drums, without restraining the space and volume they may require.

The Roland guitar synthesizer again appears on "End of the Game," the sixth track on Pat Metheny Group's 1984 album *First Circle*. Metheny's Roland playing also provides a point of heightened drama on "Dream of the Return"—a rare song with lyrics—and "Are We There Yet" from *Letter from Home* (1989). I will discuss two other Roland performances, on "The Calling" (1983) and "Endangered Species" (1986), in appendix 1. Roland guitar synthesizer solos continue to grace Metheny's albums and concerts to this day.[45]

CHAPTER 7

Drummers and Wordless Vocals

Playing Pat Metheny's Music from the Drummer's Seat:
Paul Wertico and Antonio Sanchez

Both of Danny Gottlieb's successors in the drum chair of the Pat Metheny Group—Paul Wertico (*First Circle*, 1984 through *Imaginary Day*, 1997) and, finally, Antonio Sanchez—went through periods of adjustment after joining the band. All three drummers were quite different from one another.

Paul Wertico

Paul Wertico had developed an idiosyncratic style as a young drummer. He remembers:

> When I started playing [drums], I was listening to John Coltrane and Charles Lloyd at the same time as I was listening to the Who and Cream. So, I never really differentiated between the two much. If I have a strange style, it probably comes from that. I always just heard music as music. Even back in high school, in concert or marching band, I came up with strange parts. My band director was very supportive and gave me "carte blanche" to do things. I always reacted to the music in a different way than if I had just come out of books or had a teacher who told me this is what you are supposed to do.[1]

Wertico built his early professional reputation playing around Chicago; his specialty was open improvisational (often known as "free") settings. "Mojave" and "Badland" on *Quartet* (1996) and the album *The Sign of 4* (1997)[2] provided such opportunities to play with Metheny. Wertico explained in a 2014 interview[3] that Pat Metheny first sought to hire him in 1979, and he eventually played two auditions[4] in advance of a 1983 Pat Metheny Group European tour.

Wertico and Sanchez after him were each already using flat ride cymbals before joining Metheny—Sanchez because he had been at first primarily a rock drummer and Wertico since hearing Chick Corea's *Now He Sings, Now He Sobs*, on which Roy Haynes plays them.

The biggest challenge for Wertico when he joined the PMG "was basically learning all the arrangements since there weren't that many charts" and adapting during an intense European tour that began in January 1983. "After every gig," he says, "Pat took notes and had comments for us on what we can do better on this or that, to give him what he was looking for. So that was a real on-the-job learning experience."[5] Wertico "had always played around with new sounds," including drum triggers and effects processing, and he says that adapting to playing with the sequencers "wasn't difficult for me at all," despite it being his first time. However, on that first tour, instead of

> using a click track or headphones, I had this gigantic monitor by my hi-hat that always needed to be above the volume of the rest of the band's sound—including my drums and Pat's guitar—and Pat was really loud, plus I was positioned right next to him. But, for the most part we rarely, if ever, got off with the sequencer.[6]

Having played previously with Steve Rodby in Chicago, Wertico benefited from the helpful hints the bassist would provide regarding Metheny's preferences. Singer and percussionist Pedro Aznar joined the band around the same time as Wertico, and, Wertico says, "as the new members, we really bonded" and became like a mutual support team, spending time together analyzing the music. "Later, by the time the first US tour began, things were much smoother, and Pedro and I settled much more into the music and the group."[7]

Wertico's skill set proved to be broad and adaptive, well suited to the Pat Metheny Group, as Michael Bettine and Trevor Taylor observe about *Letter from Home* (1989): "Paul's touch on the cymbals is light, floating on the top of the music. This pushes the tune without forcing it. . . . Paul has the ability to integrate his drumming into the music so that the band moves and turns with him."[8]

In contrast, on *Imaginary Day* (1997), Bettine and Taylor describe Wertico's playing as "often taking on a heavier feel to the music. . . . The floating

96   Chapter Seven

[Latin] groove is frequently replaced by straight ahead swing and even driving rock. 'The Roots of Coincidence' shows Paul laying into the drums with an energetic back beat."[9]

Antonio Sanchez

Wertico's successor, Antonio Sanchez, began his musical odyssey as a pianist and rock drummer. Sanchez says that studying piano and classical music and analyzing scores and ideas about musical structure "informs the way I see music in general and has allowed me to interpret music in a more informed way. I think it opened my ears quite a bit to melodic and harmonic material . . . [helping me] connect the dots between all kinds of music, from classical to jazz, to pop to rock, you name it."[10] He continues:

> Coming from rock or pop, as I did, it was useful for me to hear drummers like John Bonham, Neil Peart from Rush, and Stewart Copeland. Neil Peart was a master of orchestration. He would compose the parts and play the same fill every single time. I wanted to be a composite between doing that and, also, as a jazz drummer, be completely free.

Sanchez became familiar with the Pat Metheny Group when he was "a teenager growing up in Mexico City in the '80s." He recalls the DJ on radio station FM 96.9, Alejandro Gonzales Iñarritu,[11] playing "Last Train Home" on his nightly show: "I remember the haunting vocals, the melody, and the rest. I was like, 'Man, this is so different from what I've heard before.' . . . I thought, 'Wow, that's really cool.'"

Metheny first heard and spoke with Sanchez when the drummer was playing in pianist Danilo Perez's Jazz Latin trio,[12] opening for Metheny's trio with Larry Grenadier and Bill Stewart. Sanchez remembers:

> Pat was listening to us while he was having dinner backstage after his set, and the promoter asked him, "So how do you like this band?" And he said, "Yeah, I like it. I especially like the way the drummer and the percussionist play together." And then the promoter said, "It's only one guy. There's no percussion player." So, Pat stood up and went to check me out. I had a hybrid kit, a full jazz kit, but I had a bunch of percussion elements. I was doing this crazy independence thing playing the clave with my left foot, and we were doing all these time signatures the trio had been working on. I think I impressed him. Also, one of the things he told me afterwards is that for

Drummers and Wordless Vocals   97

the Pat Metheny Group, he likes somebody that comes more from playing straight-eighth-note music than swing.

Sanchez's audition session with Metheny was, like Wertico's, an hours-long duet, in this case auspiciously beginning with Ornette Coleman's "Turnaround." Sanchez recalls:

> Within a few bars I started relaxing and just enjoying the experience. . . . I remember it felt very easy and comfortable playing with him. Our time feel aligned very easily. We kept getting together every time we would both be in town and we both really seemed to enjoy the experience, although he would never reveal too much about his intentions to hire me, until around six months later when he made it official.[13]

When Sanchez first joined the group, recording *Speaking of Now* in 2001, he found that

> the band had its own language and syntax. It was like playing jazz while not playing jazz, if that makes any sense. We had to play and interact as if we were playing swing and bebop, but in the Pat Metheny Group straight-eighth-note style, which changed the whole equation.
>
> I was really trying to emulate the sound and vocabulary that both Danny and Paul had created while trying to inject my style into the mix, but at that point I definitely hadn't found my own voice within the group. It took months of touring for everybody to start feeling comfortable with me. I had never been in a situation where I came into a band that had been around for so long and that had such an extensive catalog and history. It was a great learning experience. . . . With the new material, it was no problem because nobody had played the music prior to me. . . . Pat and the whole band started getting used to me, getting used to my sound, to my touch, my feel. Then, all of a sudden, everything we were trying to do started becoming a lot more effortless.

Metheny offered helpful hints early on, and later, the two discussed choices of cymbals and snare drums. Having studied piano and classical music, Sanchez was already attuned to thinking in terms of orchestration. As a result, he says, "my drums had started expanding, [so I could] have more orchestrational choices and more colors. Pat's music was definitely one of the best places I could really bring all this in."

One challenge for each of the drummers in the Pat Metheny Group was the long duration of the shows and intense volume level of the band. Antonio Sanchez notes that the *Speaking of Now* tour started out with nearly four-hour nightly sets: "That was a brutal one." Within a couple weeks, the shows shortened a bit, which "seemed like a vacation. It was so intense. I didn't really know how to pace myself back then, and I was playing too hard. I was too eager." Sanchez particularly enjoyed playing "Roots of Coincidence" from *Imaginary Day* (first recorded in 1997) on that tour; after playing the composed sections, he says, "the solo section is super open, and it's as if you're playing bop, but heavy metal bop. . . . That's all I could ask for as a drummer, a gig where I could use all my abilities." Using a click track with in-ear monitors — one cannot hear the sound of the hall — was a new experience but one that Sanchez adapted to over time. He discovered just how loud the actual volume was once during an encore, when he removed a failing monitor from his ear.

The next Pat Metheny project that included Antonio Sanchez was the extended work *The Way Up* (2005) by the Pat Metheny Group, the topic of chapter 8. In between his two recordings with the PMG, Sanchez joined Metheny's trio with Christian McBride (*Day Trip* and *Tokyo Day Trip* [both 2008]). Metheny came to view Sanchez as a primary musical partner in much of his work, which has included a reunion band with Gary Burton (*Quartet Live* [2009]); the three Unity group albums *Unity Band*, *Kin* (←→), and *Unity Sessions* (2012–2015); and the *Evening with Pat Metheny* band with pianist Gwilyn Simcock and bassist Linda Han Oh, which recorded *From This Place* in 2020. Sanchez reflects:

> I could see that Pat liked having me around because I was easy to work with, and I was incredibly committed to anything he was doing. I was eager to play with him more. I love touring with him, so after a while, he would just let me be myself.

Soon, Metheny started welcoming Sanchez to invent his own drum parts. "I had already learned how to speak his musical language, so everything I played usually kind of fit right in. Pat would usually leave it wide open for me to just see what I would hear."

As an ensemble player, Antonio Sanchez strives for

> a very good balance between proposing and imposing. I think there are a lot of drummers and other musicians that impose, and I like to try to be one of the ones who propose. . . . if you propose an idea and it doesn't really fly and

nobody takes it, then you abort. Every time you play, micro decisions are happening in split seconds.

At the same time, he applies to the role of the drummer the metaphor of "a Persian rug,"

> where everybody thinks "Wow! This is such a beautiful rug. I'm gonna stand on it, and it feels so comfortable." And then they take off their shoes, and they start walking around and think, "Man, this is the greatest rug ever!" And then I like to pull the rug out and shake it, so while they remain comfortable, there's always something happening for them to react to.

Sanchez's ability to successfully *propose*, amid performance, shifts in musical dynamics, rhythmic feel, intensity, complexity, and other dynamics, depends not only on acceptance on the fly by Pat Metheny, but importantly, upon bassist Steve Rodby's holding the center while improvisationally making even the most subtle adaptations. Sanchez has excelled by being flexible when called for, continuing to provide stability, but "proposing" when there is space and mutual agreement. He, like Pat Metheny, knows that

> as a drummer, you have a lot of power over the band. . . . That's why [Pat] says that the drummer is always the leader . . . you can really steer things using dynamics, tempo, and time feel, in ways that other instruments can't. Being aware of that power, you really must be careful about how you use it.

Dynamic contrast, variation in the range of volume from barely audible to very loud, has, as Steve Rodby observes, "always been a huge part of Pat's aesthetic, and therefore of the band's performance." This musical attribute has factored into how Metheny constructs set lists, and it is a feature within his multisection compositions. We have seen the depth to which drummers Paul Wertico and Antonio Sanchez each attended to dynamic contrast in their playing.

Wordless Vocals

In contrast to the dynamics of drums and other instrumental sounds of the Pat Metheny Group, the voices that entered the sonic blend in the early 1980s provide a unique nuance within the musical fabric. Gradations of vocal qualities are apparent in the grainy, wispy low notes that hover between emotive expression and disintegration; in the towering, extroverted long tones high up in the falsetto range that project pathos and hope; and in the introverted innocence of the more hushed, rounded midrange tones.

I first experienced these vocal qualities when listening to Brazilian singer Milton Nascimento on Wayne Shorter's *Native Dancer* (1975). This led me to Nascimento's own albums, *Milton* (1976), then *Courage* (1969), and many more. I didn't yet realize that Nascimento's folklike melodies, complex harmonies, and evocative lyrics were connected to a much broader expanse of Brazilian popular music that intersected with American jazz musicians. When I saw Pat Metheny Group perform in 1984, Brazilian percussionist and singer Naná Vasconcelos helped bring this home for me.

It took me a while to realize that the music of Nascimento and Vasconcelos shared a Brazilian origin with music my father loved, that of Antônio Carlos Jobim, João Gilberto (including *Getz/Gilberto*, American jazz saxophonist Stan Getz's collaboration with the Brazilian songwriter),[14] and Sergio Mendes, at the time when bossa nova and samba were sweeping America in the early and mid-1960s. The music ranged from up-tempo melodies whose words zipped by at a rapid clip, to breezily unhurried, deeply emotional love songs. It was the latter that my dad loved the most; it was there where he could sing along and express his own very private emotions.

Pat Metheny's guiding musical concept has always been the idea that musical forms should support an expansive narrative arc. Metheny's *Bright Size Life* served as a template for the subsequent unfolding of this concept. All that was missing from that first iteration, he felt, was "a bit of synth orchestration, some percussion and wordless vocals."[15] Metheny understood that the voice could add a unique depth of expression to his music, even on its rapid, angular melodic lines. His conception had been to produce, with a small instrumental ensemble, a big, orchestrated sound on stage using digital synthesizers. But what was sonically missing was, he says, "breath. When I write the tunes, I think 'in trumpet.'"[16] A stream of breath is at the core of performing any wind instrument. A human singer can malleably shape not only the articulation but also the contours of a note as it emerges from the breath. Vowel sounds can subtly shift in qualities as a singer adjusts the shape of the mouth cavity. Consonants manifest upon engagement of the teeth, tongue, and lips.

Notes produced by the acoustic instruments in Metheny's band naturally decay, but adding voices allowed for more sustained pitches. Yet maybe even more important to Metheny was a desire to balance the increasing presence of electric and electronic instruments: "Having a strong and front-facing 'acoustic' balance to it all in the form of singing was essential to balance it out."[17]

While Vasconcelos was Brazilian and elements of Brazilian song had long influenced Metheny,[18] the key to understanding Metheny's use of vocalists (who have been from a variety of countries) isn't Brazil per se but simply the voice itself.

The role of wordless singers began when Naná Vasconcelos joined the band, providing merimbau, hand percussion, and unusual vocalizations in the Metheny/Mays joint project *As Falls Wichita, So Falls Wichita Falls* (1981) and then on *Offramp* (1982) and *Travels* (1983). Pedro Aznar succeeded Vasconcelos as Pat Metheny Group's vocalist. Aznar, bassist and multi-instrumentalist, hails from Argentina and is often associated with Argentine rock music.[19]

The pivotal moment that opened the conceptual door for Metheny to fully realize what he imagined possible with a singer unfolded when he met Aznar:

> When he gave me his demo tape, singing and playing all the instruments, when I met him in Brazil at a festival, it immediately changed the set of possibilities that might emerge with the band, and I don't think there could have been any individual then or now that would provide what he was able to provide. He could sing anything and to this day is one of the greatest technical singers I have ever heard, and it just opened up a whole new world of possibilities for me as a composer. Having him in the band was what allowed me to write *First Circle* and all the others that happened with him in there and set the stage even for what was possible later.[20]

Attentive Listening to the Vocalists

I have selected for listening ten recorded compositions that span the roster of Pat Metheny Group singers. I will explore each example considering Metheny's usage of wordless syllables[21] and how each singer approaches their role. Each of these examples is easily accessible, and the musical scores are all published. Most may be found in *The Pat Metheny Real Book*[22] or *The Pat Metheny Song Book: The Complete Collection—167 Compositions*.[23]

Wordless Vocals in Metheny's Up-Tempo, Dramatic Works

"The First Circle" (First Circle [1984], Vocal by Pedro Aznar)
This is a work that demands much from vocalist Pedro Aznar. The breadth of his singing skill set is exemplified by the variety of material in the score that he must deliver, from the opening declarative melody that leaps down and back up a fifth, to the stately, stepwise theme that follows. Even further, Aznar shifts

102   Chapter Seven

into the soaring falsetto conclusion of this three-part thematic structure. At every point when Aznar is singing full out, there's more to come.

"The First Circle,"[24] an expansive, dramatic, and ecstatic work, is a *happening*. Rhythmic patterns featuring handclaps, in units of two and three beats, open the piece with an unusual 22/8 meter. A repeated single note played on synthesizer provides a counterrhythm. Pedro Aznar enters, singing the calm yet anthem-like first theme that introduces a steadily unfolding structure (Figure 13, marker A). The clapping continues, joined by other rhythmic patterns on synthesizers. An acoustic guitar passage ebbs and flows with the rising and falling of cymbals. A countermelody on orchestra bells[25] adds another layer, creating a rich counterpoint.

The listener is guided to the second, more rhythmically insistent vocal melody at 2:28 (rehearsal mark C in the published score; Figure 13 in this book begins partway into the melody, at 2:45). Tambourine shakes add texture. Emotional tension increases as Aznar's vocal melody, doubled by a synthesizer line, leaps to a high G in falsetto range, and then descends (at 2:53, Figure 13, marker D; and repeated at at 8:16, marker H in the published score). The tension continues to build as the entire second melody is repeated. At the height of the piece, Aznar sings at nearly full capacity, pressed on by drumming that continues to grow in intensity.

Lyle Mays's acoustic piano solo begins at 4:45, calm at first, building around 6:00. Rich synthesizer orchestration and heavily accented drumming recap the second melodic theme at 7:00, which at 7:35[26] is rejoined by Aznar and Mays's thickly chordal acoustic piano. An overdubbed countermelody leads to the coda, at 8:40, with Aznar singing full out. The clapping returns for one cycle, leading to the sudden, dramatic conclusion.

"Tell It All"[27] (First Circle [1984], Vocal by Pedro Aznar)

Pedro Aznar delivers the opening melody as a forcefully stated folk melody. As in "The First Circle," Aznar reaches high in his chest-voice register. Despite the strength of his falsetto range, he remains in chest voice, producing a more textured sound. The second theme could easily be a trumpet line, demanding another act of endurance that Aznar achieves in an emotionally satisfying manner.

Like "The First Circle," "Tell It All" opens with a rhythmic pattern, this time played by cowbell in an asymmetrical 4/4 pattern, suggestive of a Latin percussion band. A gentle melodic theme with a folk quality is sung by Pedro Aznar over the rhythmic patterns. Aznar is singing at the top of his range without entering falsetto (Figure 13). Pat Metheny's electric guitar solo begins at 0:52, backed by drums and bass and, periodically, figures on tuned

Figure 13 Up-tempo Metheny compositions with wordless vocals: "The First Circle" and "Tell It All"

percussion (go-go bells). A minute and a half into his solo, Metheny alternates high-register octaves and rapid runs.

The guitar solo gives way to an interlude, a chordal pattern (at marker C in the published score; subsequent markers may also be found in that score), to which Aznar's singing adds another layer at 3:29, thickening the density (at marker D). Mays's piano solo begins at 3:50, in single notes at first, then growing into breath-long phrases. At 5:00 he begins to build momentum, supported by the drummer's forceful cymbal play, leading to rapid piano runs and eventually chordal structures. The chordal melody (interlude D) returns on voice, guitar, and piano, leading into the coda (at 6:15), this time with the addition of accented rhythmic hits on the go-go- bells. As the bells continue, Aznar's vocal returns at 6:35 (at A, now labeled F—Outro), and the piece reaches its conclusion with go-go bells alone.

"Third Wind" (Still Life [Talking] [1987] and The Road to You *[1993],[28] Vocals by David Blamires and Mark Ledford)*

This composition demands a vocal quality akin to a trumpet, relentlessly declaring the opening melodic theme. The rapid-fire descent that opens each segment of the second theme requires precision and a consistently strong voice. Metheny asks that the singer produce a consistently Olympic performance; this unfolding work requires endurance.

An exuberant mix of drum kit, timbales, and acoustic piano set the stage for Pat Metheny's electric guitar entrance with the first theme. Vocalists David Blamires and Mark Ledford join in repetitions of the theme, beginning at 0:29 (Figure 14, marker C; in the published score, also at marker D), ending with a long sustained note. Metheny's guitar solo suddenly begins at 1:34, actively and rhythmically comped by driving percussion. A quick cut at 3:07 shifts the music to a quietly rhythmic ticking synthesizer pattern, overlaid with timbale hits.

The second theme, presented by voice and synthesizer at 3:20 (and again at 4:22), presents a rapidly descending contrasting melody. Repetitions of the melody, first at 3:48, are interspersed with rhythm breaks, most markedly with layered, stuttering rhythmic synthesizer patterns. When these patterns return, they will be briefly doubled by the vocals. Following another drum break at 5:10, a growing mass of sustained synthesizer notes crescendos, emerging in a melody.

Suddenly, Mays plays a chordal cycle at 5:34, which is soon joined by a vocal return of the second theme (at 5:55, Figure 14, marker R; in the published score, also at marker S). With each repetition, the layers increase in

Figure 14 Up-tempo Metheny compositions with wordless vocals: "Third Wind" and "Have You Heard"

number. Cutting through them, Metheny suddenly carves a soaring Roland guitar synthesizer solo. Toward the conclusion, the melody comes forward in the mix, concluding on a sustained pitch, as "Third Wind" dramatically ends on an accented note.

"Have You Heard"[29] (Letter from Home [1989] and The Road to You *[1993], Vocals by David Blamires and Mark Ledford)*
Again, the vocal lines here are trumpet-like and demanding for a singer. The opening melody, first played by electric guitar and synthesizer, rises and falls in steady eighth notes, spanning a two-octave range. At one point, the voice and electric guitar play in unison, while a trumpet provides a contrapuntal line. The variety of timbres enriches the sound. At a later point, voice and trumpet play in unison, backed by a synthesized horn section. This is a useful exemplar of a small band producing a large, highly orchestrated sound.

Following a two-bar syncopated rhythmic cycle in 7/4 (the meter subsequently alternates between 5/4, 3/4, and 4/4), the first of three themes is introduced. The initial one is a steadily flowing angular melody played on electric guitar, concluding with a brief accented rhythmic figure. It is a study in how angularity can be tuneful. Blamires doubles the guitar on the theme, beginning at 1:00 (Figure 14, marker A). Upon its repetition, the theme is juxtaposed with a trumpet countermelody. Metheny plays an interlude at 1:51, backed by synthesizer, piano, and rhythm section, providing a segue to his guitar solo. Metheny is spurred on by Steve Rodby's driving bass line and joined periodically by a string accompaniment.

A trumpet, played by Mark Ledford, and synthesizer horn section heighten the intensity of the latter portion of the solo. A brief melodic interlude returns us to the vocal melody, at 4:33, with David Blamires and Mark Ledford's combined voices doubled by the synthesizer. The horns return and the melody concludes with a long sustained note. The rhythmic pattern of the opening returns. This time it is orchestrated with voice, trumpet, synthesizers, and piano, and the performance concludes on a sustained Dm^9 chord.

Wordless Vocals in Medium-Tempo Works: Many Moods and Dynamics

"Every Summer Night" (Letter from Home [1989],[30] Vocal by Pedro Aznar)
In this performance, Pedro Aznar's voice is layered with Pat Metheny's electric guitar, adding a warmth and buoyancy to a spirited melody. When Aznar

106   Chapter Seven

returns late in the performance, he sings in the high end of his natural range (not entering falsetto), conveying heightened emotion.

Atop an evenly accented 4/4 rhythm—every eighth note is accented—the catchy first melodic theme of "Every Summer Night" is played on Mays's synthesizer's "harmonica" timbre, backed by funk-inflected organ and piano. The lilting second theme, sung by Pedro Aznar (at 1:05, Figure 15, marker B) doubled by harmonica and electric guitar, gives way to a more lightly ticking 3/4 feel. This melody has a gentle, almost waltz-like sway. The first melody returns at 1:33, again on "harmonica," this time doubled by a second synthesizer line. A third melody, a lyrical continuation of the second theme, is introduced at 2:15, still in 4/4.

Pat Metheny's electric guitar solo begins at 2:24, backed by a steady in-the-pocket beat; entering during the second chorus is a layer of strings. It is followed at 3:25 by Mays's piano solo, which at 3:55 is joined by funky organ comping. The sequence of melodies is repeated starting at 4:42, with Aznar singing the second theme at 5:12. His voice has a grittier quality this time around, as he sings in the upper register of his chest voice. Mays's chordal passage leads us to a final round of the third melody and into a very brief organ chorale conclusion.

"Afternoon" (Speaking of Now [2002], Vocal by Richard Bona)

Richard Bona pivots from an upbeat, breezy use of his voice in the opening melody to a sound of great intensity, repositioning from a strong chest voice to finely shaped falsetto. Later in the performance, when he alternates between the two sections of the melody, Bona increases the expressive depth, interpreting the melodies (particularly the second) in a manner that suggests an improvisational quality.

This catchy, moderate-tempo tune is aptly titled. The accompaniment has a backbeat, while it projects a funk sensibility. The opening melody, gentle and lilting, is played on electric guitar backed by vibraphone, drums, bass, and strings. The speech-like rhythm suggests a "lazy" restful day—the first two notes of the melody are followed by a brief pause before the continuation of each phrase.

Richard Bona's vocal begins during the second section, providing an impassioned response to the opening. This part of the melody is prefaced with a rapidly moving passage (at 0:29, Figure 15, marker B, "Verse #1"). Halfway through this second section, Bona shifts into a beautiful falsetto. He joins Metheny in a repetition of the opening melody (at 1:23, Figure 15, marker C, "Chorus").

Figure 15 Medium-tempo Metheny compositions with wordless vocals: "Every Summer Night" and "Afternoon"

The performance continues by alternating between the two sections of the melody. Bona's vocalization grows increasingly expressive, and he adds subtle variations within his lines, improvisationally interpreting the melody. For a time, Bona sings with rubato, but toward the close of each melody, he more emphatically lands on the beat.

Pat Metheny's electric guitar solo begins at 3:00; a half minute later, the constantly repeating melodic themes return and continue through the conclusion, accompanied by Metheny's mellifluous guitar.

"On Her Way" (Speaking of Now [2002], Vocal by Richard Bona)

In this performance, Richard Bona displays contrasting aspects of his singing, first providing a quiet backdrop, then, during the second theme, intensely and powerfully singing an anthem.

"On Her Way" opens with an upbeat, up-tempo melody played on electric guitar, quietly accompanied by acoustic guitar. After the drums enter at 0:35, Richard Bona quietly doubles the guitar. A third contrapuntal layer adds to the unfolding perpetual motion; the steadily building synthesizer orchestration leads to Bona's confident introduction of the second theme, an anthemic melody (at 1:05, Figure 16, marker C).

Metheny's guitar solo begins at 1:49. Toward the end of the solo, the accompanying orchestration grows in intensity. Bona reprises the anthemic melody at 3:00, with the orchestration increasing in density upon its repetition. A second guitar solo bridges to the outro (at 4:07, Figure 16, marker J). Mays's synthesizer lines echo Bona's singing of the melody, with Metheny's guitar weaving in and out, accompanied by a celebratory mix of organ, piano, bass, and drums.

"Something to Remind You"[31] (We Live Here [1995], Vocals by David Blamires and Mark Ledford[32])

David Blamires and Mark Ledford together provide a strong, lovely doubling of an upbeat melody. This contributes to a sense of grandeur as the climax of the performance unfolds.

"Something to Remind You" begins with an upbeat rhythm track, as if introducing a slow dance tune, lushly scored with a string section. Its catchy sensibility, however, foreshadows a second theme for which we will have to wait until the two-minute mark.

When Pat Metheny introduces the melody of the first theme on guitar (in the published score at rehearsal mark B),[33] the emotional quality is far gentler, even yearning. Metheny's note slides add a deeply emotional, human vocal quality. Orchestra bells double the guitar and piano orchestration, leading to the entrance of an upbeat countermelody by the singers at 2:02, backed by acoustic piano and synthesizer. This returns us to the sunny mood evoked by the rhythm section at the opening of this track.

Pat Metheny's solo begins at 2:24. The strings and, periodically, orchestra bells gain strength in the mix, as the solo continues at 3:36 with rapid runs and

Figure 16 Medium-tempo Metheny compositions with wordless vocals: "On Her Way" and "Something to Remind You"

then languid melodicism. Mays's organ crescendos, starting at 4:15, bridge the return of the vocalized countermelody at 4:23 (Figure 16, marker F). This is tightly backed by funky piano and sustained lush strings. Reverberant drum backbeat hits provide a more laid-back feel. The melody repeats again and again, transposing upward, and is joined by synthesized horns. The melody, voices, and horns call to mind the band Earth, Wind & Fire at its height.

Wordless Vocals in Metheny Ballads

"Goodbye" (Travels [1983], Vocal by Naná Vasconcelos)[34]

The fragility of Vasconcelos's voice is the vocal feature that most lends to the emotive qualities of this piece. Vasconcelos gently lengthens many of the syllables in the middle of phrases, a technique he shares with Milton Nascimento. This heightens the way he proffers an impassioned plea, as Vasconcelos transits through a series of moods.

After a brief introduction—synthesizer pad, orchestra bells, and electric guitar—Vasconcelos sings the understated melodic theme beginning at 0:44, continuing where it is notated at 1:17 (Figure 17, after marker B, continuing into C). Each of the successive three sections of the melody builds upon or responds to its predecessor. Metheny's electric guitar solo emerges from the band's gentle comping. The optimistic mood of this solo contrasts with the bittersweet yearning of the melody, as Metheny makes use of the extended form of the chord changes to craft a long, connected melodic and chordal solo arc. This solo returns us to the melody, sung again by Vasconcelos at 5:30 (the notated portion is at 6:05), the band building momentum as the singer turns to long tones in the final moments. "Goodbye" concludes with a lovely melodic passage played by Mays employing a vibraphone timbre.

"You" (Speaking of Now [2002], Vocal by Richard Bona[35]*)*

Richard Bona pairs an expressive voice with uniquely crafted vocal syllables. In the lower and middle ranges, Bona's carefully shaped syllables set a languid mood. His falsetto register offers a rich timbre and tonal clarity. In various sections of this work, particularly across repetitions of melody, Bona builds vocal intensity, which he maintains throughout long sustained notes.

Following Pat Metheny's quiet introduction on finger-picked acoustic guitar, Richard Bona begins the gently swaying melody of "You" at the lower end of his range. (at 0:12, Figure 17, marker A; at 0:31, marker B). The next section reaches into a higher register, Bona carefully shaping the tones in his falsetto range (at 0:53, Figure 17, marker C), The melody returns to Bona's lower register at 1:01, finding resolution on a sustained final note in falsetto,

Figure 17 Metheny ballads with wordless vocals: "Goodbye" and "You"

at 1:23, leading into a brief electric guitar bridge. This returns us to the opening melody at 1:44, an octave higher. This is accompanied by a rich-sounding backdrop of piano, acoustic guitar, and strings. The latter section of the composition ebbs and flows, enriched by a second layer of Bona's voice.

The lilting melody segment at 2:48 (Figure 17, marker G) culminates in Bona's upward reach to a high E, followed by a sustained D one step below (at rehearsal mark H in the published score[36]). The long sustained notes of the melody ascend stepwise at 3:12. The composite sound of Bona's falsetto voice and the instrumentals are oceanic. At 3:32 the music shifts to a synthesizer and voice duet that continues until Metheny's guitar solo begins at 3:55. The solo is backed by strummed acoustic guitar and makes use of the chord cycle to traverse varying moods. At 5:18 Lyle Mays's piano solo begins. Bona returns to the opening melody at 6:18, singing long tones at 7:00 in full voice, as the orchestration steadily builds to a climax. From 7:30 onward, Bona's vocalizations continue as the sound of the band slowly fades.

Observations about Metheny's Music with Wordless Vocals, Composition, and Performance

Pat Metheny utilizes vocalists in multiple ways within his orchestration. To achieve his goals, Metheny sought to choose singers who shared at least two attributes: strong, expressive voices, and substantial stamina.

One of Metheny's compositional strategies in setting music with wordless vocals is, of course, found in his ballads. Metheny has composed numerous ballads without a vocalist. But when a wordless singer is part of the orchestration, Metheny draws upon his knowledge that differences in tone quality between low and high portions of a singer's range, and between chest voice and falsetto, produce differences in timbre, vocal strength, and tonal clarity. We experienced these contrasts in Naná Vasconcelos's treatment of "Goodbye," and it is a strong feature of Richard Bona's performance of "You."

We have witnessed some of the contrasting qualities of sound and emotion that singers can produce by selective use of chest voice and falsetto. Pedro Aznar's rendition of "Every Summer Night" and Richard Bona's interpretation of "Afternoon" are useful examples. Bona also displays the strong contrast between relative calm and powered singing on "On Her Way." These are qualities that can be found in both Milton Nascimento and Toninho Horta's work, pairing vocal fragility and melodic emotionality with grainier sounds in the lower registers, declarative sounds higher in the chest voice, and a deep emotional richness in the falsetto range.

Another attribute of Pat Metheny's medium-tempo compositions that are orchestrated with vocalists is the distinctly human combination of buoyancy and confident joy. We heard this in each of Pedro Aznar's musical examples, and in David Blamires and Mark Ledford's performance on "Something to Remind You."

A third strategy Metheny employs is to treat the vocalist as if he were a trumpet. In these settings, the singer is expected to produce a steady, powerful vocal line, sometimes maintained over extended periods of time. The melodies can periodically take the form of continuous streams of notes. Performing works of this kind has been a strength of each of Metheny's singers, notably the duo of Mark Ledford and David Blamires.

The tremendous demands that Metheny places on singers expected to function akin to a trumpeter are most apparent in his multisection works. On "The First Circle," Pedro Aznar makes trumpet-like melodic leaps between registers, intensely pushing his vocal capacities in the more anthemic passages. The harder Aznar presses, the deeper the fragility of his singing, even when projecting an anthemic melodic theme. "Tell It All" is another Aznar example. David Blamires and Mark Ledford's performance of the equally demanding "Third Wind" and "Have You Heard" in both studio and live recording settings delivers tremendous vocal power in a way that seems almost effortless.

Metheny could easily have chosen a trumpeter rather than a singer for many of these compositions. In fact, the Pat Metheny Group has included two trumpeters. But what Metheny has gained from his vocalists is their ability to convey emotional power with a hint of vulnerability. Pedro Aznar's singing in the upper reaches of his chest voice exemplifies this attribute.

The choice of a vocalist rather than (or in addition to) a trumpeter has the advantage of employing an instrument (the voice) to shift between performance practices and qualities of emotion during the same piece. At times, Metheny's music demands different musical modalities in different sections of a composition. One theme can be declarative, while another is lyrical and another exudes warmth and buoyancy. The range of timbral possibilities for a singer is notably broad and variable. The addition of a wordless singer helped expand the expressive potential of an ensemble with electric and electronic instruments, more fully realizing the breadth of the performances of Metheny's compositions.

CHAPTER 8

The Way Up (2005) and Reflections on the Pat Metheny Group

Expanding Form

The most expansive work by the classic formation of the Pat Metheny Group is the album-length piece *The Way Up* (2005). Pat Metheny contemporaneously described this work as "sort of a zone that I think we've been leading to all along. We've always been interested in pushing form and trying to expand what the core meaning of the group could be in terms of the structures that we play."[1] *The Way Up* is, however, out of the norm in the history of the Pat Metheny Group since, even with the numerous solo sections, it is seamlessly through-composed. It has more in common with a Stravinsky piano concerto, the Who's *Tommy*, or Duke Ellington's "Black and Tan Fantasy" than it does a head-solo-solo-head bop band performance or a jazz or rock show's set list of a dozen unrelated tunes.

The idea of "pushing form" and "expanding . . . core meaning . . . in terms of structures" is really the story of Pat Metheny's compositional career—just not on this scale or to this degree of thematic continuity. *Bright Size Life* (1976), Metheny's first recording, introduced his concept of composing structures that facilitate improvisation, unconstrained by the harmonic guardrails of bebop song forms. Many of the tunes on that album were composed during Metheny's tenure with Gary Burton. Over the years, Metheny's compositional models grew in scale and level of detail. Some feature continuously unfolding improvisational sections that challenge the soloist to think in long arcs of time, navigating periods of drama, stasis, and disruptive change along the way, before ultimately finding resolution.

As Lyle Mays comments, the first expansion of Metheny's concept appears in the cinematic *As Falls Wichita, So Falls Wichita Falls* (1981):

> With that record we wanted to do a piece of music that was somehow away from the song form. So much of what we were doing [up to this point] were songs in which the improvisation was based on the harmonies in the song—in the jazz tradition. We wanted to try something where the improvisation happened not so much in the linear sense as in the *textural* sense.[2]

In "The First Circle" (1984), discussed in chapter 7, the compositional scale, number of contrasting sections, and diversity of sounds and textures had increased. *Secret Story* (1992) utilized a broad sonic palette including symphonic colors and a children's choir to convey a long-form story. "Half Life of Absolution" (on *The Road to You* [1993]) and "Imaginary Day" (on *Imaginary Day* [1997]) represented substantial longer-form works with an overarching structural logic.

The Way Up

The Way Up represents an organically structured four-movement musical work that draws upon a shared set of musical motifs, integrating composition and improvisation, sustained across four movements. The work is album length in scale, orchestrated utilizing a wide array of musical colors and textures.

The thematically organic nature of *The Way Up* draws from structures most often associated with classical music. Metheny comments about its "strong connections to the kind of development that one finds in [composers including Stravinsky and Debussy]."[3] But here, composed segments alternate with highly detailed structures intended to serve platforms for improvisation.

Yet *The Way Up* is not alone among twentieth-century extended works that integrate composed material and improvisation. Examples, generally assigned a "jazz" designation, include Charles Mingus's *Pithecanthropus Erectus*. Mingus recalls:

> In the summer of 1953, I had the privilege of running a series of "Jazz Workshop" concerts at the Putnam Central Club in Brooklyn which enabled various jazz musicians to get together to play new compositions written by themselves and other young composers. . . . I found out two important things from this series of concerts. First, that a jazz composition as I hear it in my mind's ear, although set down in so many notes on score paper and

precisely notated, cannot be played by a group of either jazz or classical musicians. Secondly, jazz, by its very definition, cannot be held down to written parts to be played with a feeling that goes only with blowing free. A classical musician might read all the notes correctly but play them without the correct feeling or interpretation, and a jazz musician, although he might read all the notes and play them with jazz feeling, inevitably introduces his own individual expression rather than what the composer intended. It is amazing how many ways a four-bar phrase of four beats per measure can be interpreted![4]

Mingus recognized that the performance demands of a hybrid work require musicians who are experienced across both disciplines. The composed score must be played accurately and true to the composer's intent, yet interpreted expressively, with neither distortion nor rigidity. Pat Metheny's concerns very much parallel those of Mingus:

In many ways the impulse to combine improvisation with a lot of written material is one of the most treacherous areas in jazz. It's a very difficult thing to get just the right balance particularly with a large ensemble where you wind up, on a human level, with a whole bunch of people sitting around counting rests. Somehow that basic human activity just adds a certain kind of energy to the whole proceedings that the audience notices and everybody senses.[5]

Multiple skill sets need be accompanied by an openness to the interpenetration of performing a score "as is" and improvising. This is precisely the kind of compositional approach Pat Metheny views as "a recurring and ongoing thing of interest for me," one he describes as "to blur the lines between what is written to be played and how the structures that the improvising will happen in can coexist."[6]

In creating *The Way Up*, Metheny paid as close attention to the musical form and unfolding of improvisation sections as he did to the through-composed material, as drummer Antonio Sanchez recalls:

When I started playing with Pat, every single solo was over a different harmonic structure, a different groove or time feel; everything would be different. So, it would be very challenging to keep things moving in different ways [across the sections]. As part of the band, you have to make it flow and discover what's the best thing to play in each of these sections.[7]

116   Chapter Eight

Individual segments of the music, including improvisational passages needed to be performed with an eye to the whole, as Pat Metheny commented in 2004:

[It] requires the ability to think orchestrally as well as improvisationally. It requires the capacity to see the larger picture of what the music is specifically shooting for from both the widest possible view and in microscopic detail. At the same time, you have to be loose, play with real and effective dynamics, deal with odd meters while making them sound natural and be able to play incredibly loud and incredibly soft and sound natural and convincing at all levels in between.[8]

For Sanchez, *The Way Up* required

[a delicate] balance, something Pat understands really well. Dynamic balance, harmonic and melodic balance . . . [unlike] a lot of jazz that just sounds very complex and very dense — and Pat can certainly do that — then he usually balances it out with something else that, all the sudden, the music breathes a lot. . . . *The Way Up* has incredibly difficult sections — but then the next section would be this beautiful, sultry melody that made everything breathe. He can always find ways to strike that balance in just a perfect way.[9]

The scale and level of detail of this work presented unusual challenges during the process of preparation and recording, as Sanchez recalls in an article about Pat Metheny Group drummers:

[It was] a very intricate piece of music to learn. . . . We went into the studio before they started writing the actual piece so that I could record a bunch of different grooves and feels for them to get ideas from. They would suggest what kind of things they were looking for and I would just start improvising and building upon the grooves I was playing and then they used some of the demos to build upon and compose. For example, the groove that you hear in the very beginning of the album is something that I improvised during that initial session. . . .

We recorded it in sections, so we didn't have to actually learn it until we were going to go on tour much later. Once I had the final master with me, I just kept listening to it every day for months so that it would just sip into my subconscious. By the time we started rehearsing it was already saved to my brain's hard drive but then we had to learn how to play it together which was a whole other ballgame. We rehearsed for 4–5 days only and then we had the first gig. One of the scariest experiences in all of our collective lives.

For the album recording, we all had demos that we checked out ahead of time but amazingly we didn't get to rehearse before the actual session because Pat and Lyle had just actually finished writing the whole piece, so we were assembling the music as we went along. I recorded all my parts in a week, but they were in the studio for much longer doing tons of post-production and overdubs.[10]

A detailed discussion of the form of this work may be found in appendix 2.

In this book, we've traversed a wide range of Pat Metheny's compositions, from brief ballads to extended works such as "The First Circle," *The Way Up*, and "America Undefined." Metheny relates the following story: "Someone came up to me and said, 'You know, one "Farmer's Trust" is worth 100 *The Way Ups*.'"[11] Indeed, there is a point to be made in favor of the elegant and brief musical statement that "says" all that needs to be articulated in a few dozen bars. This is in fact an argument I made earlier in this book regarding the strength of Metheny's ballads.

As a musician who knows this music from having played it and listened to it, I find the succinct elegance of the main motifs of *The Way Up*, their artful development, and the carefully etched solo forms to comprise an engaging and exciting work; the more closely one listens, the more crystalline detail becomes audible.

Reflections on the Pat Metheny Group and Its Place in the Career of Its Leader

Pat Metheny is always thinking about his present and upcoming projects more than he ponders those of the past. Yet while working on new forward-looking projects, he has been engaged for several years in a retrospective project, revising all fifty years of his compositions with a rotating crew of young musicians. Having seen two iterations of his Side Eye project band perform, it is nothing akin to a "cover band." Rather, it is a vehicle of rediscovery and consideration about what the music might mean now, and how it might be interpreted in a new era.

With hundreds of compositions, Pat Metheny's collaboration with this group, mining his entire body of music presents him an opportunity to learn something *new* from his own music. There are elements of one's work that cannot be apparent in one's earlier years but await discovery in the presence and imagination of a younger generation. Metheny's 2023–24 solo tour reflects yet another reexamination of the breadth and depth of five decades of his repertoire.

In the introduction to a collection of essays by guitarist Joel Harrison, Metheny writes:

> I would be happy to play any of these tunes from any period even now. It has always felt to me like those earliest *Real Book* tunes were the first rooms in an ever-expanding house that I have been adding onto for years and that is now a sprawling estate that contains a lifetime of experiences. I don't read through these tunes and feel that I should start tearing everything down and starting over. They still seem true and worth looking at even as my experiences as a musician and in life have filled in so much over the years. They seem to work together as a single thing—almost like chapters in a long running book.[12]

Complexities of Band Leadership and Authorship

Pat Metheny made the early decision to project an image of collectivity and shared compositional credit, rather than more clearly identifying the band as his band and the music as his music. He felt "that everyone felt like they had a stake in it all, particularly in the early going when we were really working hard," leading him to insist that on the cover of *Pat Metheny Group* (1978) "everyone's name be on the front, in the same size type as mine, despite being heavily advised against doing that by the record company, and by my manager Ted Kurland and others."[13] Indeed, the band members felt a strong stake in helping realize the success of this uncertain but promising enterprise through their impassioned playing and seemingly endless travel.

At the same time, the classic formation of PMG was always a vehicle to realize compositional ideas Metheny had been working on beginning prior to forming the band and continuing throughout. Some of those ideas have been performed and recorded by PMG and others by Metheny ensembles with other personnel and band names. Metheny views his projects, duos, trios, quartets, and other ensembles, along with his compositional repertoire, as all of one piece, although the PMG classic formation is his longest-standing ensemble to date.

Yet composing credits were presented by Metheny during the lifespan of this classic PMG formation, particularly in the earlier years, as a "joint, equal collaboration" between himself and Lyle Mays, while only four compositions in the PMG repertoire were distinctly penned by Mays.[14] An appendix to the first substantive *Pat Metheny Song Book* compilation (2000)[15] details the evolution of many compositions performed by the PMG. The commentary shows a complex interplay between Metheny's (and in some cases Mays's) initial ideas, and the evolution, additions, and distance traveled to realize final versions.

To offer two examples, Metheny comments that the Metheny composition "The First Circle" contained notable contributions by Mays: "Together we came up with an ending, with Lyle writing the great counterpart line to the final statement of the melody." Similarly, while the Mays composition "Across the Sky" was completed with "just a few melodic contributions from me, mainly the tag at the end of the main melody," that concluding phrase substantially changes the character and sense of direction of the entire melody. It may well have been that this kind of processing of the music in progress fed the impression that composition of music played by PMG was a collaborative process. Compositional credits were, nonetheless, on Metheny's mind as early as 1993, when he wrote in an essay published in a Gil Goldstein compilation about composition, "I was really liberal with the credits of things for what very often was a minimal amount of added content."[16]

In the post-2000 era, *The Way Up* (2005) was, of course, a substantial collaborative effort between Metheny and Mays. In Metheny's recent *The Pat Metheny Real Book*, "On Her Way" (*Speaking of Now* [2000]) represents what was otherwise an anomaly as a composition credited "by Pat Metheny and Lyle Mays."

Metheny had discovered early on that Mays's gifts were substantive, albeit in a different vein than his own: Mays was skilled at fine-tuning and further developing Metheny compositions in progress, adding and subtracting, and helping reorganize their forms. As Metheny wrote in the Goldstein book:

> Usually, I'll sit down with a little idea and write it down. If something comes of it that's great. But, after five minutes if I don't get something happening, I'll just say it was a dead end. What Lyle does is take my little dead ends and mixes them up with his stuff to make them into something. . . . "San Lorenzo" grew out of his kind of collaboration. I had three or four different licks in a twelve-string tuning and a basic tempo. Lyle took those licks and formed them into a composition. That's the way we work more often than not. I'll have a melody or two and a basic groove and he'll come up with a

way of presenting it in a more formal way. I tend to write heads and he tends to write compositions, so it works out well. . . . But most of the time our compositions center around tunes that I have, and that he fills out.[17]

Metheny's remembrance of Lyle Mays reflects his enduring appreciation:

There was never a time that I brought Lyle in to work on something that whatever it was didn't get better. And as you certainly well know, that is pretty much what good piano players do. Whether we call it arranging or composing, or just playing good and being great at voice leading or just being a really great piano player—he was a bad dude that I feel very lucky to have had in my band for thirty-plus years. And in the area of synth orchestration, along with [Joe] Zawinul, he was the best of that era for sure. It is still hard to find folks who can do that kind of thing as well as he did back then.[18]

In 2022, in the process of interviews for this book, Metheny felt more acutely that the time had come for clarify about what had become a widely accepted mythos:

[Early on] I somehow got it in my mind that by making it feel like a Lennon/McCartney sort of thing in the presentation of it all, it could go that way, and I even started talking about like that in press kits and such. I figured that a way to encourage that would be to share in the credits, even if the "tune" was 80 or 90 percent mine and we sort of arranged it together by adding a section or an intro or whatever polish it needed to fit into a program. So, following up with that idea, on *Offramp*, I decided to do a blanket credit—all music by Pat Metheny/Lyle Mays, and it was kind of my hope even at that early date that it might one day be like that going forward. But it just wasn't.[19]

For some, like Lennon and McCartney, attribution of songwriting credits seemed, at least at the time, unimportant. The importance placed on attribution varies between composers, irrespective of the copyright issues that dominate the conversation in our era. In chapter 3, we traced the early foundation of Pat Metheny's core musical ideas that represent important elements within the DNA of his work. For Metheny, the musical ideas are crucial; hence, clarity about authorship matters.

While Metheny's model of leader/composer/performer contrasts with that of Gary Burton (who assembled a repertoire composed by others),

Metheny's concept has been more akin to Duke Ellington's,[20] as Metheny observes that "in my case I also have been the guy writing almost all of the music to serve that set of current interests in a specific way. . . . In that sense, again, Duke was a model."

The role of bandleader is never simple, particularly in a jazz-related setting where the music depends upon a significant degree of interplay between players. The perspective of the leader, particularly one who is director, composer, and performer, is going to be inherently different than the experience of the members of the band s/he leads. For Pat Metheny, each of the bands he has assembled, led, and borne primary responsibility for—as I remarked in the preface—could have had the name Pat Metheny Group, particularly the larger-scale projects. But even so, the more than three decades of the classic PMG formation (touring for its last time in 2010) was unusual, if not remarkable. For Steve Rodby, what was particularly notable of that experience was

> the absolutely astoundingly high standards that Pat and the band had, every tune, every set, every night, every city, every tour, every record. This way of living and breathing music seemed to fit well with something inside of me, and as anyone who's been in that kind of artistic environment will testify, however hard it may be, it's also a privilege to be part of that, to aspire to those heights. . . . My entire time with the Pat Metheny Group, across three decades, was so wild and challenging and creative, it's hard to describe without seeming to exaggerate. It was beyond anything I could have imagined.[21]

Metheny's creative output continues unabated, with future touring headed toward an indefinite horizon. The sheer number of Metheny's projects, past, present, and potentially future, blur distinctions between one band and another, however different may be the profile of their personnel and sonic profile.

CHAPTER 9

Listening Interpretively

"America Undefined" and "Is This America?
(katrina 2005)"

> I want to live in the whole world of music.
> HENRY COWELL[1]

> Overall, I think the main thing a musician would like to do is to give a picture to the listener of the many wonderful things he knows of and senses in the universe. That's what music is to me—it's just another way of saying this is a big, beautiful universe we live in, that's been given to us, and here's an example of just how magnificent and encompassing it is.
> JOHN COLTRANE[2]

In 1958, conductor Leonard Bernstein sat at the piano before the New York Philharmonic and faced the audience at his first televised Young People's Concert. Here's what he said:

> If I play a note on the piano, just one note [plays one] and I hold it for a long time, it has no meaning at all. But let's say I play the note and then I move to another note [plays the note and then yet another, this time a leap upward]. Right away, there's a meaning. A meaning we can't name. A sort of stretch, a pulling, a pushing, something like that. But it's there. The meaning is in the way those two notes move. And it makes something happen inside of you.

Listening Interpretively   123

If I move from the first note to another note, like this [plays an interval of a major seventh], the meaning changes. Something else happens inside of you. The stretch is bigger somehow, and stronger.[3]

When Bernstein speaks of "a meaning we can't name," he points to the ineffable quality of music, its inability to communicate specific meanings[4] akin to the way language represents concrete ideas or identifies objects. Bernstein's point is that when we listen, we feel something unnamable in response to a sequence of notes or sounds. Something happens for us, something different than the effect of language. But music has such power because of the deep a connection one can make between what we hear and what we feel in response. The metaphor we use when we say that we *resonate* to music reflects something we all experience in one way or another.

In this sense, music communicates. While I view emotion in music as inherently subjective, this is in fact one of its wondrous features. The same work can mean quite varied things to different people or even the same person at different moments.

Bernstein's observation is salient when we seek to understand composer and guitarist Pat Metheny. We discussed Metheny's ideas about music and communication in chapter 2. At the core, Metheny, like Bernstein, asks us to listen closely and allow ourselves to experience music personally. Recognizing how difficult it is to talk meaningfully about music, he draws, time and time again, an analogy between musical perception and what happens "when you go to see a good movie, or see a painting you like, or hear somebody talk to you."[5] Metheny means that our primary experience of music is in the realm of sensation and emotion, a "place" shared with other evocative experiences we can discuss more easily.

Pat Metheny's work is expansive in scope and range. His shorter compositions, two of which are discussed in chapter 2, provide a useful place to begin an examination of his work because of their concision. Metheny's more complex works often maintain a surface level of accessibility. This suggests that simplicity and complexity are not binary. Melodic and harmonic ideas reminiscent of "popular" music can be drawn upon in service of crafting complex compositions, and complex structures can be drawn upon in service of accessible communication; virtuosic lines are not presented for the sake of virtuosic display. The ballads and Metheny's more extended—and at times abstract—pieces may provide entry points different in approach from his brief compositions, yet he maintains the same goal of communicating musical

124   Chapter Nine

ideas of substance that can be digested and reflected upon by potentially any listener. As drummer Antonio Sanchez observes of one of these works, "The First Circle":

> You can be humming the tune, and you don't know if it's in 7/8, or 7/4, or what meter. You don't care; you're just humming it because it's a beautiful, incredibly well written melody. And then underneath there's a lot of sophisticated things going on rhythmically and harmonically. . . . [In the 2005 work *The Way Up*,] I could see the charts, and I could see all the crazy chords in there, and all the rhythmic stuff, and then you would hear the melody, it would draw a straight line, a very clear, straight line over all that that harmonic and rhythmic complexity. And I think that's part of Pat's success.[6]

"America Undefined"

To turn to a work far more expansive and complex than "The Bat" or "Farmer's Trust," as discussed in chapter 4, Pat Metheny's *From This Place* (2020) is a ten-section through-composed suite presenting contrasting forms and conflicting moods. Allowing ample space for improvisational solos, the piece is richly layered in post-production with collaged recorded sounds and orchestration. The recorded performance features drummer Antonio Sanchez, bassist Linda May Han Oh, and pianist Gwilym Simcock alongside Pat Metheny.

"America Undefined" includes far more referential and suggestive material than the two ballads referenced above. One can infer that Metheny brought more programmatic ideas to this work than to the ballads. Notice this, while paying primary attention to your own listening experience and the inherent subjectivity of musical expression.

One might hear the opening track of *From This Place*, "America Undefined,"[7] more than thirteen minutes in length, as a testament to survival and persistence in a time of strife and uncertainty. Certainly, the album's cover image of a cyclone hulking over a large field conveys a sense of menace and anxiety. The emotional edge of this track is tempered by the pensive "You Are" (track 3), repeated sounds of uplift and hope in the title and several other tracks, and stately grace in "The Past in Us" (track 6). The rousing, joyful, uptempo "Everything Explained" (track 7) offers an assertive response, if at least for a moment. Where "Everything Explained" is brief and to the point, "America Undefined" is a complex work marked by the ebb and flow of its phrases. Its melody repeatedly emerges from silence and returns to silence. Phrases pause before continuing, repeating, or reappearing with slight variation.

Listening Interpretively   125

"America Undefined" opens with a soft cymbal crescendo, a leitmotif that returns whenever the melody arises from silence, often heralded by a suggestive *whoosh* and *sizzle* of cymbals. At the close of phrases, the cymbals ebb. Ornate piano filigree provides sonic glue between one phrase and the next, as each emerges and retreats from the silence.

Thinking metaphorically about "America Undefined," we can all remember how it feels to embark on a difficult endeavor. Unsure of ourselves, we take one step after another, sometimes wavering and taking a step back. Moving ahead can evoke ambivalence because we cannot know what is before us, what obstacles may intervene, whether we will prevail, or even what exactly it is that we seek. Perseverance teaches us about our limitations and the value of patience, as we muster what resolve we may. We can lose and regain hope and discern but then forget who we are. We cannot always know what may be possible. We try our hardest to maintain our resolve and not allow fear to dampen our spirits. We can seize moments to celebrate no matter what. We persist with guarded determination despite ambivalence, hesitance, and hopelessness, "from this place" in which we stand.

The title of "America Undefined" calls to mind the name of a much earlier Metheny composition, "Missouri Uncompromised." It appears on his first album, *Bright Size Life* (1976). "Uncompromised" reads as a response to the notorious "Missouri Compromise" of 1820, which brought the former territory into the United States on the condition that the new state maintain slavery as a legal institution. "Uncompromised" suggests the dual meaning of the work. While at the core of the state's history is a compromise that appeased multiple contending parties, its enduring human and moral cost cannot go unchallenged. Ultimately, freedom cannot be compromised.

The title "Undefined" similarly suggests to this listener a malaise within a nation defined as a democracy, a land of equality and justice. When that definition of America is called into question, America becomes "undefined," under contention, the outcome no longer assured, its moral restoration remaining in the balance. The challenge of the day, to my mind, is to find the determination to strive to reassert America's moral core. As a listener to this music, while music cannot articulate concrete ideas, I find myself sensing a series of questions: Are we collectively moving ahead together? Is the road ahead knowable? If it is not, then how can we cope with uncertainty and anxiety? Where is a source of connection with others, and of the possibility for hope?

The melodic melody line of "America Undefined" is simple, yet enigmatic and searching. The melody inches slowly upward, pitch by pitch, sometimes repeating the same pitch before ascending, and then reaching its apex before moving back down ever so slightly and pausing. The melody begins again just a tiny bit higher and repeats the pattern. The motion is alternately insistent and hesitant; the 5/8 meter adds a degree of tension and instability. Ultimately, fragments of the phrase repeat this stepwise movement, capped by a final motif that descends from a higher note, responding with a sense of determination and providing temporary resolution. Silence returns.

Beneath the surface of all this activity stir constantly moving arpeggio figures, played by the bass. Although relatively quiet within the sound mix, their intensely active presence is felt.

The melody for this opening section is played first on a gritty, bowed bass. Its fragile, highly textured, and raw sound heightens the tentative, self-questioning mood. Underneath, a bass line and supporting piano harmonies provide a slightly dissonant foundation; the melody includes the upper notes of the chords, bringing forth a feeling of unease and tension, until more consonant chords at the conclusion of phrases provide momentary resolution. Again, the music pauses.

After further piano filigree, the melody is taken up an octave higher by the bright timbre of Metheny's electric guitar, emphasized by the high-frequency zing of the cymbals. We are now at the half-minute point and perceive the pace of the music increasing. The music presses forward toward a transition section that continues to ascend, slightly higher in pitch than the main melody. The final phrase reaches even higher in pitch. By beginning and ending on the same chord, this section frames the entire melody, providing a provisional sense of arriving home.

Piano filigree continues to weave through and segue between segments of the melodic phrases soon after the one-minute mark. The guitar offers the first of two repetitions of the melody. The musical landscape gradually grows in density as a string orchestra and flutes are added to the mix. In between guitar repetitions, a temporary holding pattern arises; the harmony is grounded by a C# pedal tone. The guitar then insistently articulates an E before reaching for a high G# and repeatedly asserting that note. Beneath that gesture is a two-chord harmonic cycle, alternating between $A^{maj7}{\sharp}^{11}$ and $F{\sharp}m^7$; there is a syncopated pattern in the bass; the section concludes with the arrival of a sustained D pedal tone.

The overall pattern of the opening portion of "America Undefined" is a determined yet hesitant upward ascent of the melody. The sensation of restlessness, periodically resolved, leaves the listener with a feeling of unease. The melodic patterns of "America Undefined" have been analogous to the rising and falling of ocean waves, and now, each of the two soloists, piano and then guitar, will ride the surf, each in their distinct way.

The core idea within Gwilym Simcock's piano solo is a distinctive, downward-arching phrase. This is a reversal of the upward, stepwise movement of the melody of "America Undefined," and it contrasts the stalwart feel of the melody with the pianist's rapidly paced lyricism. Simcock adds a distinctive rhythmic profile to the motif, a figure from which he creates sequences of repetition and transposition, constructed from either scale material or arpeggios. A highlight is a lyrical episode around the 2:50 mark that extends deeply into the bass register and seemingly into another sound world, leading to a series of instantaneous motivic variants, constantly morphing the material from which the solo is woven.

A dramatic climax arrives at 3:45, when a fragment of the melody is played in octaves. The strings then begin a sustained G♯ that extends nearly until the conclusion of the piano solo. During this closing segment, Simcock builds momentum by dressing the motivic fragment in thirds and fifths, and then in octaves. Serpentine lines, ultimately descending, point toward the solo's end on a climactic sustained note, driven fiercely by drummer Antonio Sanchez and giving way to Pat Metheny's guitar solo.

Simcock's piano solo barrels so rapidly and with such drama through its nearly two-and-a-half-minute lifespan that one can barely track its twists and turns without repeated listening. Metheny's solo, in contrast, begins in a light-hearted, optimistic mood.

Metheny draws upon three motifs to construct his guitar solo, maintaining coherence from beginning to end or, as the guitarist might say, across his "story." The first is a delicate, three-note, ascending scale; repetition of the final note is followed by a descending leap down a fifth. I experience it as conveying a hopeful attitude; the motif returns, with variations, throughout the solo.[8] The second motif draws upon the scale-based aspect of the first motif, morphing it into multiple shapes and forms: some variants ascend or descend or utilize whole-tone or pentatonic scales for material. This motif generally remains aligned with the chord changes. The third motif is a rapidly repeating trill-like figure or note bend that provides textural flourish, contrast, or a holding pattern.

As the solo unfolds, it becomes increasingly chromatic and melodically complex. Metheny seems to be engaged in a path of inquiry, seeking greater nuance of emotion as the solo proceeds. Metheny observes:

There have been times when I play a lot of notes, but there are ways to play simply using a lot of notes. It goes beyond the quantity. It is the atmosphere that you create on a narrative level that separates musicians that are improvisers who can manifest images as opposed to just notes, they can make a sound have an almost literal meaning. It can be done a lot of different ways.[9]

Antonio Sanchez reflects on the importance of allowing Metheny the space he needs to construct his solos. While these comments address a 2003 trio setting, they apply equally here:

Pat is a very conscientious soloist. He really tries to have an arc and a story whenever he plays. So, we would sometimes have discussions, even with Christian McBride, where he would be like "Okay, I'm playing over this ballad, and I'm thinking of a really long arc. So, if you guys are interacting with me with every little thing, then I have to react to what you guys are doing, and it's hard for me to play that arc." And then in some other instances it would be completely free, and he'd be very receptive to the interaction. So, I think it depends on each particular situation, on the song, on the context, on the band. Of course, because I know him so well after playing with him so much, I think I've managed to find a good balance between understanding the arc of what he is trying to do, and just try to kind of lift that arc up, without getting in the way. Pat doesn't have to worry about that because we know each other.[10]

The chord changes of "America Undefined" form a continuous backdrop during both solos. This idea of continuous melody upon which other musical events are juxtaposed is a time-tested device; it is found in Bach cantatas, Wayne Shorter's "Nefertiti," and Ornette Coleman's "Broken Shadows." In addition, three-quarters of the way through Pat Metheny's guitar solo, the melody resurfaces, near the 6:00 mark. This reappearance heightens the drama of the solo.

The sonic density of "America Undefined" increases at this point. Piano and strings articulate the ascending theme, moving toward the foreground of the mix. Metheny responds by driving his solo guitar with greater intensity, his spiraling lines bobbing upward and down, then ascending in a manner reminiscent of the melody, as he reaches for notes near the upper reaches of his instrument. The bass line also ascends from C to D, finally resolving on G, helping bring this section to a place of resolution. The strings and piano ebb as the guitar solo concludes. The main theme of "America Undefined" returns as the 7:00 mark approaches, on bowed bass and then guitar. Soon, the strings and horn double the guitar and move to the fore. This section has a triumphant, confident quality, and the melody quickly ebbs into near silence a minute later.

The confident mood passes as the strings, barely audible, sustain a single note; a pulsing sound is heard. The opening phrase of a new, more hopeful, ascending theme returns, first quietly but then more ominous in tone. Horns and strings repeatedly assert the theme as they crescendo and decrescendo. A complex collage of sounds and textures unfolds at 9:00 as the theme quietly continues in the backdrop. Quiet pulsing rhythms on percussion blend and collide with recorded train sounds. Voices are heard in the distance, and at 10:00 a wailing guitar resounds, maybe sounding an alarm, maybe offering an elegy. The strings crescendo, culminating in a grand rising arpeggio in unison. The strings begin again, more quietly, soon joined by multiple train sounds, a sonic feature found throughout Metheny's music[11]—trains on tracks, bells at intersections—filling the sound space, joined by drums that drive the repeated ascending melody onward.

Shortly after 11:00, there is a pause, maybe a breath; a train horn blares, heralding a dramatic shift into high gear. The ascending melody returns more triumphantly, repeated again and again, each time growing fuller in orchestration. The guitar wail returns, and drums mark a defined beat, almost a march, as the melody is played with great intensity, concluding in a climactic sustained unified sound.

Yet despite drum rolls, everything begins to come apart at the seams at 12:30, giving way to a chaotic tapestry of rapid figures almost randomly articulated by small cadres of instruments. Fragments of the ascending melody in the strings take on a more somber tone as a brief fragment drawn from the opening melody is somberly heard in the background. "America Undefined" concludes lacking any sense of triumph; what remains is sustained sadness.

Among the challenges of composing and improvising music is finding a balance between imagining an overall musical conception and filling it out with exquisite attention to the musical detail that realizes that scheme. These can all be very heady endeavors. At the same time, if music is to convey emotional meaning to its listeners, what lies within the macro and the micro levels must convey something of the imaginative realm of the musician. It is easy to become caught in abstractions and details.

Making it all work as a narrative whole means stitching together its many layers and parts. Drummer Antonio Sanchez speaks about how he approached his role in this goal:

My job was to make the music as seamless as possible. I enjoy that challenge quite a bit, because to go from A to Z and make it into something that makes total sense [required me] to try to make sense of whatever was put in front of me and create transitions and the different kinds of grooves for different sections of the song would be in agreement with what Pat was looking for. Sometimes I would surprise him with things that sounded better than what how he had imagined them.[12]

If Bernstein is right, and the power of music lies in its ineffable yet communicative qualities, then the project of making music is really one of translation. Yet how is it possible to convey that which carries no concrete meaning? This is the question I introduced in chapter 2, and it is one that Pat Metheny addresses musically in "America Undefined." He may have specific ideas about the turmoil that has time and time again faced this country. He may also have a vision about what qualities of character enable this country to persist as one people. But narrating those ideas is not his task as a composer. Rather, his task is to project musical ideas that in general terms may suggest sensation and emotion, while cohering musically so that we can perceive them as one unified whole. Metheny commented in 2006:

I think music occupies a unique spot in humanity. It is unlike anything else, and therefore difficult to measure. But I think somewhere in almost everyone, music is kind of a necessity. I have often thought of music as a kind of vapor that occupies that same frequency of human response as those other unquantifiables that we all seem to need—love and faith.[13]

The challenge of listening to a composition with the structural intricacy of "America Undefined," and improvised solo lines that are ornate and cascading, is that one can lose the forest through the trees. If Metheny has a goal, it is to strive for coherence and clarity such that complexity and detail serve a useful purpose without obscuring his overarching musical message.

The first task I have taken on in this chapter is to draw upon my musical experience to narrate musical detail. But I have gone further, taking a leap of faith to project what my own imagination suggests to me as I attempt to capture something of the emotional content I perceive in this work. This is not intended to provide a fixed conception of what Pat Metheny presents. Nothing of the sort is possible. Another scholar, Wayne Goins, writing about the perception of emotion in music posits a different position, that listeners to a work by Metheny (in his case, *Secret Story*) can consistently perceive specific emotions.[14] I disagree. I may hear something very different in any work of music while listening in one setting or another, as may other listeners. My perceptions are colored by my time and place, personality, and life experiences. It is my belief that Pat Metheny is searching for the listener who will attend with open ears and curiosity.

Closing Reflections: "Is This America? (katrina 2005)"

"Is This America? (katrina 2005)"[15] is a ballad included on the trio album *Day Trip* (2008), with drummer Antonio Sanchez and bassist Christian McBride. The lilting melody recalls the nineteenth-century North American folk song "Shenandoah," a well-known shanty recorded by an array of musicians including Bob Dylan, Arlo Guthrie, Glen Campbell, Paul Robeson, Keith Jarrett, and Charlie Haden. I am not suggesting that this was a model for Pat Metheny's own composition but just that in my imagination, I find a relationship.

The lyrics to "Shenandoah," as first sung by Midwestern river sailors, contain the refrain "across the wide Missouri." The song narrates the love of a trader of unnamed European extraction for an Oneida Iroquois woman, the daughter of Chief Shenandoah. In some early versions of the lyrics, the trader longs for impossible, unrequited love, while in others, the trader tricks the chief and steals his daughter.[16]

I don't know if singers and instrumentalists pay close attention to these lyrics, their history, or the issues with which the song grapples. For me, while listening, I am making a loose association between elements of the two melodies, or so I think. I'm not thinking about "Shenandoah" considering any specific associations, such as Pat Metheny being a child of Missouri or the tragedy of the massive flooding and needless human loss in the wake of Hurricane Katrina.

What I feel in response to the music, as one listener on one morning, is something of the coexistence of the bitter and the sweet. My listening plan for this morning was not to have an emotional experience but to ponder compositional ideas, musical forms, and concepts! But any such notion fell away once the performance began. What I realized later in the day is this: at the heart of things, what "Is This America?" and "Shenandoah" share is not really about melody—many songs are reminiscent of other songs—but intimations of longing.

If I had to put words to my experience, it might go like this: "Why is this not a better world? How do people persevere in light of pain and loss? Why is my overriding feeling one of hope when the title conveys such sadness?" I want to look away from what the title and other associations suggest, to just listen to the pretty melody and engage my analytical mind. But the music will have none of this. It urges me to remain with my thoughts and feelings, however conflicting, inchoate, and unrelated to ideas about musical form.

I *do* notice a few details: this is a well-crafted song and, as performed by a highly virtuosic trio, spare and to the point. The music conveys much information—I know this because I feel it deeply. Yet nothing of that information really translates into words because the song consists of music, not language. What I believe Pat Metheny wants from us, his listeners, is to listen and to feel, to gain the sense that we have gone on a meaningful journey. It matters less whether we cognitively understand it. There's never a better time to listen with focus, attention, and curiosity than right now.

APPENDIX 1

Remarkable Sounds

Manzer Guitars, the Roland Guitar Synthesizer in
Non-PMG Settings, and Sonic Density

Manzer Guitars

Beginning in the early 1980s, a fortunate encounter with Canadian luthier
Linda Manzer shaped Metheny's choices of guitars:

> [She] came to one of our shows as guitar makers often do. About every six or
> seven shows a guitar maker will come up afterward with some instruments
> to show me. I have accumulated more guitars over the years than I would
> ever have the chance to play.... With Linda's guitars, something happened
> that made me hear things differently. They really fit with my conception of
> sound, and I can't begin to explain why. The necks were easily playable for
> me.... She is a very meticulous person, and [she] was very interested in
> the details about what I liked and didn't like about the instrument. I had
> some ideas about instruments and in the back of my mind I was looking
> for someone to make them real. We started a journey that has gone on for a
> while with her building me everything from [eight-string] sitar-type guitars
> and fretless nylon strings, to baritones and miniature guitars. She has made
> 14 for me now.[1]

> The first one I got from her [the "Linda Six"] is what I used on the *First
> Circle* album and on the tune "Lonely Woman" on the *Rejoicing* album. It is
> what I have played most anytime I have played a steel six-string over the past
> 14 years.... It is kind of like a Steinway piano. There is a distinctiveness to
> the notes and something about how they interact. Clarity is a good descrip-

134   Appendix One

tion; it doesn't have any mid-range woofiness which you run into with guitars that sustain a lot."[2]

In addition to this first Linda 6 steel-string acoustic, Linda Manzer's guitars that have remained constants on Pat Metheny's recordings and tours include a nylon-string acoustic, a fretless nylon, two baritones, and the highly unusual forty-two-string Pikasso.

The importance of the Linda [fretted] nylon-string acoustic guitar to Pat Metheny is highlighted in Andre Cholmondeley's description of Metheny's pre-concert warm-up routine on recent tours:

> Typically, he arrives on stage to begin sound check an hour before the rest of the band. He plays every guitar that's in the show, just a real quick check on each one of them. He first usually grabs his Ibanez electric. He sits right down, plays some scales, chromatic stuff, just warming up, and then he'll start playing some changes, maybe some standards. *Anything* can happen for a few minutes. but once he's warmed up, he then tries the other guitars. When he gets to that last one, it gets into a real creative zone where he will run through just about anything. He'll just randomly play a song from the 1980s, or he'll do some standards, or some new stuff he's working on. It's a meditative period of the day and a really great time for sitting and listening. This will all take about twenty-five minutes.
>
> But then he finishes with his Linda Manzer nylon-string guitar. He'll sit with it for a half hour or so. He stays with that guitar because he loves it, it plays really well, it rarely needs any adjustment. It just sounds amazing. It seems to me the guitar's aesthetic, its sound, is very inspiring to him, he just disappears into it. It just feels like home. It's very comfortable. At that point, when the hour is up, Pat's warmed up.[3]

Manzer guitars are an important feature of several Metheny albums: the baritone appears on two solo recordings, *One Quiet Night* (2003) and *What's It All About* (2011); and the fretless nylon and Pikasso were introduced on the Pat Metheny Group's 1997 album *Imaginary Day*. Metheny describes the fretless nylon as

> a fretless classical guitar with an almost cello-like bridge. Ironically, I wound up running it through a fuzz tone to get the sound I like. . . . It offers me a set of new possibilities, in terms of phrasing and sonic colors. It ends up sounding a little like a slide guitar, but with me getting around the instrument a bit

more than slide technique would normally allow and trying not to play the usual blues phrases associated with that instrument.[4]

Linda Manzer's sitar guitar is similar in timbre to the Coral electric sitar[5] that Metheny previously played. The Manzer design is closer in appearance to a conventional acoustic guitar, while the best-known Coral had a teardrop shape. Metheny refers to *Beyond the Missouri Sky*, his duet recording with Charlie Haden, as "like a Linda Manzer demo record—with a lot of Linda's classical guitars, the acoustic sitar guitar, and that Linda 6 is one of the main voices throughout that album."[6] The legacy of Metheny's early interest in tuning systems also remains the baritone Manzer guitars.

Which brings us to the forty-two-string Pikasso. . . . Manzer recalls that when Metheny commissioned the Pikasso in 1984, he requested that the guitar have "'as many strings as possible.' I settled on 42 . . . with four necks. Two sound holes. Two access doors."[7] To accommodate such an unusual combination of necks and sets of strings, Manzer had to taper the shape of the guitar so that Metheny could see all the strings and rest the instrument comfortably under his arm.

Metheny himself rather modestly describes the Pikasso as

basically . . . a conventional guitar that's flanked by three other sets of multiple strings that cross underneath and over the main body of the instrument. So, you can be playing a regular guitar but have these other areas on the same playing surface where you can have ringing notes, some of which are higher than the regular guitar and some of which are lower. It's really the closest I've come to something like a piano that's also a guitar; you can really have a lot of notes ringing and sustaining over other notes without using any kind of electronics.[8]

Jonathan De Souza offers useful commentary about Metheny's performance technique on the Pikasso:

Here Metheny's hands are independent, selecting and activating pitches in a single gesture: the left hand plays the baritone neck, always using hammerons and pull-offs; the right hand plays the other areas, either fingerstyle or strumming with a pick. The left hand . . . mainly provides accompaniment to a higher right-hand melody. Even so, the Pikasso is also unlike a piano: the right hand is functionally differentiated from the left, dealing with fixed, nonchromatic pitch collections.[9]

136   Appendix One

This would be a useful moment to listen to "Into the Dream" the opening track to *Imaginary Day*, or, even better, to view it on the live performance video.[10] What is striking about this 1998 concert performance and the many subsequent concerts that have included a solo piece for Pikasso is the musicality involved in navigating such a complex instrument, such that it becomes one integrated whole. This calls to mind an observation by Metheny in 1995 about equipment: "For me, gear is just stuff, and a guitar is something with some strings. The music is conceptual, and it's what you do with what you've got. . . . I'm more interested in what people do with what they've got, rather than the gear they use."[11]

All of these Manzer instruments, plus the Ibanez electric and its multidirectional sound system, as well as the Roland guitar synthesizer, have become well integrated within individual organically organized performances on tour. It may all seem overwhelming, but these have been for years the ingredients of an average day on the job for Pat Metheny. To highlight how all of these elements can fit together, let's return to guitar tech Andre Cholmondeley's narration. Cholmondeley describes Metheny's overall "guitar world" in this way:

1.   The first is his jazz guitar, which for twenty-plus years has been his Ibanez Pat Metheny signature model. Before that it was the Gibson ES-175. That's one area of his playing, the main "Pat Metheny sound."

2.   The second area is the Roland synthesizer, which is in two parts, the GR 303 guitar, and the GR 300 synthesizer floor box. They are connected by a twenty-four-pin cable, which sends separate signals from each string of the guitar. It is not a MIDI synth or a MIDI guitar, although it gets lumped in by many people with MIDI guitar, as all synths are lumped in, even when they are not utilizing MIDI. It's an important distinction. It's amazing how consistent his use of this one sound has been, over forty years. But as soon as you pick up this guitar, it instantly sounds "like" Pat Metheny!

3.   The third area is expressed in two words: Linda Manzer. There is the old classic nylon-string Ovation, and some custom electrics, also a modern Ibanez with a whammy bar that's only used on the tune "Lodger."

4.   But virtually all the other guitars in use on tour are Manzer guitars. The most famous one is the forty-two-string Pikasso. His favorite nylon-string is a Linda Manzer. His two favorite baritone guitars are Linda Manzers, as is the steel-string acoustic Linda 6. He has approximately twenty-five guitars made by her. She's great about picking great woods, getting the woods properly dried . . . her designs are traditional yet futur-

istic in little details. Then they do the number-one thing a guitar needs to do aside from sound good: stay in tune. They're roadworthy and the quality is astounding. Some of these guitars have been on the road for decades. For the summer 2022 tour, the Pikasso was in storage for a few weeks and then traveled across the ocean, then flew with us to South America. At the first gig, I took it out, and while a couple strings out of forty-two were out, there was a ridiculously high percentage of strings perfectly in tune.[12]

The Roland Guitar Synthesizer

The original Roland GR-300 has remained a favorite instrument of Metheny's for performances and recordings to this day, playing an important role in Pat Metheny Group albums,[13] in the "Unity" projects of the 2010s,[14] and during his 2020–2022 trio and quartet tours, documented on *Side Eye NYC V1, IV* (2021).[15]

In the mid-2000s, Metheny reflected on his aging yet vital Roland guitar synthesizer: "The GR-300 still has a certain kind of funk, you don't get from any other synth. It also responds in an organic way that I think other synths usually don't."[16]

Antonio Sanchez offers a fitting overarching statement about his experiences playing with Pat Metheny at the moments when the Roland guitar synthesizer was in play:

> The Roland synthesizer is of my favorite aspects of playing with Pat. . . . I've always loved that Elvin Jones–John Coltrane relationship, when they would play duo, and they would just go completely nuts. Trane would be playing sheets of sound. It was kind of the same thing with that guitar synthesizer when Pat could reach these heights where a regular electric guitar could not possibly go. When he would take out that guitar [synthesizer], I could also go into seventh gear. . . . Sometimes we were pretty close to blowing the roof off . . . as close to a speed metal concert as you could with that amount of raw energy.[17]

Musical Example: "The Calling" (1983)

The same year as *Travels* (1983), Pat Metheny recorded *Rejoicing*, a trio album with bassist Charlie Haden and drummer Billy Higgins, both Ornette Coleman alumni. This was his second project with musicians associated with

138 Appendix One

Coleman, and as in its predecessor, *80/81* (1981),[18] Metheny (almost) exclusively plays acoustic guitar. The Roland guitar synthesizer makes a surprise appearance on "The Calling," the penultimate track of *Rejoicing*. The contrast between the synthesizer textures and sounds and those of the acoustic guitar that prevails on the album is striking. But so are the Roland's pitch bending, microtonal qualities that are associated with Ornette Coleman's approach to intonation on his alto saxophone.

The melodic theme of "The Calling" combines two simultaneously played lines on the Roland guitar synthesizer, an idea first introduced in "Offramp" (1981), discussed in chapter 7. Metheny details the technique as "using the open B string as a kind of drone, and playing around it on other strings."[19] These begin in unison, accompanied by Haden's sustained arco bass and Higgins's changing snare drum roll patterns. Played a little faster on a hollow-body electric, the melody might evoke a cross between an uplifting hymn and a fiddle tune. The combined weight of the sustained guitar synthesizer and arco bass, along with Higgins's allusions to a military funeral march, conveys a dirgelike quality. Is the mood of this tune hopeful or mournful? It is something of each before it arrives at a point of calm resolution following an extended improvisation.

When Metheny begins his solo around the 1:30 mark, the actively moving guitar synthesizer line diverges from the sustained droning string, with the intervals between the two continually changing. There is here a hint of the double stops employed in Bach's sonatas and partitas for solo violin. Haden's sustained bowed notes gravitate from one pitch to another, suggesting a gradually changing drone. Metheny's transposition of brief motifs hints at Ornette Coleman's playbook. Even as these increase in abstraction, a sense of tonality remains.

Around 3:30, Metheny picks up the pace and angularity of his lines. They remain grounded in Haden's slowly moving long tones and the resulting changing harmonic relationships. Around the 4:00 mark, Haden rises into the higher register of his bass, as Metheny's brief, breath-length phrases continue. This time each contains many rapidly played notes.

By 4:30, the timbre of Haden's bowing sounds scratchier, and he and Metheny send out a collective alarm. They return to unison, but only fleetingly. Suddenly, Metheny shifts from guitar synthesizer to electric guitar (recall that the Roland can accommodate both on the same instrument), with furiously articulated pointillistic notes and clusters, the pitches often unidentifiable. Higgins follows the guitarist closely, increasing the energy of his snare drum patterns, as Metheny moves into the upper register. Metheny eventually returns to the guitar synthesizer and the contrapuntal double-stop duet in the upper register. "The Calling" moves toward a conclusion, a sustained pitch in unison with Charlie Haden.

Pat Metheny and Ornette Coleman: The Roland Guitar Synthesizer on "Endangered Species" (1986)

One day, Ornette Coleman came to hear Pat Metheny's trio with two of Coleman's musical partners of many years. As Metheny tells the story:

> Charlie Haden, Billy Higgins, and I were playing a week [stand] at the Village Vanguard. Ornette came down one night, then the next night, and then yet again the night after that. It was then that the idea emerged as something concrete. I knew that when I left ECM to go to Geffen Records that this would be the first record I wanted to do. I had a meeting with David Geffen and told him that. He asked me if I thought that it might produce a "CHR hit" [contemporary hit radio]. I said "Probably not," but they were cool. Geffen never thought of me as a "jazz" artist—just a musician who had a fan base and, in the end, *Song X* sold more than a hundred thousand copies.[20]

This collaboration seems, in retrospect, inevitable. Metheny describes *Song X* (1986), his joint album with Coleman, as "a record that dealt with density; Ornette wanted to have this dense thing, and it was a challenge for me, harmonically."[21]

The track that Metheny believes worked most effectively in this respect is "Endangered Species"; Metheny plays Roland guitar synthesizer. The recording reunited Metheny with Charlie Haden and Jack DeJohnette, plus Ornette Coleman and his son, drummer Denardo Coleman.

Following a brief unison high-pitched cry, the first section is something like a rapid-fire duet dance between Metheny and Coleman. True to Coleman's *harmolodic* concept, they both repeatedly play the same brief motif but not exactly in unison. In an article in *DownBeat* magazine, Coleman explained his idea:

> Harmolodics is the use of the physical and mental of one's own logic made into an expression of sound to bring about the musical sensation of unison executed by a single person or with a group. Harmony, melody, speed,

140   Appendix One

rhythm, time, and phrases all have equal position in the results that come from the placing and spacing of ideas. This is the motive and action of Harmolodics.[22]

Or, as Jari Perkiömäki observes, the central idea is "the equality of different musical elements and the spontaneous and honest expression of the individuals making music."[23] Matt Lavelle adds:

> [As Coleman] is pointing out, the challenge is to see music as a human act, more than something based on the intellect. It is assumed that the intellect is already understood. Once you know what the root [of a chord] is, you are not beholden to it. Playing this way calls for intuition, trust of yourself, and others, all very human things.[24]

It is the blend of individuality and collectivity that fascinated Coleman. The harmolodic qualities of this performance of "Endangered Species" include a few ideas: that the sum of each individual player's personal conception and realization of a musical idea—timing or which note a melody begins on—can be thought of as playing in unison. The exact same pitch relations can be understood in multiple ways and thus subjectively. There is no fixed answer to a musical question.

At the one-minute mark, Coleman and Metheny play a rhythmically asymmetrical, accented phrase, precisely in rhythmic sync, and then shift to yet another phrase, also synchronized. The two drummers play in a highly energetic manner, playing off each other.

Following a full repetition, Coleman solos, while Metheny plays a steady stream of rapid notes, sometimes continually invented anew, and at other times repeating patterns. At five minutes, they briefly coalesce with longer, higher-pitched tones, Metheny plays in ascending octaves, only to return to intense perpetual motion. The two performers again coalesce around seven minutes. A repeating rhythmic electronic spring-like timbre makes its first of several appearances at this point.

The density of Metheny's playing increases, suggesting a second layer of guitar, while Coleman plays slower, repetitive phrases. Coleman's altissimo-range cries are met with higher-intensity drumming and guitar. Shortly after eight and a half minutes, Coleman plays longer tones, allowing Metheny's gestures to move toward the foreground, but not for long. After Metheny plays several staccato chords, as if comping, the previous ecstatic stasis returns, pairing Coleman's repeated patterns with Metheny's furiously rapid notes. Several drum hits provide a unifying feature as the parallel play of the melodic instruments continues. A minute-long drum break at 9:30 returns us to the initial spiraling duet theme. The drums continue, joined by a sequence of electronic sounds, bringing the piece to a close.

Drummer Antonio Sanchez reflects on the importance of Ornette Coleman to Pat Metheny and his music:

> Ornette was always a ubiquitous presence in pretty much everything Pat did. It was especially the case when we would do duo [i.e., moments when only Metheny and Sanchez were playing], which we started during the Unity Band. . . . A lot of times it was one of Pat's tunes, but then we would sprinkle it with Ornette stuff. And every time I would hear it, I'd go like "Oh, I know he's what he's doing," and then we'd go into these other directions, and then sometimes we would just play free. He would start quoting Ornette things, and it was always a lot of fun. . . . Ornette's compositions . . . were really playful, but they were very deep at the same time."[25]

In "Endangered Species," the Roland guitar synthesizer proves to be a useful instrument to generate rapid-fire note patterns and high-register piercing sounds of sufficient volume and density to match Ornette Coleman's steady-stream solo lines. They fill every ounce of available sonic space. This piece demands a very different approach to the Roland than Metheny had utilized previously, little of the lyricism, the long sustained notes and pitch bends. The timbre of the instrument transforms what on an electric guitar would have been perpetual motion in which individual notes could more easily be discerned. What is created here is more a sculpted sound mass, within which overall shapes are more discernible than individual details.

Sonic Density: *Zero Tolerance for Silence* (1994) and *Secret Story* (1992)

Another way Pat Metheny has addressed intensity in his music has been achieved through treating sonic density as a core musical element, contrasting the varying densities crafted as sums of layered materials. The guitar solo *Zero Tolerance for Silence* (1994)[26] is a full album composed using guitar-generated sound and distortion.

Zero Tolerance for Silence can be experienced by some as an unrelenting barrage of sound. Interestingly, Metheny recalls that a Japanese interviewer experienced it as another angle on Metheny's yearslong imagery of a "scene with a river flowing through it." In this case, instead of looking, as it were, at the river, the listener felt "immersed" within it. Agreeing with this assessment, Metheny articulated the difference as looking "from a different angle, or with different filters on the lenses."[27] In contrast to his general preference for albums with a broad sound palette, on this album, Metheny sought to create an album that was "mono-chromatic, two-dimensional, kind of black and white music . . . very flat."[28]

"Monochromatic" is not the same as static; this album treats sonic detail with limited materials but a maximalist treatment of density. Metheny once said:

> For me sound and the expression through sound is always about melody. To me, melody appears in many different ways. Every conversation, every experience of walking on the street, every experience of hearing an airplane take off, trash cans falling down a flight of stairs, I perceive all of it as melody. This has become more and more acute as time has gone by. You can find melody anyplace that you look for it.[29]

From this perspective, might Metheny's broad understanding of "melody" suggest that this work isn't necessarily devoid of melody but offers a highly reduced version of it?

Maybe *Zero Tolerance for Silence* is a version of a sound world without distillation, less differentiated, the result of "try[ing] to show what the whole thing was . . . the sound that I have going on all the time."[30]

Zero Tolerance for Silence, which limits the listener's ability to differentiate between elements within a sound mass, can be contrasted with a very different kind of album that treats density in a manner abundant in its clarity of materials: the lushly orchestrated, strikingly melodious *Secret Story* (1992).[31] The latter ranges from highly minimal, delicate ballads ("Always and Forever," "Antonia," and "As a Flower Blossoms [I Am Running to You]") to multilayered orchestration ("Above the Treetops," featuring a Cambodian children's choir and string orchestra)[32] and sonically rich eight-piece brass ("See the World"). Tracks that percolate with pulsing rhythms and danceable grooves contrast with near silence. Despite the obvious differences between the two albums, *Zero Tolerance for Silence* and *Secret Story* are each "explorations of sonic density."[33]

By placing these two recordings side by side, we can highlight Metheny's gradual shift from the lower-density *Watercolors*, where "it was always as much about space and silence and the spaces in between the notes as the notes themselves . . ." to the high-density *Zero Tolerance for Silence*. On the latter work, Metheny says "I really wanted to try for a sound where there wouldn't even be one speck of white left on the canvas."[34] In between these two extremes lies *Secret Story*, which treats a wide breadth of density.

While the Roland guitar synthesizer can cut through or soar across seemingly any musical texture, *Zero Tolerance for Silence* suggests a maximal sound mass that might resist the razor edge of any synthesizer, even that one. Placing *Secret Story* in the middle, we discern the fullness of Pat Metheny's treatment of sonic art, within which the Roland finds its logical placement.

APPENDIX 2

The Way Up
A Closer Look at an Extended Form

The ambitious sixty-eight-minute, four-movement composition *The Way Up*[1] introduced in chapter 8, is organized around one primary melodic motif. Multiple variations derived from that core musical material are the DNA of additional melodies and themes that constitute the work. Multiple layers of interlocking arpeggios and broken-chord patterns serve as the raw materials of complex textures, and these become, like the themes themselves, sources of continuity.

It is instructive to glance at the form of "Part One." This is the second movement of this work, following an overture-like "Opening." "Part One" begins with through-composed material but quickly integrates brief instances of guitar improvisation. As the momentum of the music builds, the instruments engage in "hocketing," a form of call and response found in African and European cultures[2] that was also a prominent feature of Renaissance-era European art music. A phrase or segments of a phrase are repeated, one instrument following another, akin to passing a baton in a relay race. Hockets become a familiar reference point for the listener who takes in the entirety of *The Way Up*.

Another compositional technique found in *The Way Up* is contrary motion, in which two melodic lines move simultaneously in opposite directions. *The Way Up* utilizes a variation on this idea: ascending chords, rather than a melodic line, are juxtaposed with a descending bass line. A similar idea is a feature of Metheny's subsequent composition "America Undefined" (*From This Place* [2020]), discussed in chapter 9. In each of these cases, this is a further development of Metheny's career-long interest in stepwise bass motion, as is his use of pedal points, sustained (or at times here, slowly changing) pitches

The Way Up: A Closer Look at an Extended Form   145

generally assigned to the bass. Another harmonic juxtaposition employed in these works is slash chords, which were discussed in chapter 3 in tracing the early development of many of these elements within Metheny's harmonic language.

Each of the four solo sections of "Part One" is self-contained. The solo segments are often harmonically and thematically related to the fully through-composed sections, at times alluding to the harmony and melody of the core motifs but in other moments provide contrast. During each solo section, the instrumentalist is tasked with responding to a specific harmonic structure, in a personalized, distinctive way.

A detailed narration of the first twelve minutes of "Part One" follows, and then I jump ahead to the second of two Metheny guitar solos (beginning at 21:19).

Opening and Motif A (0:00)[3]

"Part One" begins with a lovely melodic motif played on kalimba, a thumb piano, soon joined by electric guitar. The melody has a childlike quality in its singsong simplicity. The melody is repeated, extended, and varied, gradually cohering as an unfolding melodic line. Soon, this motif will be transposed again and again, steadily building drama.

Hocket patterns again emerge as the melody, played by Metheny on electric guitar, is answered by his electric sitar. This hocket model will provide cohesion throughout as the opening motif unfolds. Brief chord cycles bridge repetitions of the melodies. Around the one-minute mark,[4] a lyrical guitar interlude provides a bridge to a return of the opening motif, played by a grouping of instruments. The harmonies that support the melody grow in richness and depth of orchestration.

A drum machine steadily ticks, quietly joined by electronic percussion and more atmospheric sounds, multi-delayed trumpet breaths. A pattern built on the opening motif is played by electric piano. Similar electronic patterns will return later in "Part One."

This six-minute-plus opening section is through-composed. Passages drawing upon the opening motif are constantly reharmonized. These passages are separated by brief electric guitar improvisations and variations. The bass line descends stepwise and enters a repeated ascending loop near the conclusion of the second guitar solo, before again descending and coming to rest. The opening motif returns.[5]

The instrumentation and densities of the layered accompaniment highlight

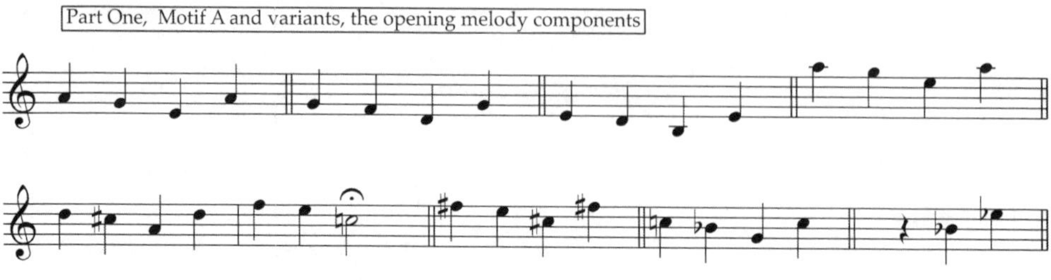

146   Appendix Two

Part One, Motif A and variants, the opening melody components

Figure 18 *The Way Up,* "Part One," Motif A and variants

the dynamism and variability of this work. Tension and drama are built and released by increasing the number of layers, particularly of contrasting guitar sounds—acoustic, various electrics, electric sitar, and, just before the four-minute mark, guitar synthesizer. At various points, hockets pass melodic fragments between the players, like a baton in a relay race, jumping from electric sitar to acoustic piano and, after the five-minute mark, back again.

Chorale (6:20)[6]

Emerging out of near silence, a very quiet mix of wind chimes and other sound design elements emerges at 6:20. These sounds dramatically contrast with the richly orchestrated previous sections. A simple and elegant Bach-like chorale, repeated twice, begins with layers of acoustic guitars, adding harmonica on the repetition. Spare drumming adds texture. A quiet mélange of voices, electronic sounds, percussion, and electric guitar, as if in the distance, bring the chorale to a close. Its final note is extended by a sustained pedal point, leading into the next section.

Interlude and Motif B (8:40)[7]

A half-minute-long interlude begins with rhythmically pulsing notes, leading into a rhythmically lively chordal segment with alternating pairs of slash chords that share the same bass note. A contrary-motion passage—as the chords ascend, the bass line descends—brings this section to a close.

At 9:20,[8] a second motif, upbeat and buoyant in character, is introduced on electric guitar and trumpet, punctuated by sudden interpolations by the rhythm section. A minute later, a flange-treated acoustic guitar plays broken-chord patterns. A second layer, brief variants of the first motif, is added by a second acoustic guitar. The mood grows more assertive and rhythmically active as this second motif continues. The harmonies shift from an A pedal to a

C pedal.[9] Layers of acoustic interlocking guitar broken chords return, and with them, more fragments of Motif A (Figure 18). The energy level heightens.

Motif C (11:08)

A new motif, with breakneck-speed scalar runs,[10] emerges out of the active melodic fragments. These are interrupted multiple times by brief chord patterns—again constructed from subtly shifting chords paired with pedal points—and by energetic drum breaks. Tension continues to build across the frenzy, coming to a head on a sustained, harmonically unstable $D\flat^{13\sharp11}/F$ chord.[11]

We now skip from the 12:00 mark, past a section that leads into a series of three solos,[12] to Pat Metheny's second guitar solo and the conclusion of "Part One."

Second Guitar Solo, First Half (21:19)[13]

Emerging from a foundation of broken-chord patterns on acoustic guitar, the structure of this portion of the solo is grounded in a series of brief cadential harmonic patterns accompanied by bass and drums. The warm tone of the electric guitar is paralleled by the sunny disposition of Metheny's phrases. A countermelody, Motif A—with electric sitar hockets and glissandi—returns at 22:22.[14]

This solo is one of the clearest examples of how Metheny constructs a harmonic form that shapes not the details of his note choices or phrasing but the emotional contours of a solo. Metheny's first solo required him to navigate a path that was defined more by its approach to the listener's perception of motion: forward, stalling, and forward toward a cadence. This second solo has a lighter tone, suited to its placement toward the conclusion of an extended movement.[15]

The optimistic mood builds at 22:53,[16] as the harmonization that previously underlay Motif A (cycles of $D^{maj7\sharp11}-F\sharp m^7$) shapes its disposition. The slowly unfolding form then provides a relaxed feeling: each chord lasts two bars across a twenty-bar segment. A brief darkening of the mood builds tension, which is released by a cadence, leading to a return of the Motif A harmonies.

At 23:22,[17] the joyous, upbeat quality of the solo is heightened by the appearance of a countermelody, overlaid by a second guitar track played in octaves (Figure 19). A similar kind of overlay appeared in Metheny's first solo, but at that earlier point, it emulated an accompanying big-band horn section.

Figure 19 Four excerpts from *The Way Up*, guitar solo 2, with "big-band shout" countermelody

This time we hear just an echo of that technique, more subtly integrated and played exclusively on electric guitar.

The harmonic foundation undergoes several subtle transpositions from the G^{maj7}–$F\sharp^{sus}$ chord cycle, leading to an emotionally satisfying series of patterns that begin with stepwise bass lines but quickly lead to cadences, at 23:22 and then 23:34:[18]

23:22: Em^9–$F\sharp m$–G^{maj7}–B^{sus}–B^7–Em^7
23:34: C^{maj7}–A/B–$F\sharp^7$–G^{maj7}–A/B–B^9–Em^9

This pattern—the sequence of chord changes that lead to a stepwise bass line-to-cadence pattern, with slash chords strategically employed—is at the center of the form undergirding Metheny's solo. But with each repetition of the pattern, the cadence resolves in a new key, one step higher. Our literal experience of this continual "rise/relax into simple chord changes/rise again" cycle offers an unfolding of a metaphorical "way up." The drama steadily builds as Metheny's solo fluently flows without calling obvious attention to the constant changes in key. These steady shifts, however, subtly but markedly redefine the harmonic and emotional context of his phrases. He reaches a peak beginning at the twenty-four-minute mark, the harmony steadily rising and rising.

Second Guitar Solo, Second Half (24:20)[19]

Pat Metheny's guitar solo suddenly shifts to a double-time feel, entering a new direction, more like a bop blowing session. Steve Rodby's walking bass lines and Antonio Sanchez's cymbal rides contribute to the open space for Metheny to sail through. There is a new chordal pattern, this time punctuated by a staccato emphasized chord and, after a pause, a sustained chord on the downbeat. Instances of contrary motion are sprinkled about.

Tension builds at 24:50[20] when the changing chords are juxtaposed for ten seconds with a G pedal. New harmonically complex sets of hurdles appear for Metheny to navigate, rapidly and with fluency. Two final sets of rhythmic chord patterns — intersected by heavily accented chords — conclude with a sustained, multiply layered chord. Throughout this time, Metheny teases out intricate implications and chromatic extensions of the chords.

Motif E and Conclusion (25:22)

Suddenly we enter the final segment of "Part One." A composed ascending melodic line rises from the lowest register of the guitar, doubled in the bass[21] (Figure 20). After descending, it ascends once again, this time in octaves, countered by heavily accented chords and high-intensity drumming, which gives way to a drum break.

The final iteration of the steadily ascending melodic line,[22] this time beginning on E♭, is accompanied by a descending bass line — in contrary motion. The final chord is a sustained multiply stacked slash chord (E♭/D♭/C), played with piano tremolo (a "rolling chord"), followed by a final explosive array of percussion, as the rolling chord gradually fades to conclude "Part One."

Concluding Observations about *The Way Up*

The Way Up represents Pat Metheny's deepest integration of through-composition and improvisation during his Pat Metheny Group period. Yet neither of these approaches to making music is privileged over the other. The two are integral elements of the whole. As Metheny has said on many

Figure 20 *The Way Up*, Motif E at 25:22

occasions, each is a methodology of composition; the difference between the two is that improvisation unfolds "at a higher temperature" and with greater immediacy.

For Pat Metheny, composition and improvisation each represent a broad canvas within which one engages a panoply of features, among them sonic, melodic, dynamic, juxtapositional, and temporal. His compositional work represents a decades-long evolution initiated by a desire to explore musical forms that allowed him the space to approach improvisation in ways that weren't overly determined by conventions dominant within the jazz forms of his teen years.

NOTES

Introduction

1. In addition, I cite Goins, *Emotional Response to Music*, which addresses Pat Metheny's album *Secret Story* (192) from the perspective of music and emotions. Two biographies published in Europe—Viva, *Pat Metheny, Lyle Mays e la storia del Pat Metheny Group* and Segala, *Pat Metheny: Artiste multiplunique*—are unavailable in English translation.

2. Vella, "Phase Dancing."

Chapter 1

1. Harrison, "Interview with Pat Metheny."

2. Chiu, "4th & Broadway: When Tower Records Was Church."

3. For example, Wes Montgomery, *A Day in the Life* (A&M, 2001), Stanley Turrentine, Sugar (CTI, 1971), Hubert Laws, *The Rite of Spring* (CTI, 1972), Milt Jackson, *Sunflower* (CTI, 1973). See Jazz Discography Project, "CTI Records Discography Project."

4. Harrison, "Interview with Pat Metheny."

5. "I feel kind of unaligned or nonaligned." Interview with Bob Gluck, January 12, 2021. The term "nonaligned" gained currency during the Cold War as a way for countries seeking geopolitical neutrality in face of the United States–Soviet Union power struggle to define their identity.

6. Woodard, "In Search of Pat Metheny."

7. Metheny, *Pat Metheny: Selected Recordings*, liner notes. In his liner notes about "New Chautauqua," he details his ancestral musical history.

8. "I always associated phrasing more with the saxophone for instance than the guitar, with two major exceptions—Jim Hall and Wes Montgomery for instance." Costa, "Pat Metheny: Learning, Teaching & Expanding the Art of Improvisation."

152   Notes to Pages 7–8

9. In particular the Max Roach–Clifford Brown Quintet *Live At Basin Street.*

10. *New York Is Now* (1968) was Metheny's first Ornette Coleman, album and it represented an introduction to his music. See Rush, *Free Jazz, Harmolodics, and Ornette Coleman*; based on interviews with Coleman, this work includes among its study of Coleman compositions the Coleman-Metheny collaboration "Kathelin Gray."

11. Steinberg, Interview with Pat Metheny, KKSF 103.7 FM. "The Girl from Ipanema" was the second song Metheny learned to play on guitar. Many years later, he spent several weeks in Brazil, meeting its important songwriters, and the country became a second home for him in the late 1980s.

12. The festival (1964–1972) was part of a hoped-for rejuvenation of jazz in a city that had been one of the national centers of the music from the 1920s until the late 1940s.

13. Montgomery actually grew up in Indianapolis, not New York.

14. Ratliff, "Listening to CD's with: Pat Metheny."

15. Ellington wrote in his memoir: "'Jazz' is only a word and really has no meaning. We stopped using it in 1943. To keep the whole thing clear, once and for all, I don't believe in categories of any kind." Ellington, "Interpretations in Jazz," 452.

16. Also see Walton, *Music: Black, White, and Blue.*

17. For a recent example, Esperanza Spalding said: "Jazz music . . . is full of changes, because it was born of a people who were constantly grappling with the dynamic shifts of oppression and found a way to create a through line of beauty and coherency through those changes. That's part of why you hear a lot of movement, a lot of chord changes in quote unquote, jazz music." *New York Times*, "50 Years Ago, Stevie Wonder Heard the Future.".

18. Among these is the playful, freewheeling call-and-response technique that Samuel Floyd refers to as "signifyin." The term draws upon the literary analysis of Henry Louis Gates Jr. in *The Signifying Monkey*. See Floyd, "Ring Shout!" Relevant jazz performance practices might include intricate rhythmic interplay between players, trading fours, cross-rhythms, solos that elaborate upon or vary motifs drawn from the tune, and the idea that musicians should cultivate their own unique sound. Also see Wilson, "The Heterogeneous Sound Ideal in African American Music." The cluster of musical values are articulated and exemplified in Wilson, "Black Music as an Art Form," and Monson, "Doubleness and Jazz Improvisation."

19. Archie Shepp commented, in the mid-1960s, that the legacy of racism is the "too many problems involved with the social and historical relationship of the two peoples [Black and white]" resulting in a "difficulty for white audiences . . . to accept jazz and the Negro as its true innovator." Baraka, *Black Music*, 151.

20. Archie Shepp and William Parker are examples. See Kofsky, *Black Nationalism and the Revolution in Music.*

21. Billy Taylor is generally considered the initiator of this idea. See Taylor, "America's Classical Music." The idea was recast and, in some ways, reshaped by Wynton Marsalis and Stanley Crouch. See Arnold-Forster, "Dr. Billy Taylor."

22. Lewis, "Foreword: Who Is Jazz," ix.

23. Such debates have been prominent among Black musicians such as Archie

Shepp in the 1960s and, more recently, Nicholas Payton, who prefers to speak of "Black American music" instead of "jazz" or other genre terminology. See Payton, "Black American Music and the Jazz Tradition." Among white writers, see Gerard, *Jazz in Black & White*. Embedded within Gerard's argument against the position that jazz is fundamentally an art form of Black America is the comment that "bebop was the first jazz style in which African Americans got the credit for being the leaders and creators of the music" (23).

24. Metheny has recorded jazz standards, often in small ensemble settings. Included among them are "All the Things You Are" (Jerome Kern) on Metheny's *Question and Answer* and *Trio → Live*, as well as the Heath Brothers' *All the Things You Are*; "Giant Steps" (John Coltrane) on *Trio 99 → 00* and *Trio → Live*; "Summertime" (George Gershwin) on *Jim Hall & Pat Metheny* and *Dream Teams*; and "Lonely Woman" (Horace Silver) on *Rejoicing* and *Dream Teams*. *Question and Answer* also includes "Solar" (Miles Davis) and "Old Folks" (Willard Robison); the Heath Brothers' album also includes "Autumn Leaves" (Joseph Kosma) and "My Foolish Heart" (Victor Young). Another small-group jazz setting, *Parallel Realities* by John DeJohnette with Herbie Hancock and Pat Metheny, features compositions by DeJohnette.

25. One might argue that the interests of marketing, booking, sustaining venues, building a following, and other practical concerns have become a more salient determinant of which "home" a musician's work is said to inhabit.

26. Specific dates of these and subsequent gigs are documented in Morvan, "The Pat Metheny Database."

27. Also on the program were headliner Stan Kenton, the Louis Bellson Orchestra, Clark Terry & Bob Brookmeyer, and Marilyn Maye, among others.

28. Fellezs, *Birds of Fire*, 5. "[They] created an explicitly transgeneric form of music, sounding out the gaps between musical difference as spaces where individual might reshape musical traditions, conventions, and assumptions." Fellezs, 4.

29. Burton was scheduled to appear as a soloist with the Wichita State College Band, and he invited Metheny to sit in. Metheny recalls that he knew Burton's music very well: "When they booked Gary Burton to play, festival producer Maxine Adams called me in Miami (I was teaching by then) and said Burton would be playing. I took the bus there on the off chance I might get to meet him. After he heard me at the afternoon rehearsal I wound up playing a couple of tunes in a quartet with him." Pat Metheny, interview with Bob Gluck, May 30, 2023. Metheny had appeared in that festival in previous years. (For background about the festival, see its website at https://www.wichitajazzfestival.com/history-and-past-festivals-copy.) Burton remembers Metheny as "one of those rare players . . . he had a flair in his playing and a personal charm. He was not yet a polished player, but I knew he had a lot going." Tesser, *Reunion*, liner notes.

30. Herbie Hancock's exploratory Afrocentric Mwandishi band would give way to his funk-inflected Headhunters. John McLaughlin was pursuing a meeting place for Indian spiritual discipline alongside two differing musical paths. One was highly electric, with a fever pitch of volume, speed, and intensity; another, acoustic, empha-

sized McLaughlin's interest in Hindustani raga forms. Chick Corea was in transit from a more exploratory band that included Anthony Braxton a member of the Association for the Advancement of Creative Musicians, and was moving through one with a Brazilian inflection en route to yet another that embraced electric sounds and synthesizers.

31. Woodard, "In Search of Pat Metheny." Gunther Schuller drew upon this mantra when he wrote, "We must begin to think of form as a verb" (George Russell, *Jazz Workshop* liner notes). Amiri Baraka (then Leroi Jones) explores the idea of jazz as a verb in *Blues People*, especially chap. 10, "Swing—from Verb to Noun."

Metheny's observation is also echoed in a reflection by Wayne Shorter: "The word 'jazz' to me means 'creative music.' Also, the extended meaning means really no category." Shorter adds that simple terms are needed to teach children. Brodacki, "The Original Batman," 26.

32. Among the musicians on Pat Metheny's roster would be Duke Ellington, Charlie Parker, John Coltrane, Ornette Coleman, Miles Davis, Herbie Hancock, Wes Montgomery, Sonny Rollins, Gary Burton, and a cluster of Kansas City–area musicians.

33. Steinberg, Interview with Pat Metheny, KKSF 103.7 FM.

34. Pat Metheny, interview by Bob Gluck, May 17, 2022.

35. Haynes is one of the most influential drummers in jazz history. His career highlights include working with Charlie Parker, Sonny Rollins, John Coltrane, Chick Corea, and—most relevant here—Stan Getz and, in 1967, the Gary Burton Quartet. He joined Dave Holland on the Pat Metheny trio recording *Question and Answer* (1990), and he is part of the Gary Burton album *Like Minds* (1998), with Pat Metheny, Chick Corea, and Dave Holland.

36. Pat Metheny, interview by Bob Gluck, May 30, 2023.

37. This practice emerges in the Miles Davis Quintet of the 1960s, particularly in Herbie Hancock's approach to the piano.

38. Greenbaum, "Pat Metheny and Lyle Mays: *First Circle*," 30.

39. Fagien, "The Pat Metheny Interview."

40. Metheny adds: "Jobim especially, because I was learning those classic 10 or 15 songs right around the same time I was learning bebop and standards." Vasconcelos, "Interview with Pat Metheny." Metheny reminds us also that Brazilian-American musical relationships have been reciprocal: Antônio Carlos Jobim, Milton Nascimento, and Ivan Lins were engaged in a cross-fertilization with American musicians. For instance, Nascimento's collaborators, beginning in the early 1970s, included Wayne Shorter and Herbie Hancock (on Shorter's *Native Dancer* [1975] and Milton Nascimento's *Courage* [1969] and *Milton* [1970]), as well as Metheny himself.

41. Fordham, "Getting Things Down Pat."

Chapter 2

1. Darling, "The Spiritual Significance of Music."

2. Kay, "Pat Metheny."

3. Pat Metheny, interview with Bob Gluck, May 25, 2021.

Notes to Pages 16–26   155

4. Ibid.

5. Ibid.

6. Tauss, "A Piece of the Puzzle."

7. Weston and Jenkins, *African Rhythms*, 1.

8. Floyd, "Ring Shout!," 265–87; Monson, *Saying Something*, 73–104.

9. Lewis, "Improvised Music since 1960," 93.

10. Ibid, 117. Vijay Iyer holds that a musician's "story" encompasses the fullness of their personality, sound, and embodied performance practices. For Iyer, it lies "also in the microscopic musical details, as well as in the inherent structure of the performance itself. . . . The story is revealed not as a simple linear narrative, but as a fractured, exploded one." Iyer, "Exploding the Narrative in Jazz Improvisation," 395.

11. *New York Times*, "50 Years Ago, Stevie Wonder Heard the Future."

12. Barron, quoted in Berliner, *Thinking in Jazz*, 201.

13. The storytelling metaphor is also used by tabla player Badal Roy, known for his performances with John McLaughlin and Miles Davis, and with classical Indian musicians. Consider this exchange with an interviewer (Kompanek, "Badal Roy: Keeping the Groove"):

> *Questioner*: "Your solos have such a great dramatic arch to them. You build up tension and let it go."
>
> *Roy*: "By doing that, I'm telling a story. That's the main thing. When you write about me, say Badal Roy is telling a story. And I'm checking it out, which drum is giving me a sound I really appreciate at that moment. I go with the groove, and then go free."

14. Pat Metheny, interview with Bob Gluck, May 25, 2021.

15. Metheny Music Foundation, "Our History: The Lee's Summit–Metheny Connection."

16. *Just Jazz Guitar*, "Guitarist Interview with Pat Metheny."

17. Kay, "Pat Metheny."

18. Cooke, *Pat Metheny: The ECM Years*, 16–17.

19. Pat Metheny, interview with Bob Gluck, August 4, 2022.

20. Ibid.

21. Metheny, "Imaginary Day: About the Tracks."

22. Forte, "The Pat Metheny Group—Jazz's Foremost Garage Band."

23. Composed by Hugh Williams and Jimmy Kennedy in 1935.

24. Pat Metheny, interview with Bob Gluck, May 25, 2021.

25. Takemitsu, *Confronting Silence*, 51. See also Cal Performances, "The Silk Road Ensemble with Yo-Yo-Ma," program notes.

26. Jankelevitch, *Music and the Ineffable*, 74–75. A survey of the substantive literature about music and meaning within European "classical" musical practices is beyond the scope of this book, but among notable contributors are Peter Kivy (*Sound and Semblance* and *Music Alone*) and Suzanne Langer (*Feeling and Form*), who characterizes music in this way: "Feeling, life, motion and emotion constitute its import" (51).

156   Notes to Pages 26–32

27. Lakoff and Johnson, *Metaphors We Live By*, 5.

28. *Merriam-Webster Dictionary*, "Metaphor."

29. As Lawrence Zbikowski explains, correspondences between verticality and pitch are examples of "cross-domain mapping." Zbikowski, "Conceptual Models and Cross-Domain Mapping."

30. Zbikowski describes this as a kinesthetic metaphor, the sensation "of tightening and relaxing our muscles; of narrowness and constraint yielding to that of expansion (as when a physical restraint is removed) . . ." Zbikowski, "Conceptual Models and Cross-Domain Mapping," 3.

31. Lakoff and Johnson, *Metaphors We Live By*, 5.

32. As Mark Johnson points out: "[The patterns of our *ongoing ordering activities*] emerge as meaningful structures for us chiefly at the level of our bodily movements through space, our manipulation of objects, and our perceptual interactions. . . . I conceive of them as *structures for organizing* our experience and comprehension." Johnson, *The Body in the Mind*, 29.

33. Pat Metheny, interview by Bob Gluck, May 17, 2022.

34. Ellington, *Music Is My Mistress*, 460.

35. Baraka, *Black Music*, 152.

36. Pat Metheny, interview by Bob Gluck, May 17, 2022.

37. Ibid.

38. Peterson, *Music and the Creative Spirit* (italics added).

39. Pat Metheny, interview by Bob Gluck, May 17, 2022.

40. Form in "The Bat" is discussed in chapter 3. Metheny's solo on *Trio → Live* (2000) is discussed in chapter 4.

41. Pat Metheny, *80/81* (1981). A version called "The Bat Part II" appears on *Offramp* (1981).

42. On Pat Metheny Group, *Travels* (1983). Also on *Jim Hall & Pat Metheny* (1999).

43. Among the many others similarly worth noting are the title track of *Letter from Home* (1989) and "Naked Moon" on *the Road to You* (1993f). Motifs in the Metheny solo to "Always and Forever" from *Secret Story* (1992) may be found in chapter 4.

44. In Metheny's published score, these are the first two bars of the "B" section. Metheny, *The Pat Metheny Real Book*, 37.

45. These strike me as reminiscent of a favorite phrase of Ornette Coleman, used to offer one example, in the closing section of "Broken Shadows," first released on Coleman's live album, *Crisis*.

Chapter 3

1. Pat Metheny, interview with Bob Gluck, May 25, 2021.

2. Rubin, *McCartney 3, 2, 1*, season 1, episode 3, "The People We Loved Were Loving Us!," 7:35–7:17.

3. Ibid., 8:50–9:05. McCartney speaks further about "funky folk" later in this episode.

Notes to Pages 32–36   157

4. Ibid., 4:45–5:05.

5. "Yesterday" was recorded and released in the United Kingdom in 1965, on *Help*, but released the next year in North America, on *Yesterday and Today*.

6. One could also think of "Penny Lane" (1966) and "While My Guitar Gently Weeps" (1968) as vamps, a device more typical in rock songs, because of the repetitions in the bass.

7. Rubin, *McCartney 3, 2, 1*, season 1, episode 4, "Like Professors in a Laboratory," 4:25–4:41 and 4:44–5:15.

8. Remnick, "Paul McCartney Doesn't Really Want to Stop the Show."

9. Examples include Wilson Pickett and Steve Cropper's "In the Midnight Hour" (1965); and Berry Gordy, Hal David, Willie Hutch, and Bob West's "I Want You Back" (1969) and "I'll Be There" (1970), performed by the Jackson 5. One other popular song of the 1950s worthy of note for its use of this device is "Let It Be Me," an English-language translation of "Je t'appartiens," by Gilbert Becaud.

10. For example, Brian Wilson's "God Only Knows" (the Beach Boys, 1966); Gary Booker's "A Whiter Shade of Pale" (Procol Harem, 1967), whose organ motif originates in Bach's Cantata 140 ("Sleeper's Awake"); Jimmy Page and Robert Plant's "'Stairway to Heaven" (Led Zeppelin, 1971); Billy Joel's "The Piano Man" (1973), and Jerry Jeff Walker's show tune "Mr. Bojangles" (1968).

11. *Miles Smiles, Sorcerer,* and *Nefertiti*.

12. The personnel on *Unity* includes tenor saxophonist Joe Henderson, trumpeter Woody Shaw, and drummer Elvin Jones; on *Lifetime*, Young joined electric guitarist John McLaughlin. The Hancock Sextet would at one point in its development also include Henderson and Shaw.

13. Beato, "The Gary Burton Interview."

14. Ibid.

15. The band included drummer Bob Moses (who would subsequently join the Gary Burton Quartet), saxophonist Jim Pepper, and bassist Chris Hills. Free Spirits, *Out of Sight and Sound* (1967).

16. A live recording of the band, *Live at the Scene February 22nd 1967* was released in 2011 on Sunbeam Records.

17. Keepnews, "Larry Coryell, Guitarist of Fusion." Also see Barth, *Voices in Jazz Guitar*, 141–57.

18. Gitler and Morgenstern, "Newport '69: Bad Trip." The mayhem caused by rock audiences seeking to break through the fences to gain free admission certainly added fuel to the fire, as Gitler continues: "In 1969, Wein went for rock and railed to meet the demands that the extra attendance (no doubt expected) placed upon him and his security staff. Next year he won't have rock, thanks to the decision of the Newport City Council, an edict I agree with esthetically but not morally." The next, final day of the festival featured James Brown.

19. Ibid.

20. Ibid. See also Beato, "The Gary Burton Interview."

21. The music by Keith Jarrett and Chick Corea first appears on Burton's duet

158 Notes to Pages 36–37

albums *Gary Burton & Keith Jarrett* (1971)—with a rhythm section that includes Steve Swallow—and *Crystal Silence*, with Chick Corea (1973). Steve Swallow's "Falling Grace" is included on the Corea-Burton album, along with several Corea compositions, most relevant here being "Desert Air" and "Crystal Silence." Corea's "Sea Journey" is included on *Passengers* by the Gary Burton Quintet with Eberhard Weber (1977). Burton's *The New Quartet* (1973, with guitarist Mick Goodrick) includes Corea's "Open Your Eyes You Can Fly," Jarrett's "Coral," and Carla Bley's "Olhos de Gato." Bley's work continues to be part of Burton's records: "Silent Spring" features on *Ring* by the Gary Burton Quintet with Eberhard Weber (1974); her music comprises the entire set of the Gary Burton Quartet's *Dreams So Real: Music of Carla Bley* (1976).

22. Pat Metheny recalls: "At the time, Gary Burton was beginning to kind of take over a role that later became what he did as dean of the school, by bringing in actual players rather than pure educators. Steve Swallow joined the faculty at the same time I did, as did pianist James Williams, who had been a good friend since jazz camp in 1968. We were roommates that first spring of 1974." Metheny, interview with Bob Gluck, May 30, 2023.

23. Vasconcelos, "Interview with Pat Metheny."

24. The Starfire replaced his initial Fender Coronado. Forte, "Pat Metheny: Jazz Voice of the '80s."

25. Metheny attributes this lacuna in part to the limited number of skillful and innovative players, and to an inherent design dilemma in the instrument: "I mean it has a small dynamic range, especially the jazz guitar sound and jazz is the music of dynamics. You start thinking about a saxophone player like Sonny Rollins, or any great saxophone player, the difference between their softest note in a phrase and their loudest note is probably a ratio of 15 to 1, with a guitar, without changing the volume, the softest to loudest ratio is maybe 2 to 1, 3 to 1, tops, maybe more if you have a real good touch, but it's still nowhere near, I mean you're talking about Art Blakey who's going to really blap. To me, that's what makes jazz swing and there are very few guitar players who can really swing." Webb, "Interview with Pat Metheny."

26. Jim Hall performed on Burton's *Something's Coming* (1964). Burton's first quintet included guitarist Larry Coryell, whose successors were Sam Brown and Jerry Hahn, producing *Duster* (1967) and three more albums. Burton's interest in the electric guitar was renewed with his *The New Quartet*, with Mick Goodrick (1973).

27. Gary Burton Quintet with Eberhard Weber (1974), with Weber joined by Steve Swallow on bass and Bob Moses on drums.

28. Gary Burton Quintet, with Steve Swallow on bass and Bob Moses on drums (1974).

29. With Steve Swallow and Eberhard Weber on bass and Danny Gottlieb on drums (1977).

30. Vasconcelos, "Interview with Pat Metheny."

31. Niles, *The Pat Metheny Interviews*, 31.

32. *Just Jazz Guitar*, "Guitarist Interview with Pat Metheny."

33. Ibid.

Notes to Pages 38–40   159

34. Harrison, "Interview with Pat Metheny."

35. Cooke, *Pat Metheny: The ECM Years*, 40–48.

36. Metheny's first recordings with Burton were *Ring*, by the Gary Burton Quintet with Eberhard Weber (1974), and then the Gary Burton Quartet's *Dreams So Real: Music of Carla Bley* (1976). Metheny is the sole guitarist on *Passengers* by the Gary Burton Quintet with Eberhard Weber (1977). *Passengers* includes, in addition to Corea's "Sea Journey," compositions by Pat Metheny ("Nacada," "The Whopper," and "B & G [Midwestern Nights Dream]"), Steve Swallow ("Claude and Betty"), and Eberhard Weber ("Yellow Fields").

37. Harrison, "Interview with Pat Metheny."

38. Chronologically, when one considers these two streams of music—vamp-influenced and triads-plus-stepwise-bass-lines—it is the latter, in Gary Burton's initial period of discovery in 1966–1974, that emerged first as a 1970s phenomenon, and then the two streams coexisted throughout that decade. Of course, vamps had a long jazz history prior to this period, in music of the big bands and in the R&B- and gospel-inflected "hard bop."

39. Two of the tracks on *The Inner Mounting Flame* (1971), "The Noonward Race" and "Vital Transformation," each build upon a vamp reminiscent of Jimi Hendrix's "Purple Haze": da-da-DAH, da-da-DAH, da-da-DAH, (then ascending) da-da-da-da . . . above which soar McLaughlin's guitar lines. Along a parallel model, on Return to Forever's *Hymn of the Seventh Galaxy* (1973), electric guitarist Bill Connors's solo soars above a multiply repeated nine-note vamp played by Chick Corea's electric piano and drummer Lenny White's and electric bassist Stanley Clarke's driving rhythms.

40. Joe Zawinul's imaginative layering of a plethora of the sounds from synthesizers and sonic elements from other cultures left its imprint on Metheny, but less so its vamp-based model. "Boogie Woogie Waltz," the opening track on Weather Report's third album, *Sweetnighter* (1973), juxtaposes an infectious three-beat shuffle with a syncopated bass riff: da-dah-dah dit-dit-[breath]-dah da-dah-dah, against which Zawinul punches and zigzags on a wah-wah Fender Rhodes.

41. Pat Metheny, interview with Bob Gluck, May 25, 2021.

42. "Ictus," for example, is a whirlwind-paced piece in which an idiosyncratic melody predominates; yet again, harmony largely consists of triads.

43. *Just Jazz Guitar*, "Guitarist Interview with Pat Metheny."

44. Pat Metheny, interview with Bob Gluck, May 25, 2021.

45. In "April Joy," discussed below, C/B♭ could be heard as a C^{11} (a dominant seventh plus a ninth and eleventh). Herbie Hancock's tune "Maiden Voyage" employs the eleventh-chord spelling. Metheny chose, like Shorter, to notate simply, with slash chords, emphasizing the harmonic ambiguity.

46. Miles Davis, *Miles in The Sky* (1968).

47. The difference in spelling is owed to the harmonic context of each chord. With the root spelled as D♭, the E♮ in the melody forms the top note of a D♭^{9} chord; with the root spelled as C♯ in the subsequent measure, the F♯ melody note becomes the top note of a C♯^{11} chord.

160   Notes to Pages 40–47

48. Steven Strunk considers various stylistic elements within Wayne Shorter's compositions but doesn't address "Paraphernalia." Strunk, "Notes on Harmony in Wayne Shorter's Compositions."

49. First recorded by Hubert Laws and Dave Friedman, but subsequently recorded on *Pat Metheny Group* (1978).

50. An A^7/D chord places a suspended fourth in the bass (or it can be thought of as a Dm^{13} chord).

51. In the bridge section, Evans crafted a series of chord substitutions for the chord progression $D^7-G^7-C^7-F^7$, placing the chromatically descending $G\flat-F-E-E\flat$ on the bottom. A second substitution occurs in a subsequent passage. See Ahnert, "Bill Evans' Bridge on Oleo." Evans was noted for his tendency to leave out the roots of chords, following in the tradition of Bud Powell.

52. Included on Gillespie's *Afro* (1954).

53. "Falling Grace" is also included on Gary Burton and Chick Corea's duet recording, *Crystal Silence*, recorded in November 1972 and released in 1973.

54. The recording includes the Beatles' "Norwegian Wood"; Mike Gibbs's "Ballet," "Sweet Rain," and "Liturgy"; Steve Swallow's "Portsmouth Figurations" and "General Mojo's Well Laid Plan"; Carla Bley's "Sing Me Softly of the Blues"; Gary Burton's "Response"; and Burton and Larry Coryell's "One, Two, 1-2-3-4."

55. Unlike Steve Swallow's own published score, the much-circulated *Real Book* does not include the $A\flat$ that begins this segment of the bass line.

56. The $A\flat^{maj7}$ chord also clarifies why the piece doesn't begin with an $A\natural$ chord, and initiating a ii–V–I progression.

57. Credited to Miles Davis on the album *Kind of Blue* (1959). Swallow's reference to "Blue in Green" is unsurprising, as Swallow has noted, "I was thinking about Bill Evans, and trying to write a song in his idiom." Pat Metheny adopted a related circular model in "April Joy" on his first Pat Metheny Group album (1978).

58. Goldstein, *Jazz Composers Companion*, 107.

59. Pat Metheny, interview with Bob Gluck, May 23, 2021.

60. Ibid.

61. *Just Jazz Guitar*, "Interview with Pat Metheny."

62. Pat Metheny, interview with Bob Gluck, May 23, 2021.

63. Notated charts can be found in Metheny, *The Pat Metheny Real Book*.

64. Among Metheny's up-tempo compositions using these devices are "Question and Answer" (from *Question and Answer*, 1990) and "80/81" (*80/81*, 1980); they are also found in the extended multisectional works *The Way Up* (2005) and "America Undefined" (*From This Place*, 2020).

65. Pat Metheny, interview with Bob Gluck, May 25, 2021.

Chapter 4

1. Pat Metheny, interview with Bob Gluck, May 25, 2021.

2. Coltrane began using this technique during his time in Thelonious Monk's band

Notes to Pages 47–58   161

in 1957–58; his solo in "Epistrophy," documented on Monk's recorded 1957 Carnegie Hall concert, encapsulates his early use of repetition, expansion, and variation of motivic material. His discovery that motivic development was also a core principle of Hindustani classical music helped spark his work from 1961 to the end of his life, most famously on display in *A Love Supreme* (1964). For more on "Epistrophy," see Bertholf, "John Coltrane: Jazz Improvisation, Performance, and Transcription"; Porter, *John Coltrane: His Life and Music* (123, 226, 279); and Ratliff, *Coltrane: The Story of a Sound* (35–60).

3. Wynton Kelly Trio with Wes Montgomery, *Smokin' at the Half Note* (1965).

4. *Just Jazz Guitar*, "Interview with Pat Metheny."

5. Hamilton, "Paul Bley: Time Must Have a Stop."

6. Ornette Coleman, *The Shape of Jazz to Come* (1959).

7. Jost, *Free Jazz*, 48, 59–60.

8. Live at Club 7, Oslo, Norway; November 25, 1976. There is no official recording, but video of the concert circulates on the internet.

9. The lead sheet can be found in Metheny, *The Pat Metheny Real Book*, 18–19.

10. *Trio → Live* (2000).

11. *80/81* (1980) was performed by a group of top-flight musicians, two of them associated with Ornette Coleman's band.

12. Pat Metheny, *Trio → Live* (2000).

13. The notation of motifs within this solo is drawn from Alejandro Moro's published transcription of the entire solo in *Pat Metheny Trio → Live*. The published version has no bar numbering. Notated material in Figure 10 is not complete, nor is every measure included. The focus is on the three selected motifs. Although some bars are skipped, each bar is identified with its correct number, beginning with bar 1 (which aligns with Moro's second system on p. 104 of the published transcription). To correlate numbering in the figures of this book with the published score, note that p. 104 of the score (one system above the section marked "B") includes bars 1–7; p. 105 includes bars 8–19; p. 106 includes bars 20–31; p. 107 includes bars 32–43; and p. 108 includes bars 44–53.

14. Variations may be found in bar 26, where the motif begins on a different scale degree, and in bars 13 and 32, where it is inverted. Also, repeated-note figures hint at the motif in bars 37–38 and 48–49.

15. Instances where motif B appears over ii–V–I (or I^{maj7}) cadences can be found in bars 2–8, 30, and 48–49. The pattern is altered slightly in bar 36, where it ends on vi^7. At other times, it lies across stepwise bass movement, for example in bars 17, 23–24, 34, and 51–52. At times resolution of the cadence is delayed slightly.

16. The pattern continues in bars 3, 6, 21, 31, 33, and 35 and is extended in 47.

17. Schuller, "Sonny Rollins and the Challenge of Thematic Improvisation."

18. "Jazz improvisation became through the years a more or less unfettered, melodic-rhythmic extemporaneous composing process in which the sole organizing determinant was the underlying chord pattern." Schuller, ibid.

19. Sonny Rollins, *Saxophone Colossus* (1956).

162   Notes to Pages 58–60

20. Walser, "Deep Jazz."

21. Walser, *Keeping Time*, introduction to chap. 36, "Musings: The Musical Worlds of Gunther Schuller"; and Walser, "Deep Jazz," 285–89.

22. Monson, *Saying Something*, 135–36.

23. Givan holds that the example contains only two passages that might be said to include motifs but are actually variants of preexisting, commonly used licks that first appear in the third cycle of the solo. Givan, "Gunther Schuller and the Challenge of Sonny Rollins."

24. Gioia views Rollins as "more a master of spontaneity, creativity, and coherence than a formalist," but one who "built his improvisations the old-fashioned way, phrase by phrase. This gave them a solidity, a strength, much like a house built carefully, one brick at a time." Gioia adds that thematic development appears as early in jazz history as the 1920s, with trumpeter King Oliver's solo on "Dippermouth Blues." Gioia, *The History of Jazz*, 310.

25. A little-known Italian release documents one of these shows, unfortunately not the best one. Pat Metheny with Sonny Rollins, *Dream Teams* (1994). The two-CD set draws upon two separate concerts with different rhythm sections: Alphonso Johnson and Jack DeJohnette in Japan, 1983, and Charlie Haden and Billy Higgins in Italy, 1986. For more information, refer to Discogs.com: https://www.discogs.com/release/4474290-Pat-Metheny-With-Sonny-Rollins-With-His-Trio-Dream-Teams.

26. Pat Metheny, interview with Bob Gluck, May 25, 2021.

27. James Dean notated in guitar tablature recorded performances in search of finger movements for chromatic runs and various embellishments. Dean, "Pat Metheny's Finger Routes," 68. Dean concludes: "Much in Metheny's playing . . . defies this type of analytical approach . . . that is original and inspired in the moment of the performance itself," while "faster passages can tend to be less purely improvised, the technique often relying more on variations of a set of muscle memories in rhythmically denser passages of music, and . . . these muscle memories [can have] impact on the melodies. . . . Some sections of the music are reliant on well-developed finger-guided phrases." Dean, 70. Dean notes that similar questions have been studied regarding Wes Montgomery in Van Der Bliek, "Wes Montgomery: A Study of Coherence in Jazz Improvisation," 153. Andy Smith asks the opposite question: In what ways do Pat Metheny's solos, particularly in the context of his performances of historical repertoire, influence his composing. Smith, "Pat Metheny: Composing to Exploit the Sound of the Guitar."

28. Steve Larson found a well-practiced familiarity with the harmonic and rhythmic environment that guides his improvisations, sometimes even rehearsing his solos. Larson's examples are from the triple-tracked album by Bill Evans *Conversations with Myself*, particularly Thelonious Monk's "'Round Midnight" and Victor Young's "Stella by Starlight." Larson observes: "Some improvisations are best regarded as composition. Other improvisations are not. Some compositions are best regarded as recorded improvisations. Other compositions are not. Some aleatoric music, often cited as an example of music that is both composed and improvised, may be neither. And I suspect that all enduring music is created by improvisation, whether or not it is recorded in

Notes to Pages 60–64   163

notation." Larson concludes that there is no static, firm line between composition and improvisation. Larson, "Composition versus Improvisation?"

29. See Dean, "Pat Metheny's Finger Routes."

30. Cooke offers a thorough analysis and discussion of *As Falls Wichita, So Falls Wichita Falls* in *Pat Metheny: The ECM Years*, 171–87.

31. Pat Metheny, interview with Bob Gluck, May 25, 2021.

Chapter 5

1. Fagien, "The Pat Metheny Interview."

2. Bienstock, "Meet the Beatles Guitars."

3. Huber, "The History of John Lennon's Rickenbacker 325 Guitars."

4. Lowe, *"Turn Me Loose White Man,"* vol. 2, 140. Audio example on accompanying CD 21, track 22.

5. Webb, "Interview with Pat Metheny." The historic moment was an important American watershed. The baby boomers were adolescents and teens. 1964 heralded an era of not only electric but electronic instruments, in particular the first Moog synthesizer; culturally it was the year of the launch of the New York World's Fair and the Whisky a Go Go nightclub in Los Angeles; Kodak Instamatic cameras were selling like hotcakes. Politically, 1964 marked the first stirrings of the Berkeley free speech movement, Lyndon Johnson's Great Society, the first expansion of the war in Vietnam, and victories for the civil rights movement on a national level amid violence against activists.

6. Niles, *The Pat Metheny Interviews*, 9.

7. Niles, 9–10.

8. *Just Jazz Guitar*, "Guitarist Interview with Pat Metheny."

9. Ibid.

10. Metheny Music Foundation, "Our History: The Lee's Summit–Metheny Connection."

11. Milward, "Wandering Minstrel." Milward confuses the ES-140 with Metheny's subsequent ES-175 and states that the 175 was the guitar advertised in the *Star*. Among other sources, Carolyn Glenn Brewer correctly identifies it in *Beneath Missouri Skies*, 12.

12. Metheny finds his choice of the latter song ironic given, as he articulates it, "the way things have gone," meaning his subsequent strong interest in Brazilian music and also his subsequent decision to live "in the country for several years." *Digital Interviews*, "Pat Metheny."

13. It was destroyed in the baggage carrier of an airplane and initially replaced with a Fender Mustang.

14. The signature models have included PM 100 and PM 120. Adler, "Pat Metheny: The Advancing Guitarist."

15. Wynton Kelly Trio with Wes Montgomery, *Smokin' at the Half Note* (1965).

16. *Just Jazz Guitar*, "Guitarist Interview with Pat Metheny."

17. Wes Montgomery, *Down Here on the Ground* (1968).

18. *Just Jazz Guitar*, "Guitarist Interview with Pat Metheny."

19. Metheny, *Wes Montgomery Live in '65*, liner notes.

20. Fagien, "Interview with Pat Metheny." Metheny adds: "Django had the kind of conviction and power in each phrase that made his solos add up to more than just a string of ideas—they all seemed to be of one piece."

21. Melvyn Cooke, quoting Ken Micallef, "Jim Hall and Pat Metheny: Mutual Admiration Society" (1998), formerly available on guitar.com. Cooke, *Pat Metheny: The ECM Years*, 24–25.

22. Ratliff, "Listening to CD's with: Pat Metheny."

23. Among the more sonically conservative, yet excellent guitarists of that era are Herb Ellis, Joe Pass, Tal Farlow, Kenny Burrell, Barnie Kessel, Grant Green, Charlie Byrd, and, subsequently, Larry Carlton, Earl Klugh, George Benson, Pat Martino, Philip Catherine, Lee Ritenour, Gabor Szabo, and Steve Kahn.

24. Brown plays on Gary Burton Quartet, *Live in Tokyo*, (1971, released in Japan), and on *Gary Burton & Keith Jarrett* (1971).

25. Goodrick's tenure began on Gary Burton, *The New Quartet* (1973).

26. Meltzer, "Pat Metheny—Mick Goodrick: Gary Burton's Star Guitarists."

27. The album, its music, and its cover design are discussed in depth in Cooke, *Pat Metheny: The ECM Years*, 73.

28. The Pat Metheny Group would consist of most of the same personnel from *Watercolors*: drummer Danny Gottlieb and pianist Lyle Mays, with bassist Mark Egan replacing Eberhard Weber.

29. Costa, "Pat Metheny: Learning, Teaching & Expanding the Art of Improvisation."

30. Meltzer, "Pat Metheny—Mick Goodrick: Gary Burton's Star Guitarists."

31. *Jazz Improv*, "Pat Metheny: In Depth Explorations."

32. Barth, *Voices in Jazz Guitar*, 314.

33. Ratliff, *Coltrane: The Story of a Sound*, x.

34. Pat Metheny, interview with Bob Gluck, May 30, 2023.

35. Curtis Roads explains that the technology "requires that there be small differences between the various voices of the simulated ensemble, including slight delays, alternations of fundamental frequency (resulting in beating effects), and asynchronous vibrato." Roads, *The Computer Music Tutorial*, 439.

36. A delay captures a sound signal, shifts the time of that signal, and then replays it. This can be perceived as a simple repetition of a sound or, with feedback, as a more complex sonic construction.

37. Fagien, "The Pat Metheny Interview."

38. Ibid.

39. Antonio Sanchez, interview with Bob Gluck, December 9, 2022.

40. Metheny, "Question and Answer."

41. Ibid.

42. *Just Jazz Guitar*, "Guitarist Interview with Pat Metheny."

43. Small, "Face to Face with Pat Metheny."

Notes to Pages 69–77   165

44. Ibid.

45. Metheny continued, "I'm using a Coral Electric Sitar on one tune, which has a real cool sound, and an Ibanez electric twelve string, tuned real weird. I think that's it." Webb, "Interview with Pat Metheny."

46. In 1980, Metheny commented that his twelve-string guitars included "an Epiphone 12-string, a Fender, a Guild, and an Ibanez," with the acoustic guitar on *Phase Dance*, the Pat Metheny Group's first album, being "a Guild D-40C, in Nashville tuning, with a Bill Lawrence pickup." Forte, "The Pat Metheny Group—Jazz's Foremost Garage Band."

47. Small, "Face to Face with Pat Metheny."

48. This is the same idea as in "Icefire" on *Watercolors*.

49. Forte, "The Pat Metheny Group—Jazz's Foremost Garage Band."

50. Webb, "Interview with Pat Metheny."

51. Ibid. Metheny explains his technique: "[Restring with] the lightest gauge you can get away with, i.e., 008, tune that to the G that's actually higher in pitch than the E string, the D string you do the same and it becomes the D one step below the E string. The A becomes a fifth below the E string, and the lower E instead of being 2 octaves lower is now only one octave lower than the E string, which means that you can play all the normal grips but the voicings come out backwards, more or less. The lower part of the neck is actually as high or higher in pitch than the top part of the neck." Kay, "Pat Metheny."

52. *Just Jazz Guitar*, "Guitarist Interview with Pat Metheny."

53. Metheny, *Pat Metheny: Selected Recordings*, liner notes, speaking about "New Chautauqua," from *New Chautauqua* (1978).

54. Ibid.

55. Ibid.

56. *Just Jazz Guitar*, "Guitarist Interview with Pat Metheny."

Chapter 6

1. Except where otherwise noted, all Pat Metheny quotations in this chapter are drawn from his interview with Bob Gluck, December 23, 2022.

2. Pat Metheny, interview with Bob Gluck, January 2, 2023.

3. See Wilson and Weston, "Edward Kennedy Ellington as a Cultural Icon," 69.

4. Simonini, "An Interview with Pat Metheny."

5. Metheny notes that prior to his and Gottlieb's year together with Gary Burton, "during my year or so in Miami [September 1972–December 1973) where we met, we did our share of B-lister show gigs like Kaye Stevens, Frankie Laine, and others, a highlight being a week with Dick Shawn at a supper club, with Jaco [Pastorius] on bass."

6. Joe Morello is widely known as the drummer in the Dave Brubeck Quartet.

7. Although Weber's pianist Rainer Brüninghaus, already familiar to ECM, had been another appealing option.

8. Ellington, "Interpretations in Jazz."

166   Notes to Pages 77–81

9. Vella, "Something Left Unsaid."

10. Ibid.

11. Among the few jazz drummers to adopt a feel more commonly found in rock and pop music are Tony Williams, Paul Motian in Keith Jarrett's American Quartet, and drummers in the electric bands led by Miles Davis alumni—Billy Cobham in John McLaughlin's Mahavishnu Orchestra; Alphonze Mouzon, Eric Gravatt, Ishmael Wilburn, and others in Weather Report; and Lenny White in Chick Corea's Return to Forever.

12. Vella, "Something Left Unsaid."

13. Wertico, "Flat Ride Cymbals."

14. Vella, "Something Left Unsaid."

15. Ibid.

16. Forte, "The Pat Metheny Group—Jazz's Foremost Garage Band."

17. The echoplex achieved at least three different sonic transformations: a delayed repetition (sometimes multiply) of what had just been played, which could overlap with what was subsequently played; a rapid delay resulting in a blurred sound; and a pitch shift.

18. A ring modulator electronically alters the waveform and thus the sound of the instrument played by creating complex frequencies different from that of the note played, among them sums and differences of the instrument's waveform and a "modulating" frequency generated by the specialized circuitry.

19. A history of the adoption of the electric piano can be found in Gluck, *You'll Know When You Get There*, 63–70; "Electric Piano as a Sound Design Instrument" is the topic of discussion on 71–72 in the same book, including an observation by Pat Metheny. The unanticipated but logical next step of adding synthesist Patrick Gleeson to the band is addressed on 127–32. Chick Corea's parallel and arguably more radical addition of the ring modulator to electronically transform the sound of the electric piano is discussed in Gluck, *The Miles Davis Lost Quintet*, 99–100. Following Hendrix, Zawinul and Corea also treated their electric pianos with fuzz boxes, with Zawinul and Hancock also using wah-wah pedals.

20. Bianchi, *Elegant People*. For more on Joe Zawinul's adoption of the ARP 2600, see Bianchi, 105–6; for the Oberheim, see 207–8.

21. Brodowski and Szprot, "Interview with Lyle Mays."

22. Except where otherwise noted, all Steve Rodby quotations are from his interview with Bob Gluck, February 28, 2023.

23. Dyas, "Aebersold: A Jazz Icon's Journey."

24. Jamey Aebersold recalled: "Myself, David Baker [Metheny's mentor in Kansas City], Dan Haerle and Jerry Coker were at the forefront of these new combo jazz camps. Their popularity grew and grew, and we added faculty to where we had 70 teachers and 15 staff. . . . Our jazz camps have always welcomed young and old, playing all instruments. We've had everything from harp to tuba to harmonica enroll. We've had people come 25 years in a row." Dyas, ibid.

25. Dyas quotes Jamey Aebersold: "At the beginning of the week, you may limit

Notes to Pages 84–89   167

the number of choruses per person or the song could go on forever. After the first several rehearsals I encourage lengthening each person's solo and remind them they are taking the listeners' ears on a musical journey. So, be in control of your solos and don't just let your fingers go flying and not be connected to your mind." Dyas, ibid.

26. Rodby recalls that "either Pat or Lyle composed . . . almost all the *cool* or fancy stuff," for instance "the beautiful bass line on 'So May It Secretly Begin,' upon which my playing is based," and brought it to life "with small but (to my sensibility) important improvisations along the way."

27. Steve Rodby, interview with Bob Gluck, June 21, 2023.

28. The published chart in *The Pat Metheny Song Book* includes only notation for the opening, but central, bass vamp.

29. Mays added a newly released Prophet five-voice synthesizer, a Yamaha CP-30 electric piano, and a Yamaha YC-20 electric organ.

30. Lyle Mays told the same interviewer: "That was Pat's [idea]. He called me up on the phone one time and said, 'Listen to this!' I have two Autoharps with the bars taken off, tuned to open chords—one is a big open D chord, which I use on 'Phase Dance'; the other I use on 'San Lorenzo' in conjunction with the tuning Pat has on his 12-string. We put a hockey puck pickup on each one, which I think is like a submarine detector or something." Forte, "The Pat Metheny Group—Jazz's Foremost Garage Band."

31. See Little, "Guitar Synthesizers: More or Less in Jazz Tradition"; and Bonzai, "Lunching with Bonzai: Pat Metheny—Jazzing It Up."

32. Forte, "The Pat Metheny Group—Jazz's Foremost Garage Band."

33. Rodby adds: "This was then, and still is, in sharp contrast to so much music that uses clock/sequence time, leaving the pace unvaried, often with a static and unmusical result."

34. Vella, "Phase Dancing."

35. Leet, "Guitar Synths—The Story So Far." New England Digital also built a prototype interface for the Synclavier that Metheny's production manager David Oakes mounted on the bottom of the Roland GR-303. Metheny used it to play FM synthesis (an early form of digital synthesis) sounds on the Synclavier. John McLaughlin used a similar setup as a regular part of his performance tool kit with his Mahavishnu band of the early 1980s. Metheny, "Question and Answer."

36. Metheny, *Pat Metheny: Selected Recordings*, liner notes, about "Are You Going with Me?" from *Travels* (1982).

37. A tracking mechanism converts the frequency of each string as it vibrates, when a pitch is played by the guitarist, to a voltage that sets the (changing) voltage of two oscillators.

38. Mullen, "Interview with Robert Fripp."

39. Wayne Scott Joness explains: "An 'E' played one octave above an open 'E' string will not only be sounding at twice the frequency, but the harmonic content will be very different as well. This is the happy consequence of the brute force synthesis used in the GR-300 . . . [which] has two oscillators, both harmonically locked to the string pitch,

but one oscillator can be offset by a range of plus or minus one octave. So it is possible to play one oscillator an octave below pitch, or to layer two oscillators together at the interval of a perfect fifth. These pitch intervals can be preset as pitch offset 'A' and 'B.' . . . and a filter is designed so that higher pitches open the filter more, making for a brighter sound." Joness, "Roland GR-300 Analog Guitar Synthesizer."

40. Webb, "Interview with Pat Metheny."

41. The Roland has two different settings, one for the synthesizer and another as an electric guitar. Cholmondeley notes: "These are superb guitars. I think it's just to get into that Les Paul guitar zone, which he's not known for except on *Zero Tolerance for Silence*. If you are playing solo, it's a great choice to have if you're looking for a little fuller tone." Andre Cholmondeley, interview with Bob Gluck, January 18, 2023.

42. Andre Cholmondeley, interview with Bob Gluck, January 18, 2023. Over the years, Pat Metheny has also made use of various newer guitar synthesizer technologies, such as the Roland VG8 guitar processor, on "The Roots of Coincidence" on *Imaginary Day* (1997) and in his 1999–2000 trio performances with bassist Larry Grenadier and drummer Bill Stewart.

43. Webb, "Interview with Pat Metheny." Metheny also came to realize that the Roland could expand his role as guitarist/bandleader: "Playing chords on the guitar synthesizer, behind everything, can make me part of a synthesizer ensemble, as well as being the guitar player."

44. Cooke, *Pat Metheny: The ECM Years*, 200–212.

45. Some examples include "The Truth Will Always Be" and the lyrical "The Longest Summer" *Secret Story* (1992); "Red Sky" and the title track on *We Live Here* (1995); "Oceana" and "Language of Time" on *Quartet* (1996); Parts 2 and 4 of *The Way Up*; two tracks on *Unity Band* (2012), most notably "Roofdogs"; and the title track of *Kin* ($\leftarrow\rightarrow$).

Chapter 7

1. Bettine and Taylor, *Percussion Profiles*, 361.

2. The latter recording documents a four-evening series of duets and quartets joining Metheny and Wertico with guitarist Derek Bailey and percussionist Gregg Bendian.

3. Cooke, *Pat Metheny: The ECM Years*, 232.

4. The first part was an hours-long jam in December 1982 and the second in early January 1983.

5. Vella, "Phase Dancing."

6. Ibid.

7. Ibid.

8. Bettine and Taylor, *Percussion Profiles* .

9. Ibid.

10. All quotations from Antonio Sanchez, except where noted, are from his interview with Bob Gluck, December 19, 2022.

Notes to Pages 96–101   169

11. Alejandro Gonzales Iñarritu later directed the film *Birdman or (The Unexpected Virtue of Ignorance)* (2014), in which Sanchez's drumming is a substantial element of the soundtrack, reflecting and driving the narrative.

12. Sanchez had recently graduated from the Berklee College of Music and done a stint, at Perez's recommendation, with Paquito D'Rivera in the United Nations Orchestra.

13. Vella, "Phase Dancing."

14. *Getz/Gilberto* (1964). The album followed Stan Getz's first two samba-inflected albums, *Jazz Samba* (1962, with guitarist Charlie Byrd) and *Big Band Bossa Nova* (1962).

15. Pat Metheny, interview with Bob Gluck, May 25, 2021. Metheny credits Gary Burton's "insistence that I search for a personal language" for leading to the creation of this model.

16. Pat Metheny, email to Bob Gluck, May 30, 2023.

17. Ibid.

18. Metheny has long-standing musical connections with Milton Nascimento and singer/songwriter/guitarist Toninho Horta. Nascimento and Horta hail from the same region of Brazil, the large inland state of Minas Gerais, inland from the coastal strip on which Rio de Janeiro and São Paulo lie just to the south. Nascimento and Horta have both lived close to the center of the state, in Belo Horizonte. For more context about the two musicians, see Murphy, *Music in Brazil*, 49–50.

19. Several singers followed his path, none of them Brazilian. David Blamires was born in England, was raised in Canada, and lives in Chicago. The late trumpeter and singer Mark Ledford was born in Detroit and lived in Los Angeles. Richard Bona, born in Cameroon, has lived in Germany, France, and New York City. Anna Maria Jopek, whose collaborative album with Metheny is titled *Upojene* (2008), is Polish. Multi-instrumentalist and singer Giulio Carmassi (on "On Day One," from *Kin (←→)*, 2014) is from Italy. What these vocalists share is a skill set well suited to the diverse qualities of vocal lines in Pat Metheny's music.

In addition to wordless vocals, Metheny's groups and recordings have also included musicians whose instruments display vocal qualities. Among these have been Vietnamese American trumpeter Cuong Vu (*Speaking of Now* [2002] and *The Way Up* [2005]), trumpeter Mark Ledford (*Still Life [Talking]*, 1987), and Belgian American harmonica player Toots Theilmans (*Secret Story* [1992]), and Swiss American harmonica player Gregoire Maret (*The Way Up* [2005] and *From This Place* [2020]).

20. Pat Metheny, email to Bob Gluck, May 30, 2023.

21. Metheny has recorded a handful of compositions that do include lyrics. Immediately coming to mind are "Mas Alla (Beyond)" on *First Circle* (1984), "Dream of the Return" and "Vadala" on *Letter from Home* (1989), and, most recently, "From This Place" on *From This Place* (2020), with Meshell Ndegeocello.

22. Metheny, *The Pat Metheny Real Book*.

23. Metheny and Mays, *Pat Metheny Song Book*.

Notes to Pages 102–115

24. A score can be found in both volumes of notated scores. While the description here follows *The Pat Metheny Real Book*, p. 82; greater detail may be found in *The Pat Metheny Song Book*, p. 160.

25. The acoustic guitar and orchestra bells are notated only in the *Pat Metheny Song Book* version, at rehearsal mark B.

26. Marked as sections G and H in the *Pat Metheny Real Book* score.

27. The notated score is published only in *The Pat Metheny Song* Book, p. 180.

28. The score in *The Pat Metheny Song Book*, p. 228, includes greater detail of "Third Wind" than is found in *The Pat Metheny Real Book*. *Still Life (Talking)* also includes vocals on "Minuano," "Last Train Home" (during the closing theme), "(It's Just) Talk," and "Beat 70." Note that "Last Train Home" and "Beat 70" are also recorded on *The Road to You* (1993).

29. There are slight differences between the versions notated in the two songbooks. In particular, in *The Pat Metheny Song Book*, p. 242, the melodic line at rehearsal marks B and D is notated one octave higher.

30. The published score appears in *The Pat Metheny Song Book*, p. 262. On *Letter from Home* (1989), Pedro Aznar's vocals without lyrics also are heard on "Spring Ain't Here," "Better Days Ahead," and "5-5-7," during the final repetitions of the main theme (notated in *The Pat Metheny Song Book*, p. 250); on "Beat 70," during the main theme and before the piano solo that comes toward the end of the performance; and on "Slip Away."

31. The score only appears in *The Pat Metheny Song Book: The Complete Collection*, p. 338.

32. Mark Ledford's wordless vocals also appear on *Secret Story* (1992), on "Finding and Believing," and relatively low in the mix on "See the World."

33. *The Pat Metheny Song Book*, 338.

34. Naná Vasconcelos's singing voice can also be heard on "Au Lait" (*Offramp*, 1982), in which he sings the main theme as a backdrop to Metheny's and Mays's mid-performance solos. Throughout this piece Vasconcelos offers reverberant vocalizations and breath sounds.

35. *Speaking of Now* (2002) also includes Richard Bona's vocals on "As It Is," "Another Life" (multitrack choral vocal at the beginning), "A Place in the World," and "Red Sky" (doubling the melody).

36. *The Pat Metheny Real Book*, 268–69.

Chapter 8

1. Rodriguez, "Reflections from Metheny," Cooke, *Pat Metheny: The ECM Years*.

2. Scheneckloth, "Pat Metheny: A Step beyond Tradition," 16.

3. Vasconcelos, "Interview with Pat Metheny." Recall also Lyle Mays's comment four years prior to *The Way Up*: "I keep going back to Brahms and Bach and Stravinsky and Ravel and Debussy. Bartok, Berg." Brannon, "Lyle Mays Interview."

4. Mingus, *Pithecanthropus Erectus*, liner notes.

Notes to Pages 115–119   171

5. Niles, *The Pat Metheny Interviews*, 47.

6. Pat Metheny, interview with Bob Gluck, May 25, 2021.

7. Antonio Sanchez, interview with Bob Gluck, December 19, 2022.

8. Fagien, "The Pat Metheny Interview."

9. Antonio Sanchez, interview with Bob Gluck, December 19, 2022.

10. Vella, "Phase Dancing."

11. Pat Metheny, interview with Bob Gluck, January 12, 2021.

12. Harrison, "Interview with Pat Metheny."

13. Pat Metheny, interview with Bob Gluck, December 23, 2022.

14. The four Mays compositions are "American Garage," "(Cross the) Heartland," "Au Lait," and "Language of Time."

15. In the 2000 *Pat Metheny Song Book*, an appendix offers descriptions of all the included compositions. Of those marked "Pat Metheny/Lyle Mays," here are the details regarding the nature of authorship. (1) Lyle Mays compositions are "Language of Time" and "Across the Sky" ("just a few melodic contributions from me [Metheny], mainly the tag and the end of the main melody"). (2) Collaborative efforts are "San Lorenzo" ("We wrote the basic arrangement, using those few phrases as the basic materials, with Lyle adding a lot of new melodic material"), "September Fifteenth" ("Lyle and I combined two tunes that we had written separately into one"), "American Garage" ("Lyle developed the piece further with the intro and the idea for the first 'A' section, and together we came up with the body of the tune and the soloing section"), "The Epic" ("We sat down with nothing, no sketches done by one or the other of us, just blank pieces of paper, and tried to write something together"), "Something to Remind You" ("one of my recent favorite collaborations with Lyle"), "The Heat of the Day" ("one of my real favorite collaborations with Lyle"), "Red Sky" ("another great Lyle 6/4 groove. We hammered out the melody"), "557" ("Lyle and I wrote the interlude section"), "Praise" ("Together we wrote the Beatle-esque middle section"), "Tell It All" ("Lyle and I really worked out the guitar-piano ensemble voicings in detail), "The First Circle" ("Together we came up with an ending, with Lyle writing the great counterpart line to the final statement of the melody"), "We Live Here" ("written the last day of our writing time together"), and "Stranger in Town" ("a tune of ours . . "). (3) Compositions by Pat Metheny where Lyle Mays made additions and edits are "Phase Dance" ("Lyle and I wrote the intro and the ending"), "Airstream" ("Lyle really was able to help me define a context for this cool little musical idea, and it found a home"), "Third Wind" ("[addition of] the fast polyrhythmic interlude and the 12/8 tag with that great, memorable hook"), "Praise" ("Lyle came up with the intro and the bridge"), "End of the Game" ("Lyle wrote a beautiful release section after the main guitar solo"), "Minuano 15/8" ("later reexamined by Lyle . . . his intro and the 'marimba' section"), "Eighteen" ("Lyle came up with the main guitar 'riff' on the guitar"), "James" ("with Lyle writing the nice introduction"), "Travels" ("I remember writing the 'A' section, Lyle coming out and checking it out and sitting down and coming up with the bridge"), "The Awakening" ("[Lyle] took the theme and did an expansion on it"), "The Girl Next Door" ("[Lyle and I wrote] the bridge/interlude section"), "And

172 Notes to Pages 119–129

Then I Knew" ("great release section by Lyle after the guitar solo"), "45/8" ("Lyle wrote a simple 8-bar phrase"), "Lone Jack" ("finished with Lyle adding the interlude/intro/outro"), and "Half Life of Absolution" ("addition of a new bridge and an extensive re-harmonization of the out melody that Lyle and I came up with"). Metheny and Mays, *Pat Metheny Song Book*, 439–45.

16. Goldstein, *Jazz Composers Companion*.

17. Goldstein, 100.

18. Pat Metheny, interview with Bob Gluck, December 23, 2022.

19. Ibid.

20. In some ways, the Ellington model is not the best analogy because for many years, Ellington had the highly accomplished composer and arranger Billy Strayhorn contributing far more substantially to the Ellington repertoire than Mays did for the PMG.

21. Steve Rodby, interview with Bob Gluck, February 28, 2023.

Chapter 9

1. Weisgall, "The Music of Henry Cowell," 498.

2. DeMichael, "John Coltrane and Eric Dolphy Answer the Jazz Critics."

3. Bernstein, *What Does Music Mean*, 46:08–46:55.

4. A discussion of the term "meaning" can be found in chapter 7.

5. Kay, "Pat Metheny."

6. Antonio Sanchez, interview with Bob Gluck, December 19, 2022.

7. The title "America Undefined" references the James Baldwin essay "The Discovery of What It Means to Be an American" (1959), in which Baldwin writes: "America's history, her aspirations, her peculiar triumphs, her even more peculiar defeats, and her position in the world—yesterday and today—are all so profoundly and stubbornly unique that the very word 'America' remains a new, almost completely undefined and extremely controversial proper noun. No one in the world seems to know exactly what it describes, not even we motley millions who call ourselves Americans." Baldwin, *Nobody Knows My Name*, 76–77.

8. Scattered throughout are a wide range of variations on this pattern, first articulated at 4:13, and then 4:21, 4:35–4:47, 5:21. 5:27, 5:56–5:58, 5:55–5:59, and elsewhere.

9. *Just Jazz Guitar*. "Guitarist Interview with Pat Metheny."

10. Antonio Sanchez, interview with Bob Gluck, December 19, 2022.

11. The sounds of trains were ubiquitous during Pat Metheny's childhood. His family lived a half hour from Kansas City in the small exurban town of Lee's Summit, through which ran the Missouri–Pacific freight train line. The town was named, Metheny recalls (Pat Metheny, interview with Bob Gluck, May 17, 2022): "from it being the highest point between Kansas City and St. Louis on that line. Although it isn't all that high, it is higher than the area around us, leading to some pretty wide views, particularly looking westward." The sights and sounds of the trains became implanted

in Metheny's consciousness from the beginning of his life. Visually, the mile-long row of train cars was a constant, "pretty much all day and night." The tracks were "really just a few yards away from my bedroom window" in the family's home. From a sonic perspective, "when we moved three blocks away, the sound of the train going through the town was still constant, and even better from a bit of a distance." The trains and train tracks of Metheny's youth are among the enduring sounds that periodically appear within his music.

12. Antonio Sanchez, interview with Bob Gluck, December 19, 2022.

13. Peterson, *Music and the Creative Spirit*.

14. Goins, *Emotional Response to Music*. Goins holds that emotion is conveyed by utilizing a grouping of "rhetorical devices" in Metheny's music, "subtle manipulation of melody, harmony, and rhythm, which often manifests itself in the form of speech-like qualities in his music." He posits in a study that a group of people listening to the same compositions can consistently align these with clusters of descriptive words, for example "calm, soothing, lyrical," and "bright, happy joyous." Goins finds overlap between his subjects' identified word clusters; he acknowledges that "exploring the exact causes and effects of mood states is a nebulous procedure at best, as evidenced by the numerous and often conflicting viewpoints presented by well-known researchers" (iv).

15. This is a different song from one with a similar title, "This is Not America" by Pat Metheny and David Bowie, an instrumental version of which is part of the soundtrack to the film *The Falcon and the Snowman*.

16. For a period in 2012, the State of Virginia considered, but ultimately demurred from, designating a revised version of "Shenandoah" as the interim state song. It would have replaced "Carry Me Back to Old Virginia," a song filled with racist references to the plantation South, a document of yet another symbol of an American history that never truly goes away. Unlike "Carry Me Back," "Shenandoah" remains an American favorite thanks to its melodic beauty and the poetry of the multiple meanings of the name Shenandoah as a symbol of longing. See "Virgina State Song."

Appendix 1

1. Small, "Face to Face with Pat Metheny." Of performing live in 1985, Metheny said, "I mainly play the Linda acoustic, that's my favorite." Webb, "Interview with Pat Metheny."

2. Metheny adds: "[Her] two miniature guitars [include] a triple, which is twelve-string with the strings in three groups of four, rather than six groups of two, and an alto guitar, which is about halfway between a regular guitar scale and this mini one." Small, "Face to Face with Pat Metheny."

3. Andre Chomondeley, interview with Bob Gluck, January 18, 2023. Chomondeley frames this portion of the pre-show routine within the fuller day schedule: "The crew tends to walk into the theater at ten a.m. to set up. The band will still be at the hotel or on the bus. We always check stuff at two p.m., and then Pat's always going to get there at three, and the band gets there at four. We do a long check of the levels for

each guitar in the show before Pat even arrives, at which point he checks them again. We have a different setting for the nylon string, a different one for the steel string, a different one for the Pikasso. All the way down, they're all different EQ, different gain stages, different types of output. So that's a really important thing that shows why the set list is important. And to that point, this is how Pat designs a set list. Usually, when we get the list, it names each guitar next to the name of a tune."

4. De Souza, "'All Sights Were Perceived as Sounds,'" 154.

5. The Coral electric sitar was first introduced to Metheny audiences on "Last Train Home" (*First Circle* [1984]). Designed by Vincent "Vinnie" Bell for Danelectro in 1967, the sitar has six playable strings plus a set of thirteen strings that vibrate sympathetically, like the acoustic sitar, but it is a portable instrument accessible to guitarists who lack the specialized knowledge and technique required to tune and play that instrument. The sitar gained currency in popular music in the mid-1960s thanks to use by George Harrison and the Beatles, who were influenced by master classical musician Ravi Shankar. A popular model of the Coral was shaped like a teardrop. It had a "Sitarmatic" bridge and "two rosewood bridges with metal saddles and metal friction pegs designed to be tuned with a harp-style wrench, three 'lipstick tube' pickups (two for the played strings, one for the drones), three Volume knobs, three Tone knobs, floating pickguard with the Bell Signature Design logo, a finish dubbed 'Textured Bombay Red,' rosewood fingerboard with dot inlays, and a Patent Pending sticker affixed to the back of the headstock." Gruhn and Jones, "Coral Electric Sitar."

6. Forte, "Pat Metheny: The Jazz Guitar Prodigy at 60."

7. Manzer, "Pikasso."

8. Metheny, "Imaginary Day: About the Instrumentation."

9. De Souza, "'All Sights Were Perceived as Sounds,'" 163,. Regarding the tuning systems, De Souza adds: "There are four sets of strings here. The 'conventional' neck has six strings, tuned as a baritone guitar a major third lower than the standard E-tuning (thus C, F, B♭, E♭, G, C). This is the only area with frets. Above this neck is a bank of twelve shorter, higher strings tuned to a G-minor pentatonic scale. Strung zither-like over the body is another set of strings: these are tuned to a C♯-minor collection that is missing a sixth. A final set of twelve sympathetic strings, which Metheny seldom plays directly, passes underneath two others; it is tuned to a G-minor chord."

10. Pat Metheny Group, *Imaginary Day Live* (1998).

11. Bonzai, "Lunching with Bonzai: Pat Metheny—Jazzing It Up."

12. Andre Cholmondeley, interview with Bob Gluck, January 18, 2023.

13. The Roland appears on various tracks on the live album *The Road to You* (1993); the title track on *We Live Here* (1995); several tracks of *Imaginary Day* (1997); "As it Is," the opening track on *Speaking of Now* (2002); and the PMG's final album, *The Way Up* (2005).

14. Pat Metheny, *Unity Band* (2012), *Kin* (←→) (2014), and *The Unity Sessions* (2016).

15. The Roland appears on "Question and Answer" (first recorded on the 1990 *Question and Answer* trio album) and "Zenith Blue."

Notes to Pages 137–147   175

16. Adelson, "Interview with Pat Metheny."

17. Antonio Sanchez, interview with Bob Gluck, December 19, 2022.

18. On *80/81* Charlie Haden was joined by fellow Coleman alumnus tenor saxophonist Dewey Redman, plus alto saxophonist Michael Brecker and drummer Jack DeJohnette.

19. Pat Metheny, email to by Bob Gluck, May 30, 2023.

20. Ibid.

21. Simon, "Pat Metheny: Ready to Tackle Tomorrow."

22. Coleman, "Prime Time for Harmolodics."

23. Perkiömäki, "Lennie and Ornette Searching for Freedom in Improvisation," 10.

24. Lavelle, "Ornette Coleman and Harmolodics," 142.

25. Antonio Sanchez, interview with Bob Gluck, December 19, 2022.

26. Pat Metheny, *Zero Tolerance for Silence* (1994).

27. *Just Jazz Guitar*, "Guitarist Interview with Pat Metheny."

28. Ibid.

29. Ibid.

30. Ibid.

31. Pat Metheny, *Secret Story* (1992).

32. The "Pinpet" orchestra of the Royal Cambodian Ballet.

33. Zweriin, "For Pat Metheny, Silence Is Awful."

34. Fagien, "The Pat Metheny Interview."

Appendix 2

1. A slightly shortened, hour-long version of the work was included on touring set lists following the recording's release.

2. See Grauer, "Echoes of Our Forgotten Ancestors," and a more populist discussion in Zeger, "The Evolution of Hocketing."

3. Footnotes regarding *The Way Up* associate this author's narrative discussion with the published score, Steve Rodby, ed., *The Way Up: A Complete Score Composed by Pat Metheny and Lyle Mays*, 45.

4. Rodby, *The Way Up*, 48.

5. The importance of motifs in Pat Metheny's compositions and solos was explored in chapter 4.

6. Rodby, *The Way Up*, 62.

7. Rodby, 62.

8. Rodby, 66.

9. Rodby, 66–68.

10. Rodby, 72.

11. Rodby, 76.

12. Including solos by guitar (at 14:24), piano (at 16:56), and trumpet (at 18:30).

13. Rodby, 103.

14. Rodby, 106.

15. Motifs in Figure 16 and guitar solo excerpts in Figure 17 were transcribed and notated by Bob Gluck, with chord changes drawn from Rodby, *The Way Up*.

16. Rodby, *The Way Up*, 107.

17. Rodby, 109.

18. Rodby, 109–10.

19. Rodby, 113.

20. Rodby, 114.

21. Rodby, 118–19.

22. Rodby, 119.

BIBLIOGRAPHY

Interviews Conducted by Bob Gluck

Cholmondeley, Andre: January 18, 2023 (over Zoom).
Metheny, Pat: January 12, 2021; May 23, 2021; June 2, 2021; May 17, 2022; May 25, 2021; August 4, 2022; September 23, 2022; and December 23, 2022 (by email).
Rodby, Steve: February 28, 2023; and May 22, 2023 (over Zoom).
Sanchez, Antonio: December 19, 2022 (over Zoom).

Other Sources

Adelson, Steve. n.d. "Interview with Pat Metheny." http://steveadelson.com/interview_metheny.php. Accessed December 8, 2020.

Adler, David. 2005. "Pat Metheny: The Advancing Guitarist." *Jazz Times*, March 1 (updated May 9, 2019). https://jazztimes.com/features/profiles/pat-metheny-the-advancing-guitarist/.

Ahnert, Seth. 2015. "Bill Evans' Bridge on Oleo." *The Jazz Language* (blog), March 4. http://thejazzlanguage.com/bill-evans-bridge-on-oleo/.

Ake, David. 2007. "The Emergence of the Rural American Ideal in Jazz: Keith Jarrett and Pat Metheny on ECM Records." *Jazz Perspectives* 1 (1): 29–59, 47.

Arnold-Forster, Tom. 2017. "Dr. Billy Taylor, 'America's Classical Music,' and the Role of the Jazz Ambassador." Journal of American Studies 51 (1): 117–39.

Baldwin, James. 1961. *Nobody Knows My Name: More Notes of a Native Son*. New York: Dial Press.

Baraka, Amiri (Leroi Jones). 1999. *Blues People: The Negro Experience in White America and the Music that Developed From It*. New York: Harper Perennial. First published 1963 by Charles Morrow and Co.

Baraka, Amiri (Leroi Jones). 2010. *Black Music*. New York: Akashic Books. First published 1968 by Charles Morrow and Co.

Baritoneguitar.org. 2016. "'Half Nashville' Tuning: Metheny Style." *Baritoneguitar.org* (blog), January 3. https://www.baritoneguitar.org/blog/half-nashville-tunning-metheny-style.

Barth, Joe. 2006. *Voices in Jazz Guitar*. Pacific, MO: Mel Bay.

Beato, Rick. 2019. "The Gary Burton Interview." May 30. https://www.youtube.com/watch?v=9VOw0oomUEY.

Berliner, Paul. 1994. *Thinking in Jazz: The Infinite Art of Improvisation*. Chicago: University of Chicago Press.

Bettine, Michael, and Trevor Taylor. 2001. *Percussion Profiles: Interviews, Articles and Discographies of 25 of the Worlds Most Creative Percussionists*. Chelmsford, UK: Soundworld.

Bianchi, Curt. 2021. *Elegant People: A History of the Band Weather Report*. Guilford, CT: Backbeat.

Bienstock, Richard. 2021. "Meet the Beatles Guitars." *Guitar Player*, October 25. https://www.guitarplayer.com/gear/meet-the-beatles-guitars.

Bernstein, Leonard. 1958. *What Does Music Mean*. Young People's Concerts broadcast 1.1 New York Philharmonic broadcast from Carnegie Hall, January 18. Transcript available at https://leonardbernstein.com/lectures/television-scripts/young-peoples-concerts/what-does-music-mean.

Bertholf, Garry J. 2006. "John Coltrane: Jazz Improvisation, Performance, and Transcription." Honors thesis, Colby College.

Bonzai, Mr. 1995. "Lunching with Bonzai: Pat Metheny—Jazzing It Up." *Mix* 19 (3): 83–90.

Brannon, Mike. 2001. "Lyle Mays Interview." *All About Jazz*, May. https://www.lylemays.com/aaj-interview-2001.

Brewer, Carolyn Glenn. 2021. *Beneath Missouri Skies: Pat Metheny in Kansas City 1964–1972*. Denton: University of North Texas Press.

Brodacki, Krystian. 1992. "The Original Batman: Wayne Shorter Remembers Miles Davis." *Jazz Forum* 132 (1): 24–29.

Brodowski, Paweł, and Janusz Szprot. 1985. "Interview with Lyle Mays." *Jazz Forum* 96 (5). Republished at https://www.lylemays.com/jazz-forum-interview.

Burton, Gary. 2013. *Learning to Listen: The Jazz Journey of Gary Burton, An Autobiography*. Boston: Berklee Press/Hal Leonard.

Cage, John. 1961. *Silence*. New York: Wesleyan University Press.

Cal Performances. 2007. "The Silk Road Ensemble with Yo-Yo-Ma," program notes. https://calperformances.org/learn/program_notes/2006/pn_Silk_Road.pdf.

Cazares, David. 2013. "Vibraphone Pioneer Gary Burton Learned to Listen to Himself—and the Music." Minnesota Public Radio, *MPRNews*, October 2. https://www.mprnews.org/story/2013/10/02/vibraphone-pioneer-gary-burton-learned-to-listen-to-himself-and-the-music.

Chiu, David. 2016. "4th & Broadway: When Tower Records Was Church." *Cuepoint* (blog), December 23. https://medium.com/cuepoint/4th-broadway-when-tower-records-was-church-65f15d7af2f7.

Cohen, Harvey G. 2010. *Duke Ellington's America*. Chicago: University of Chicago Press.

Coleman, Ornette. 1983. "Prime Time for Harmolodics." *DownBeat*, July, 54–55.

Cooke, Mervyn. 2017. *Pat Metheny: The ECM Years, 1975–1984*. New York: Oxford University Press.

Costa, J. C. 1986. "Pat Metheny: Learning, Teaching & Expanding the Art of Improvisation." *College Musician* 1 (1): 32–36.

Cott, Jonathan. 1996. "Interview with Steve Reich." *New York Magazine*. Republished at https://www.stevereich.com/jonathan-cott/.

Cross, Dominick. 2014. "Metheny's Unity Group has 'Instant Connection.'" *Daily Advertiser* (New Orleans), February 13. https://www.theadvertiser.com/story/community/2014/02/13/-methenys-unity-group-has-instant-connection-/5471971/.

Darling, David. 2008. "The Spiritual Significance of Music." Unpublished.

Dean, James. 2014. "Pat Metheny's Finger Routes: The Role of Muscle Memory in Guitar Improvisation." *Jazz Perspectives* 8 (1): 45–71.

DeMichael, Don. 1962. "John Coltrane and Eric Dolphy Answer the Jazz Critics." *DownBeat*, April 12. https://downbeat.com/microsites/prestige/dolphy-interview.html.

De Souza, Jonathan. 2016. "'All Sights Were Perceived as Sounds': Pat Metheny and the Instrumental Image." In Björn Heile, Peter Elsdon, and Jenny Doctor, eds., *Watching Jazz: Encounters with Jazz Performance on Screen*. New York: Oxford University Press.

Digital Interviews. 1999. "Pat Metheny," June. Accessed January 25, 2021; no longer available online.

Discogs. n.d. "Pat Metheny with Sonny Rollins & with His Trio—*Dream Teams*." https://www.discogs.com/release/4474290-Pat-Metheny-With-Sonny-Rollins-With-His-Trio-Dream-Teams.

Driggs, Frank, and Chuck Haddix. 2005. *Kansas City Jazz: From Ragtime to Bebop—A History*. New York: Oxford University Press.

Dyas, J. B. 2016. "Aebersold: A Jazz Icon's Journey." *Downbeat*, March, 94–96.

Ellington, Edward Kennedy. 1973. *Music Is My Mistress*. New York: Doubleday.

Ellington, Edward Kennedy. 1993. "Interpretations in Jazz: A Conference with Duke Ellington, 1947." In Mark Tucker, ed., *The Duke Ellington Reader*. New York: Oxford University Press. Originally published in *Etude*, March 1947.

Fagien, Michael. 2002. "The Pat Metheny Interview." *Jazziz*, March. https://assets.jazziz.com/uploads/2019/07/JAZZIZ-Pat-Metheny-Interviews-Special-Issue.pdf.

Fellezs, Kevin. 2011. *Birds of Fire: Jazz, Rock, Funk, and the Creation of Fusion*. Durham, NC: Duke University Press.

Floyd, Samuel A., Jr. 1991. "Ring Shout! Literary Studies, Historical Studies, and Music Inquiry." *Black Music Research Journal* 11 (2): 265–87.

180 Bibliography

Fordham, John. 1992. "Getting Things Down Pat: Mr. Metheny talks to John Fordham about Lost Love, Classical Jazz and His Latest LP Release." *Wire* 102 (August), 14–15.

Forte, Dan. 1979. "The Metheny Method: A Primer for Guitarists, Not Fusion, Not Jazz, Not Rock." *Musician* 18: 38–43.

Forte, Dan. 1980. "The Pat Metheny Group—Jazz's Foremost Garage Band." *Musicians' Industry* 2 (2): 32–41. Republished at https://www.lylemays.com/jazzs-foremost -garage-band.

Forte, Dan. 1981. "Pat Metheny: Jazz Voice of the '80s." *Guitar Player*, December, 90–94.

Forte, Dan. 2016. "Pat Metheny: The Jazz Guitar Prodigy at 60." *Vintage Guitar*, December. https://www.vintageguitar.com/26318/pat-metheny-2/.

Freeman, Mark. 1993. *Rewriting the Self: History, Memory, Narrative*. New York: Routledge.

Furlong, Bob. 2010. "Exploring Nashville Tuning." *Premier Guitar* (blog), May 18. https://www.premierguitar.com/diy/exploring-nashville-tuning.

Gates, Henry Louis, Jr. 1988. *The Signifying Monkey: A Theory of African American Literary Criticism*. New York: Oxford University Press.

Gerard, Charley. 2001. *Jazz in Black & White: Face, Culture, and Identity in the Jazz Community*, Westport, CT: Praeger.

Gioia, Ted. 1997. *The History of Jazz*. Oxford: Oxford University Press.

Gitler, Ira, and Dan Morgenstern. 1969. "Newport '69: Bad Trip." *DownBeat*, August 21, 25–31, 45.

Givan, Benjamin. 2014. "Gunther Schuller and the Challenge of Sonny Rollins: Stylistic Context, Intentionality, and Jazz Analysis." *Journal of the American Musicological Society* 67 (1): 167–237.

Gluck, Bob. 2012. *You'll Know When You Get There: Herbie Hancock and the Mwandishi Band*. Chicago: University of Chicago Press.

Gluck, Bob. 2016. *The Miles Davis Lost Quintet and Other Revolutionary Ensembles*. Chicago: University of Chicago Press.

Gluck, Bob. 2017. "Global Musical Connections: Parallels to the Long History of Globalization." *Global Synergies* 4. https://www.albany.edu/international/assets /Global-Synergies-spring17-web.pdf.

Gluck, Robert. 2008. "Between, Within and Across Cultures." *Organised Sound* 13 (2): 141–52.

Goins, Wayne E. 2001. *Emotional Response to Music: Pat Metheny's Secret Story*. Lewiston, NY: Mellen.

Goldstein, Gil. 2014 (1993). *Jazz Composers Companion*. Mainz: Advance Music.

Grauer, Victor A. 2006. "Echoes of Our Forgotten Ancestors." *World of Music* 48 (2): 5–58.

Greenbaum, Stuart. 1992. "Pat Metheny and Lyle Mays: *First Circle*: Transcription and Analysis." Master's thesis, University of Melbourne.

Gruhn, George, and Sarah Rose Jones. 2015. "Coral Electric Sitar." *Vintage Guitar*, June. https://www.vintageguitar.com/23062/coral-electric-sitar/.

Hamilton, Andy. 2007. "Paul Bley: Time Must Have a Stop." *Wire*, October. Republished at https://www.andyhamilton.org/single-post/2007/10/19/paul-bley-time-must-have-a-stop.

Harrison, Joel. 2021. "Interview with Pat Metheny," in *Guitar Talk: Conversations with Visionary Players*. Newark: Terra Nova.

Hazlett, Tim. 2015. "10 Questions for Jazz Legend, Pat Metheny." *Classical Connections* (blog), November 12. http://timhazlett.blogspot.com/2015/11/10-questions-for-jazz-legend-pat-metheny.html.

Huber, Chris. 2021. "The History of John Lennon's Rickenbacker 325 Guitars." *Extra Chill* (blog), December 4. https://extrachill.com/2021/12/john-lennon-rickenbacker-325-guitar-history.html.

Huotari, Allen. 2001. "An Interview with Pat Metheny." *All About Jazz*, April.

Iyer, Vijay. 2004. "Exploding the Narrative in Jazz Improvisation." In Robert O'Meally, Brent Edwards, Farrah Jasmine Griffin, eds. *Uptown Conversation: The New Jazz Studies*. New York: Columbia University Press.

James, Stephen D., and J. Walker James. 2014. "Conductor of Music and Men: Duke Ellington through the Eyes of His Nephew." In Edward Green, ed., *The Oxford Companion to Duke Ellington*. Cambridge: Cambridge University Press.

Jankelevitch, Vladimir. 2003. *Music and the Ineffable*. Princeton, NJ: Princeton University Press.

Jazz Discography Project. n.d. "CTI Records Discography Project." https://www.jazzdisco.org/cti-records/. Accessed May 23, 2023.

Jazz Improv. 2004. Special Issue: "Pat Metheny: In Depth Explorations." *Jazz Improv* 4 (4).

Johnson, Mark. 1986. *The Body in the Mind*. Chicago: University of Chicago Press.

Joness, Wayne Scott. n.d. "Roland GR-300 Analog Guitar Synthesizer." https://www.joness.com/gr300/GR-300.htm. Accessed December 3, 2022.

Jost, Ekkehard. 1981. *Free Jazz*. New York: Da Capo. Originally published 1974.

Just Jazz Guitar. 2001. "Guitarist Interview with Pat Metheny." *Just Jazz Guitar*, April 23. Republished at https://www.patmetheny.com/writings/full_display.cfm?id=12.

Kay, M. 1984. "Pat Metheny." *Music U.K.* 25, January 1984.

Keepnews, Peter. 2017. "Larry Coryell, Guitarist of Fusion before It Had a Name, Dies at 73." *New York Times*, February 21. https://www.nytimes.com/2017/02/21/arts/music/larry-coryell-dead-jazz-rock-guitarist.html.

Kivy, Peter. 1984. *Sound and Semblance: Reflections on Musical Representation*. Princeton, NJ: Princeton University Press.

Kivy, Peter. 1991. *Music Alone: Philosophical Reflections on the Purely Musical*. Ithaca, NY: Cornell University Press.

Klopus, Joe. 2012. "Jazz Town: Metheny Unifies His Sound." *Kansas City Star*, September 6. https://www.kansascity.com/entertainment/article308014/jazz-town-metheny-unifies-his-sound.html.

Bibliography

Kofsky, Frank. 1970. *Black Nationalism and the Revolution in Music*. New York: Pathfinder.

Kompanek, Chris. 2009. "Badal Roy: Keeping the Groove." *All About Jazz*, July 17. https://www.allaboutjazz.com/badal-roy-keeping-the-groove-badal-roy-by-chris-kompanek.

Lakoff, George, and Mark Johnson. 2003. *Metaphors We Live By*. Chicago: University of Chicago Press. Originally published 1980.

Langer, Suzanne. 1953. *Feeling and Form: A Theory of Art*. New York: Scribner.

Larkin, Cormac. 2017. "In Five Seconds My Life Changed. I Was Worse Than the Worst Jazz Snob." *Irish Times*, November 9. https://www.irishtimes.com/culture/music/in-five-seconds-my-life-changed-i-was-worse-than-the-worst-jazz-snob-1.3283078.

Larson, Steve. 2005. "Composition versus Improvisation?" *Journal of Music Theory* 49 (2): 241–75.

Lavelle, Matt. 2019. "Ornette Coleman and Harmolodics." Master's thesis, Graduate Program in Jazz History and Research, Rutgers University.

Leet, Norm. n.d. "Guitar Synths — The Story So Far." http://www.roland.co.uk/blog/guitar-synths-the-story-so-far/. Accessed February 9, 2021.

Lewis, George E. 1996. "Foreword: Who Is Jazz?" In Philip V. Bohlman and Goffredo Plastino, eds., *Jazz Worlds/World Jazz*. Chicago: University of Chicago Press.

Lewis, George E. 1996. "Improvised Music Since 1950: Afrological and Eurological Forms." *Black Music Research Journal* 16.1 (Spring), 91–119.

Little, Charles. 1985. "Guitar Synthesizers: More or Less in Jazz Tradition." *Jazziz*, March. https://assets.jazziz.com/uploads/2019/07/JAZZIZ-Pat-Metheny-Interviews-Special-Issue.pdf.

Lowe, Allen. 2021. *"Turn Me Loose White Man," Or: Appropriating Culture: How to Listen to American Music, 1900–1960*, vol. 2. New Haven: Constant Sorrow Press.

Manzer, Linda. n.d. "Pikasso." https://manzer.com/guitars/custom-models/pikasso/. Accessed November 27, 2022.

Meltzer, Michael A. 1976. "Pat Metheny — Mick Goodrick: Gary Burton's Star Guitarists." *Guitar Player* 10 (3).

Merriam-Webster Dictionary. n.d. "Metaphor." https://www.merriam-webster.com/dictionary/metaphor. Accessed May 22, 2018.

Metheny, Mike. 1995. "Q&A with . . . Pat Metheny." *Jazz Ambassadors Magazine* 9 (4): 24–31.

Metheny, Pat. 1999. "Question and Answer." https://www.patmetheny.com/qa/questionView.cfm.

Metheny, Pat. 2004. *Pat Metheny: Selected Recordings*, liner notes. ECM rarum 9, CD.

Metheny, Pat. 2006. *Pat Metheny Trio → Live*. Alejandro Moro, transcriber. Milwaukee: Hal Leonard.

Metheny, Pat. 2007. *Wes Montgomery Live in '65*, liner notes. Jazz Icons series 2. Naxos 2.119003, DVD.

Metheny, Pat. 2012. *Pat Metheny Unity Group: Kin (←→)*, lead sheets. Milwaukee: Hal Leonard.

Metheny, Pat. 2017. *The Pat Metheny Real Book*. Milwaukee: Hal Leonard.

Metheny, Pat. 2019. *Pat Metheny: Jazz Piano Solos*. Milwaukee: Hal Leonard.

Metheny, Pat. n.d. "Imaginary Day: About the Instrumentation." http://www.patmetheny.com/features/imaginary/inst.htm. Accessed December 15, 2022.

Metheny, Pat. n.d. "Imaginary Day: About the Tracks." https://www.patmetheny.com/features/imaginary/tracks.htm. Accessed November 17, 2022.

Metheny, Pat, and Lyle Mays. 2000. *Pat Metheny Song Book: The Complete Collection—167 Compositions*. Milwaukee: Hal Leonard.

Metheny Music Foundation. n.d. "Our History: The Lee's Summit–Metheny Connection." https://methenymusicfoundation.org/our-history/. Accessed December 14, 2020.

Milward, John. 1992. "Wandering Minstrel." *Boston Globe Magazine*, August 23.

Mingus, Charles. 1956. *Pithecanthropus Erectus*, liner notes. Atlantic Records 1237, LP. Republished at http://albumlinernotes.com/Pithecanthropus_Erectus.html.

Monson, Ingrid. 1994. "Doubleness and Jazz Improvisation: Irony, Parody, and Ethnomusicology." *Critical Inquiry* 20 (2): 283–313.

Monson, Ingrid. 1996. *Saying Something: Jazz Improvisation and Interaction*. Chicago: University of Chicago Press.

Moon, Tom. 1993. "Pat Metheny Gets Serious." *Jazz Times* 23 (6), 24–27, 87.

Morvan, Marc. n.d. "The Pat Metheny Database." http://marc.morvan.free.fr/pmdb/chronology/index.html. Accessed November 3, 2022.

Mullen, Tom. 1986. "Interview with Robert Fripp." *Guitar Player*, June. https://www.joness.com/gr300/fripp.htm.

Murphy, John P. 2006. *Music in Brazil*. New York: Oxford University Press.

New York Times. 2022. "50 Years Ago, Stevie Wonder Heard the Future." *New York Times*, October 27. https://www.nytimes.com/interactive/2022/10/27/arts/music/stevie-wonder-talking-book.html.

Niles, Richard. 2009. *The Pat Metheny Interviews: The Inner Workings of His Creativity Revealed*. Milwaukee: Hal Leonard.

Okamoto, David. 1992. "Pat's Profile." *Jazziz* 9 (5).

Payton, Nicholas. 2014. "Black American Music and the Jazz Tradition." *Nicholas Payton* (blog), April 30. https://nicholaspayton.wordpress.com/2014/04/30/black-american-music-and-the-jazz-tradition.

Perkiömäki, Jari. 2002. "Lennie and Ornette Searching for Freedom in Improvisation: Observations on the Music of Lennie Tristano and Ornette Coleman." Thesis, Jazz Department, Sibelius Academy, University of the Arts, Helsinki.

Peterson, Lloyd. 2006. *Music and the Creative Spirit: Innovators in Jazz, Improvisation, and the Avant Garde*. Lanham, MD: Scarecrow Press.

Porter, Lewis. 2000. *John Coltrane: His Life and Music*. Ann Arbor: University of Michigan Press.

Radano, Ronald M. 1993. *New Musical Figurations: Anthony Braxton's Cultural Critique.* Chicago: University of Chicago Press.

Radano, Ronald M. 2003. *Lying Up a Nation: Race and Black Music.* Chicago: University of Chicago Press.

Ratliff, Ben. 2005. "Listening to CD's with: Pat Metheny: An Idealist Reconnects with His Mentors." *New York Times,* February 25. https://www.nytimes.com/2005/02/25/arts/music/pat-metheny-an-idealist-reconnects-with-his-mentors.html.

Ratliff, Ben. 2007. *Coltrane: The Story of a Sound.* New York: Farrar, Straus, and Giroux.

Reich, Steve. 1987. "*Electric Counterpoint*: Composer's Notes." https://www.boosey.com/cr/music/Steve-Reich-Electric-Counterpoint/7542.

Reich, Steve. 2002. "Music as a Gradual Process," in *Writings on Music: 1965–2000.* New York: Oxford University Press.

Reich, Steve. 2007. "*Music for 18 Musicians*: Composer's Notes." https://www.boosey.com/pages/cr/catalogue/cat_detail?musicid=548.

Reid, Graham. 2020. "Pat Metheny Interviewed (2020): The Confounding Career of Pat Metheny." *Elsewhere* (blog), March 10. https://www.elsewhere.co.nz/jazz/9312/pat-metheny-interviewed-2020-the-confounding-career-of-pat-metheny/.

Remnick, David. 2021. "Paul McCartney Doesn't Really Want to Stop the Show." *The New Yorker,* October 18. https://www.newyorker.com/magazine/2021/10/18/paul-mccartney-doesnt-really-want-to-stop-the-show.

Roads, Curtis. 1996. *The Computer Music Tutorial.* Cambridge: MIT Press.

Rodby, Steve, ed. n.d. *The Way Up: A Complete Score Composed by Pat Metheny and Lyle Mays.* Milwaukee: Hal Leonard.

Rodriguez, Nathan. 2004. "Reflections from Metheny." *JamBase,* January 26.

Rubin, Rick, producer. 2021. "The People We Loved Were Loving Us!" Season 1, episode 3 of *McCartney 3, 2, 1.* Hulu.

Rush, Stephen. 2017. *Free Jazz, Harmolodics, and Ornette Coleman,* New York: Routledge.

Russell, George. 1957. *Jazz Workshop,* liner notes. RCA Victor 1372, LP.

Schuller, Gunther. 2015. "Sonny Rollins and the Challenge of Thematic Improvisation." In Robert Walser, ed., *Keeping Time: Readings in Jazz History.* New York: Oxford University Press.

Segala, Pascal. 2017. *Pat Metheny—Artiste multiplunique.* Paris: Du Layeur Editi.

Scheneckloth, Tim. 1982. "Pat Metheny: A Step beyond Tradition." *DownBeat,* November, 14–16, 66.

Shore, John. 1998. "Traveling Man, Jazz Guitarist Pat Metheny Discusses His New Album and Life on the Road." *SLAMM Magazine.*

Simon, John Alan. 1977. "Pat Metheny: Ready to Tackle Tomorrow." *DownBeat,* July 13, 23–24, 53.

Simonini, Ross. 2022. "An Interview with Pat Metheny." *The Believer,* March 7. https://www.thebeliever.net/an-interview-with-pat-metheny/.

Small, Mark L. 1997. "Face to Face with Pat Metheny." *Acoustic Guitar,* April.

Smith, Andy. 2007. "Pat Metheny: Composing to Exploit the Sound of the Guitar." Master's thesis, Massey College of Creative Arts, Massey University, Auckland.

Steinberg, Dore. 1995. Interview with Pat Metheny, KKSF 103.7 FM, San Francisco. Available at https://web.archive.org/web/20170512114741/http://hepcat1950.com/pmivkksf.html.

Strunk, Steven. 2008. "Notes on Harmony in Wayne Shorter's Compositions, 1964–67." *Journal of Music Theory* 49 (2): 301–32.

Stryker, Mark. 2022. "Chronology: Sonny Greer and Sam Woodyard Drum for the Duke." *JazzTimes*, November 10. https://jazztimes.com/features/columns/chronology-sonny-greer-and-sam-woodyard-drum-for-the-duke/.

Super Channel TV. 1993. "Talkin' Jazz" Interview with Pat Metheny. Accessed June 7, 2021, at https://www.youtube.com/watch?v=aQIWwTLGdzw, but no longer available online.

Takemitsu, Toru. 1995. *Confronting Silence: Selected Writings*. Berkley, CA: Fallen Leaf Press.

Tauss, Lucy. 1995. "A Piece of the Puzzle." *Jazziz*, February.

Taylor, Billy. 1999. "America's Classical Music." In Robert Walser, ed., *Keeping Time: Readings in Jazz History*. New York: Oxford University Press.

Tesser, Neil. 1990. Gary Burton, *Reunion*, liner notes. GRP 9598, CD.

Van Bruggen, Benjamin. 2014. "The Art of Composing: How Steve Reich's Music Has Influenced Pat Metheny's and Lyle Mays' *The Way Up*: A Research into the History of Composition Techniques." Master's thesis, Utrecht University.

Van Der Bliek, Rob. 1991. "Wes Montgomery: A Study of Coherence in Jazz Improvisation." *Jazzforschung/Jazz Research* 23.

Vasconcelos, Andre. 2012. "Interview with Pat Metheny for the Berklee Blogs." *Berklee Blogs*, October 2. https://blogs.berklee.edu/2012/10/interview-with-pat-metheny-for-the-berklee-blogs.

Veitch, Dave. 1999. "Metheny's Method." *Calgary Sun*, June 25.

Vella, Joseph. 2020. "Something Left Unsaid: Musical Musings from Lyle Mays." https://www.lylemays.com/something-left-unsaid.

Vella, Joseph. 2022. "Phase Dancing: Gottlieb, Wertico, Sanchez—The Art of Drumming in the Pat Metheny Group." *All About Jazz*, March 24. https://www.allaboutjazz.com/phase-dancing-gottlieb-wertico-sanchez-the-art-of-drumming-in-the-pat-metheny-group.

Walser, Robert. 1997. "Deep Jazz: Notes on Interiority, Race and Criticism." In Joel Pfister and Nancy Schnog, eds., *Inventing the Psychological: Toward a Cultural History of Emotional Life in America*. New Haven, CT: Yale University Press.

Walser, Robert, ed. 2015. *Keeping Time: Readings in Jazz History*, 2nd ed. New York: Oxford University Press.

Walton, Ortiz. 1972. *Music: Black, White, and Blue*. New York: William Morrow.

Webb, Nicholas. 1985. "Interview with Pat Metheny." *Guitarist Magazine*, May. Republished at https://www.joness.com/gr300/metheny.htm.

Weisgall, Hugo. 1959. "The Music of Henry Cowell." *Musical Quarterly* 45.

Welburn, Ron. 1971. "The Black Aesthetic Imperative." In Addison Gayle Jr., ed., *The Black Aesthetic*. New York: Doubleday.

Wertico, Paul. n.d. "Flat Ride Cymbals: Make Mine a Double." https://www
.paulwertico.com/articles/flatridecymbals.php, Accessed January 2, 2022.

Weston, Randy, and Willard Jenkins. 2010. *African Rhythms: The Autobiography of
Randy Weston*. Durham, NC: Duke University Press.

Whyte, Matt, and Charles Limb. 2022. "Pat Metheny: Bright Size Life."
Sing for Science podcast, March 16. https://open.spotify.com/episode
/6R0mthnY6ICt1CxHXhqMgJ.

Wilson, Olly. 1983. "Black Music as an Art Form." *Black Music Research Journal* 3:1–22.

Wilson, Olly. 1992. "The Heterogeneous Sound Ideal in African American Music." In
Josephine Wright, ed., *New Perspectives on Music: Essays in Honor of Eileen South-
ern*. Sterling Heights, MI: Harmonie Park Press.

Wilson, Olly, and Trevor Weston. 2014. "Edward Kennedy Ellington as a Cultural
Icon." In Edward Green, ed., *The Oxford Companion to Duke Ellington*. Cambridge:
Cambridge University Press.

Woodard, Josef. 1998. "In Search of Pat Metheny." *Jazziz*, January.

"Virginia State Song." *Encyclopedia Virginia*. n.d. https://encyclopediavirginia.org
/entries/virginia-state-song/. Accessed November 3, 2023.

Viva, Luigi. 2021. *Pat Metheny, Lyle Mays e La Storia Del Pat Metheny Group*. Rome:
Arcana Edizioni.

Zavada, Jack. 2022. "What Do Unity Churches Believe?" *Learn Religions*, September 2.
https://www.learnreligions.com/unity-beliefs-and-practices-700122.

Zbikowski, Lawrence M. 1997. "Conceptual Models and Cross-Domain Mapping:
New Perspectives on Theories of Music and Hierarchy." *Journal of Music Theory* 41
(2): 193–225.

Zbikowski, Lawrence M. 1997–98. "Des Herzraums Abschied: Mark Johnson's Theory
of Embodied Knowledge and Music Theory." *Theory and Practice* 22/23:1–16.

Zeger, Eli. n.d. "The Evolution of Hocketing." *Red Bull Music Academy Daily*. https://
daily.redbullmusicacademy.com/2018/02/the-evolution-of-hocketing,

Zwerin, Mike. 1994. "For Pat Metheny, Silence Is Awful: The Sound under the Sound."
New York Times, March 30. https://www.nytimes.com/1994/03/30/style/IHT
-for-pat-metheny-silence-is-awful-the-sound-under-the-sound.html.

DISCOGRAPHY

This document does not aim to represent a complete discography but rather to focus on recordings discussed in the book or that play a direct role in providing contextual background. Pat Metheny has released numerous solo and duet albums, film soundtracks, appearances on albums by other musicians, and other recordings that are not addressed in this discography.

Derek Bailey, Pat Metheny, Gregg Bendian, and Paul Wertico. 1994. *The Sign of 4.* Knitting Factory Works.

The Beatles. 1965. *Help.* Parlophone/EMI (British release).

The Beatles. 1966. *Yesterday and Today.* Capital Records (North American release).

Gary Burton. 1964. *Something's Coming.* RCA Victor.

Gary Burton. 1969. *Throb.* Atlantic.

Gary Burton. 1973. *The New Quartet.* ECM.

Gary Burton. 1990. *Reunion.* GRP.

Gary Burton and Chick Corea. 1973. *Crystal Silence.* ECM.

Gary Burton and Keith Jarrett. 1971. *Gary Burton & Keith Jarrett.* Atlantic.

Gary Burton, Pat Metheny, Chick Corea, and Dave Holland. 1998. *Like Minds.* Concord Jazz.

Gary Burton, Pat Metheny, Steve Swallow, and Antonio Sanchez. 2009. *Quartet Live!* Concord Jazz.

Gary Burton Quartet. 1967. *Duster.* RCA Victor.

Gary Burton Quartet. 1968. *Country Roads and Other Places.* RCA Victor.

Gary Burton Quartet. 1971. *Live in Tokyo.* Atlantic.

Gary Burton Quartet with Eberhard Weber. 1975. *Passengers.* ECM.

Gary Burton Quintet with Eberhard Weber. 1974. *Ring.* ECM.

Gary Burton Quintet. 1976. *Dreams So Real: Music of Carla Bley.* ECM.

188 Discography

Ornette Coleman. 1959. *The Shape of Jazz to Come*. Atlantic .
Ornette Coleman. 1960. *Change of the Century*. Atlantic.
Ornette Coleman. 1968. *New York Is Now!* Blue Note.
John Coltrane. 1964. *A Love Supreme*. Impulse!
Miles Davis. 1965. *E.S.P.* Columbia.
Miles Davis. 1966. *"Four" & More: Recorded Live in Concert*. Columbia.
Miles Davis. 1967. *Miles Smiles*. Columbia.
Miles Davis. 1967. *Sorcerer*. Columbia.
Miles Davis. 1967. *Nefertiti*. Columbia.
Miles Davis. 1968. *Filles de Kilimanjaro*. Columbia.
Miles Davis. 1968. *Miles in the Sky*. Columbia CK 48954, CD.
The Free Spirits. 1967. *Out of Sight and Sound*. ABC .
The Free Spirits. 2011. *Live at the Scene February 22nd 1967*. Sunbeam.
Dave Friedman. 1975. *Winter Love, April Joy*. East Wind.
Dizzy Gillespie and His Orchestra. 1954. *Afro*. Norgran.
Charlie Haden and Pat Metheny. 1997. *Beyond the Missouri Sky*. Verve.
Jim Hall and Pat Metheny. 1999. *Jim Hall & Pat Metheny*. Telarc.
Herbie Hancock. 1965. *Maiden Voyage*. Blue Note.
Herbie Hancock. 1971. *Mwandishi*. Warner Brothers.
Herbie Hancock. 1972. *Crossings*. Warner Brothers.
Herbie Hancock. 1973. *Sextant*. Columbia.
Wynton Kelly Trio and Wes Montgomery. 1965. *Smokin' at the Half Note*. Verve.
Mahavishnu Orchestra. 1971. *The Inner Mounting Flame*. Columbia.
Pat Metheny. 1976. *Bright Size Life*. ECM.
Pat Metheny. 1977. *Watercolors*. ECM.
Pat Metheny. 1979. *New Chautauqua*. ECM.
Pat Metheny. 1980. *80/81*. ECM.
Pat Metheny. 1984. *Rejoicing*. ECM.
Pat Metheny. 1985. *The Falcon and the Snowman*. EMI.
Pat Metheny. 1990. *Question and Answer*. Geffen.
Pat Metheny. 1992. *Secret Story*. Geffen.
Pat Metheny. 1994. *Zero Tolerance for Silence*. Geffen.
Pat Metheny. 2000. *Trio 99 → 00*. Warner Brothers.
Pat Metheny. 2000. *Trio → Live*. Warner Brothers.
Pat Metheny. 2008. *Day Trip*. Nonesuch.
Pat Metheny. 2008. *Tokyo Day Trip*. Nonesuch.
Pat Metheny. 2012. *The Orchestrion Project*. Nonesuch.
Pat Metheny. 2012. *Unity Band*. Nonesuch.
Pat Metheny. 2014. *Kin (←→)*. Nonesuch.
Pat Metheny. 2016. *The Unity Sessions*. Nonesuch.
Pat Metheny. 2020. *From This Place*. Nonesuch.
Pat Metheny. 2021. *Side-Eye NYC V1.IV*. Modern Recordings.
Pat Metheny and Ornette Coleman. 1986. *Song X*. Geffen.

Pat Metheny and Lyle Mays. 1981. *As Falls Wichita, So Falls Wichita Falls*. ECM.

Pat Metheny with Sonny Rollins and His Trio. 1994. *Dream Teams*. Bugsy.

Pat Metheny Group. 1978. *Pat Metheny Group*. ECM.

Pat Metheny Group. 1980. *American Garage*. ECM.

Pat Metheny Group. 1982. *Offramp*. ECM.

Pat Metheny Group. 1983. *Travels*. ECM.

Pat Metheny Group. 1984. *First Circle*. ECM.

Pat Metheny Group. 1987. *Still Life (Talking)*. Geffen.

Pat Metheny Group. 1989. *Letter from Home*. Geffen.

Pat Metheny Group. 1993. *The Road to You*. Geffen.

Pat Metheny Group. 1995. *We Live Here*. Geffen.

Pat Metheny Group. 1996. *Quartet*. Geffen.

Pat Metheny Group. 1997. *Imaginary Day*. Warner Brothers.

Pat Metheny Group. 2002. *Speaking of Now*. Warner Brothers.

Pat Metheny Group. 2005. *The Way Up*. Warner Brothers.

Pat Metheny Group. 2006. *Imaginary Day Live*. Eagle Eye Media, DVD.

Pat Metheny Group. 2008. *The Way Up — Live*. Eagle. Eye Media, DVD.

Thelonious Monk with John Coltrane. 1961. *Thelonious Monk with John Coltrane*. Jazzland.

Wes Montgomery. 1968. *Down Here on the Ground*. A&M.

Milton Nascimento. 1969. *Courage*. A&M.

Milton Nascimento. 1976. *Milton*. A&M.

Steve Reich. 1989. *Different Trains/Electric Counterpoint*. Elektra/Nonesuch.

Return to Forever featuring Chick Corea. 1973). *Hymn of the Seventh Galaxy*. Polydor.

Max Roach–Clifford Brown Quintet. 1956. *Live at Basin Street*. Ingo Two.

Sonny Rollins. 1957. *Saxophone Colossus*. Prestige.

Wayne Shorter. 1975. *Native Dancer*. Columbia.

Weather Report. 1973. *Sweetnighter*. Columbia.

Weather Report. 1974. *Mysterious Traveler*. Columbia.

Weather Report. 1975. *Tale Spinnin'*. Columbia.

Tony Williams Lifetime. 1969. *Emergency*. Polydor.

Larry Young. 1966. *Unity*. Blue Note.

INDEX

Aebersold, Jamey, Summer Jazz Workshops, 81–82, 166nn23–25

Aznar, Pedro: discovery expanded Metheny's vista of working with singers, 101; "Every Summer Night" (Aznar), 105–6, 170n30; joining PMG at same time as and bonding with Wertico, 95; "Tell It All" (Aznar), 102–3; wordless vocals performances with PMG on "The First Circle," 101–2

Barron, Kenny, story metaphors, 17–18

bass lines, stepwise: in Beatles' songs, 32–33; by Evans, 41, 160n51, 160n57; in compositions by Corea, Jarrett, and Metheny in repertoire of Gary Burton band, 43; in Gillespie's "Con Alma," 41, 160; juxtaposed with triads in Swallow's "Falling Grace," 42; juxtaposition with triads, 41; in Metheny's works, 43–46, 160n64; in music of Baroque era, 32; in popular songs of 1930s, 32; relevance to improvisation using motifs to build narrative arc, 46–58;

in rhythm and blues, 157n9; in rock music, 157n10

Beatles, 41, 63; stepwise bass lines in songs, 32–33. *See also* Lennon, John; McCartney, Paul

Bernstein, Leonard, Young People's Concert commentary, 122–23

Blamires, David: "Have You Heard," 105; "Something to Remind You," 108–9, 169n19; wordless vocals performances with PMG on "Third Wind," 103–4

Bley, Carla: compositions in Gary Burton band repertoire, 37–38; "Ictus," 159n42

Bona, Richard: "On Her Way," 107–8; wordless vocals performances with PMG on "Afternoon," 106–7; "You," 109–10, 169n19, 170n35

Burton, Gary, 6; albums with Metheny, 38; band, 10; Coryell's influence on, 34–35; as exploratory musician with background in bop traditions, 154n34; formation of new band integrating ideas from rock music, 35–37; with Getz, 33–34; inviting

Index

Burton, Gary (*continued*)
 Metheny to teach at Berklee School of Music and join his band, 36, 158n22; McCartney's influence on, 31, 33; meeting Metheny, 9, 153n31; as mentor and band leader to Metheny, 37–38; new choice of repertoire, 37, 42, 157n21; new ideas about musical form, 34; Swallow's "Falling Grace" as new model for form, 42, 160n53, 160n55; "telling a story" as metaphor, 18; use of electric instruments, 73, 158n26

Cholmondeley, Andre: Metheny's use of alternatives to GR-303/300 guitar synthesizer, 168n42; outline of Metheny's "guitar world," 136; on Metheny's warm-up routine before concerts, 134, 173n3
Coleman, Ornette, 7, 33–34; "Broken Shadows" as composition with continuously repeating melody, 128; compositions "Round Trip" and "Broadway Blues" on Metheny's *Bright Size Life*, 11; "Endangered Species" (*Song X*) by Metheny and, 139–41; as exploratory musician with background in bop traditions, 154n34; Harmolodic theory, 139–40; improvisation within "Lonely Woman," 49–50; as model for Metheny's Roland guitar synthesizer phrasing, 93; use of motifs in improvisation, 47, 58
Coltrane, John, 33–34; as exploratory musician with background in bop traditions, 154n34; on meaning of music, 122; as model for Gottlieb on "Offramp," 93; use of motifs in improvisation, 47, 58, 160n2
Corea, Chick, 6, 9, 38, 153n32; compositions within Gary Burton band

repertoire, 37; "Crystal Silence" and "Desert Air," 43; as exploratory musician with background in bop traditions, 154n34; use of electric and electronic instruments, 73, 80, 166nn17–19; use of triads, 38
Coryell, Larry: Free Spirits, 35, 157n15; with Gary Burton Quartet, 66; influence on Gary Burton, 34–35
Creed Taylor Incorporated (CTI), 6, 151n5

Davis, Miles, 6, 34; early 1970s albums, 38; as exploratory musician with background in bop traditions, 154n34; use of electric instruments, 73
DeJohnette, Jack: on *80/81*, 175n18; on "Endangered Species" (*Song X*), 139; with Lloyd, 34

Egan, Mark, 10, 81
Ellington, Duke, 7; discomfort with term "jazz," 152n17; multi-role model of band leading, 72–74, 121; musician as "reporter" metaphor, 27
Eye, Pete, Trio with Pat Metheny at 1972 Kansas City Jazz Festival, 39

Free Spirits. *See* Coryell, Larry
Fripp, Robert, on guitar synthesizers, 88–89

genre: concept and its critique, 5–6, 12; Metheny as "unaligned" with, 6, 12–13, 151n7
Gilberto, Astrud, 100; *Getz/Gilberto*, 169n14; "The Girl from Ipanema," 7, 152n13
Gottlieb, Danny, 10; with Burton, 158n29; connecting with Rodby, 83; playing on "Offramp," 93; selection as first drummer for PMG classic

formation, 74; trio with Metheny and Pastorius, 36, 165n5; use of digital sequencing in PMG, 88; use of flat ride cymbals and sound projection, 78–79

guitars: acoustic, 11; alternatives to Roland GR-303/300 guitar synthesizer, 167n42; Beatles' electric, 63, 163nn2–3; Burton's incorporation of electric, in bands, 66, 158n26, 164nn24–25; on "The Calling" (*Rejoicing*), 137–39; early history of electric, 63, 163n4; electric, and youth rebellion, 64, 163n5; on "Endangered Species" (*Song X*), 139–41; fretless nylon string, 19–20, 23; Goodrick with Burton band and Metheny's joining as second, 66, 159n36, 164n26, 164n30; Guild Starfire twelve-string electric, Metheny played, 36, 158n24; Hendrix and, 62–63; Ibanez electric, 136, 163n14; Metheny and developing sound on, as unique as distinctive jazz saxophonist, 65–67; Metheny's choice of acoustic, specialized techniques, strumming, and alternate tunings, 69–71; Metheny's electric, in 1980, 165nn45–46; Metheny's fascination with, 64; Metheny's favorite Wes Montgomery solo on, 64–65; Metheny's first electric Gibson ES-140 and then ES-175N, 64, 163n11, 163n13; New England Digital Synclavier interface for Roland GR-303, 167n35; other examples of Metheny's use of Roland guitar synthesizer, 93, 137–38, 168n45, 174n13; Pikasso, 135–36; projection of sound in space, 62, 68–69; Reinhardt, Burrell, and Hall and, 65, 164nn20–21, 164n23; Roland guitar synthesizer (GR-303 with

GR-300 module) and specialized performance techniques, 88–90, 136, 167n39, 168n41, 168n43; Roland on *Offramp*, 90–93; sitar, 135; sonic density on *Zero Tolerance for Silence*, 141–43; trumpet as model for articulation, 67; on 2021–23 *Side Eye* tours, 137; why use of electric, was limited in jazz, 158n25. *See also* Manzer, Linda

Haden, Charlie: *Beyond the Missouri Sky* (*Short Stories*), 29; on "The Calling" (*Rejoicing*), 139; on "Endangered Species" (*Song X*), 139; with Metheny's 80/81 band, 12, 175n18

Hancock, Herbie, 6, 9; as exploratory musician with background in bop traditions, 154n34; Herbie Hancock Sextet (1968–67), 34; Mwandishi Sextet, 38, 153n32; 1967 performance of Wayne Shorter's "Paraphernalia" with Miles Davis Quartet, 40; route to band leading, 74; use of electric and electronic instruments, 73, 80, 166nn17–19

Haynes, Roy, 10; performances with notable musicians, 154n37; use of flat ride cymbals, 95

Hendrix, Jimi, 62–63, 80

improvisation: in "Always and Forever" (Metheny), 56–58; in "April Joy" (Metheny), 53–54; in "The Bat" (Metheny, 2000 trio version), 54–56; how spontaneous is, 162nn27–28; Metheny's narrative approach to, 38; Metheny's use of motifs in Swallow's "Falling Grace," 51–53; Metheny's views on, and composition as interrelated activities, 59–62; use of motifs to build improvisational narrative arc, 46–58

194   Index

Jarrett, Keith, 3; compositions within Gary Burton band repertoire, 37; with Lloyd, 34; stepwise bass lines and triads in "Coral" and "Fortune Smiles," 43; use of triads, 38

jazz: as approach and process, 10; context of race and, 8, 17, 152nn19–22, 152n25; controversies about rock music and, 35, 157n18; Ellington's discomfort with term, 152n17; as genre and between genre, 9, 12–13, 153n30; Metheny's proficiency performing and recording, standards, 153n26; Metheny's resistance to, as identifier, 8, 12; storytelling metaphors and, 17–19, 155n13

Jobim, Antônio Carlos, 7, 100; influence on Metheny, 154n42

Kansas City Jazz Festival, 9, 39, 152n14

Ledford, Mark: "Have You Heard," 105; "Something to Remind You," 108–9, 169n19, 170n32; trumpet playing on "Have You Heard," 105, 169n19; wordless vocals performances with PMG on "Third Wind," 103–4

Lee, Bill, as dean at University of Miami, 8

Lee's Summit, Missouri, Metheny's hometown, 7

Lennon, John, Rickenbacker 325 electric guitar, 63. See also Beatles

Lloyd, Charles, 3; Forest Flower and Dream Weaver, 34

Manzer, Linda: fretless nylon-string acoustic guitar, 20, 134; "Into the Dream," 136, 173n2; Linda 6 steel-string acoustic guitar, 133–34; meeting Metheny, 133; Pikasso, 135–36, 174n9; sitar guitar, compared with Coral electric sitar, 135, 174n5. See also Cholmondeley, Andre; guitars

Mays, Lyle, 3; As Falls Wichita, So Falls Wichita Falls as a first expansive long-form Metheny/Mays composition, 114; Autoharp, 167n30; chord cycle on "Third Wind," 104; as composer of "Across The Sky," 119, 171n15; discussion and narration of The Way Up, 114–17; electronic keyboards, 79–81; Indonesian influences on "Imaginary Day," 21; at Jamey Aebersold Summer Jazz Workshops, 81–82; Metheny's reflections regarding compositional attribution and on role of, 118–20, 171nn14–15; piano solo on "Every Summer Night," 106; piano solo on "The First Circle," 101; selection as keyboardist for PMG classic formation, 75–77; solo on "Imaginary Day," 22; on Watercolors, 10, 76–77; The Way Up, for PMG, as most expansive work, 113–15

McCartney, Paul: innovations in form as inspiration for Burton and other jazz musicians, 31; stepwise bass lines and contrary motion as compositional devices, 32–33

McLaughlin, John, 9, 38, 153n32; Mahavishnu Orchestra, 38; New England Digital Synclavier interface for Roland GR-303 guitar, 167n35

meaning, music's: Bernstein's commentary on, 122–23; in European classical music aesthetics, 155n26; Goins on music and emotion, 130–31, 173n14; "Is This America? (katrina 2005)" and, 131–32; Metheny on music and perception, 123–24; Metheny on power of music, 130; music as mission, 28–29; musician as "reporter," 27–29. See also metaphor and music

metaphor and music: "America Undefined" (From This Place) approached through storytelling metaphor and narrative arc, 124–31; "America Undefined" in light of "Missouri Uncompromised" (*Bright Size Life*), 125; in *Imaginary Day*, 19–24; Lakoff and Johnson on, 26–27, 156n32; Metheny's solos on "The Bat" (on *Trio/Live*) and "Farmer's Trust" approached through storytelling metaphor, 29–30; music as "telling a story," 14–19, 25–27, 155n10; musician as "reporter," 27–28; narrative interpretation of "Is This America? (katrina 2005)" in light of folksong "Shenandoah," 131–32, 173n16; in reference to Baldwin essay, 172n7; Zbikowski on, 156n30

Metheny, Pat: on "Afternoon," 107; albums with and mentorship from Burton, 36–37; alternate configurations for PMG instrumentation, 75; alternatives to ii-V-I and vamp forms, 38, 159n39; in "Always and Forever," 56–58; *American Garage*, 11; appreciation of Hall, 65; in "April Joy," 53–54; "April Joy" representing early new compositional direction, 9, 39–41, 160n50; *As Falls Wichita, So Falls Wichita Falls* as first expansive long-form Metheny/Mays composition, 114; in "The Bat" (2000 trio version), 54–56; at Berklee School of Music, musical life in Boston, and joining Gary Burton band, 36–37; *Bright Size Life*, 9–11; *Bright Size Life* as template without orchestration, percussion, and wordless vocals, 100; collaboration with Coleman on "Endangered Species," 139–41; decision-making about release of first album of career, 75; developing approach to band leading, and multi-

role model of Ellington, 72–74; developing unique sound, 65–66; 80/81 band, 3, 12; dilemmas regarding compositional attribution, 118–20, 171nn14–15; on "Every Summer Night," 106; as faculty at Jamey Aebersold Summer Jazz Workshops, 81–82; with Gary Burton band, 6, 10, 36, 66, 159n36; with Gary Sivil Trio, 8; on "Goodbye," 109; guitar solo on "America Undefined" (*From This Place*), 127–28; "Imaginary Day" as example of storytelling metaphor, 19–24; importance of Aznar in recognizing possibilities of working with singers, 101; and importance of melody, 24; importance of Swallow's new approach form in "Falling Grace," 42–43; improvisational model Montgomery, 47–49; influence of Carlos Jobim on, 7; influence of Coleman on, 7, 152n12; influence of Davis's *"Four" & More* on, 7; influence of Montgomery on, 7; and long-form compositions, through *First Circle*, 113–14; meeting Burton, 9, 153n31; musical form structured for personal approach to improvisation, 47; musical symbiosis with drummer Sanchez, 97–98; music as mission, 28–29; musician as "reporter" metaphor, 27–29; narration and discussion of "America Undefined," 124–31; narration and discussion of "Is This America? (katrina 2005)," 131–32; *New Chautauqua*, 11; at 1972 Kansas City Jazz Festival, 9, 153n29; on "On Her Way," 107–8; *Pat Metheny Group* (album), 11; Pat Metheny Trio, 9; projection of sound through space, 62, 68; recognition that sound is not dependent upon sound projection, 68–69; reflections

Metheny, Pat (*continued*)
on Mays, 120; relationship with and selection of Rodby as new bassist, 81–84; and Roland guitar synthesizer solo on "Third Wind," 105; role as band leader in PMG, 118–21; Ruskin as mentor to, 7; *Secret Story,* 12; selecting band members and guiding PMG, 74–93; selecting drummer (Gottlieb) as primary task, 74; selection of bassist (Egan), 77–78; selection of keyboardist (Mays), 75–77; solos on "The Bat" (on *Trio/Live*) and "Farmer's Trust" as storytelling metaphor, 29–30; on "Something to Remind You," 108; stepwise bass lines juxtaposed with triads in solos on "The Bat" and "Always and Forever," 43–46; strumming on *The New Chautauqua* and *Beyond the Missouri Sky,* 70; study with Zoller, 7; "telling a story" as metaphor, 14–19, 25; on "Tell It All," 102–3; on "Third Wind," 104; on train sounds, 172n11; trumpet as model for articulation, 67; as "unaligned" musician, 6, 12–13; at University of Miami, 8, 165n5; use of and approach to acoustic guitars and specialized technique and tunings, 69–71, 165n51; use of motifs in improvisational approach, 47; use of motifs in Swallow's "Falling Grace," 51–53; views on improvisation and composition as interrelated activities, and use of hybrid forms, 59–62; *Watercolors,* 10–11; *The Way Up,* for PMG, as most expansive work, 113–15; wordless vocals as compositional and orchestration tool, 99–101; on "You," 110; *Zero Tolerance for Silence* and *Secret Story,* 141–43
Miles Davis Quintet: influence of *"Four" & More* on Metheny, 7; in 1966–67,

34; performance of "Paraphernalia" in 1967, 40
Mingus, Charles, 7; Metheny/May's *The Way Up* in relationship to, *Pithecanthropus Erectus* as long-form composition with improvisational sections, 114–15
Mitchell, Joni, 9; guitar tunings, 70
Montgomery, Wes, 7–8; as exploratory musician with background in bop traditions, 154n34; improvisation employing motifs in "If You Could See Now," 47
Moses, Bob: on *Bright Size Life,* 9–10; as exploratory musician with background in bop traditions, 154n34; in Gary Burton's band, 158nn27–28; in Pat Metheny Trio, 9
motif/motifs: by Coleman, 49–50; by Coltrane, 47, 58, 161n2; critique of Schuller's analysis of motivic development by Rollins, 58, 161–62nn17–24; employment as improvisational device, 47–58; in Metheny's "Always and Forever," 56–58; in Metheny's "April Joy," 53–54; in Metheny's "The Bat" (2000 trio version), 54–56, 161nn15–16; Metheny's use of motifs in Swallow's "Falling Grace," 51–53; by Montgomery, 47–49

Nascimento, Milton, 100; and Horta, 169n18

Oberheim polyphonic digital synthesizer, 79–80

Pastorius, Jaco: on *Bright Size Life,* 9–10; in Pat Metheny Trio in Miami and Boston, 9, 36, 165n5
Pat Metheny Group (PMG): "Afternoon" (Bona), 106–7; *American Garage,* 11;

addition of singers performing wordless vocals, 99–101, 110–12; classic formation of, 2–3, 12, 164n28; detailed narration and analysis of *The Way Up*, "Part One," 144–50; development of classic formation of, 74–93; discussion and narration of *The Way Up*, 114–17; early days on road, 79; and electronic keyboards, 79–81; "Every Summer Night" (Aznar), 105–6; *First Circle*, 12; "The First Circle" (Aznar), 101–2; "Goodbye" (Vasconcelos), 109; Gottlieb as first drummer of, 74; guitar solos in *The Way Up*, "Part One," 145, 147–49; "Have You Heard" (Blamires and Ledford), 105; *Imaginary Day*, 12, 19–24; Metheny's preference for flat ride cymbals, 78–79, 95; musical dynamics within first rhythm section, 78–79; narration and discussion of musical examples of wordless vocals in Metheny's performances with, 101–11; narration of Rodby's approach to "Red Sky," 85–87; *Offramp*, 12; "On Her Way" (Bona), 107–8; *Pat Metheny Group* (album), 11; place of Roland guitar synthesizer in, 88–93; *The Road to You*, 12; Rodby learning "legacy" tunes and touring (documented on *Travels*) and his approach to acoustic bass in, 83–85; Rodby's history with Metheny and selection as new bassist in, 81–84; Sanchez as drummer on *Speaking of Now* and *The Way Up*, 96–99; selection of bassist (Egan), 77–78; selection of keyboardist (Mays), 75–77; "Something to Remind You" (Blamires and Ledford), 108–9; "Tell It All" (Aznar), 102–3; "Third Wind" (Blamires and Ledford), 103–4; use of digital sequencing, 87–88;

Vasconcelos in first, 83, 101; Wertico as new drummer, 94–96; "You" (Bona), 109–10
"progressive" rock bands, 6

Redman, Dewey, with Pat Metheny's 80/81 band, 12
Rodby, Steve, 3; discussion of bass playing in PMG repertoire, 84–85, 167n26; function of and approach to acoustic bass in PMG, 83–84; history with Metheny and selection as new PMG bassist, 81–84; as involved in production, 84; at Jamey Aebersold Summer Jazz Workshops, 81–82; learning "legacy" tunes and touring (documented on *Travels*), 83; narration of approach to "Red Sky," 85–87; use of digital sequencing in PMG, 87
Roland guitar synthesizer, GR-303 guitar and GR-300 module. *See* guitars
Rollins, Sonny, 7; concerts with Metheny, 162n25; critique of Schuller's analysis of solo in "Blue 7" as motivic development, 18, 19, 58, 161n17, 162nn20–24; as exploratory musician with background in bop traditions, 154n34
Ruskin, Tommy: mentoring Metheny, 7; "telling a story" as metaphor, 18

Samuels, Dave, formation of quartet in Boston with Metheny, 36
Sanchez, Antonio: approach to ensemble playing, 98–99; experience of Metheny's approach to guitar sound projection, 68; familiarity with and joining PMG, 96–98; on "The First Circle," 124; first experiences with PMG on *Speaking of Now* and performance of "Roots of Coincidence," 98; learning and performing *The*

Sanchez, Antonio (*continued*)
Way Up, 115–17, 124, 149; participation on subsequent Metheny bands (trio, Unity projects, and *From This Place*), 98; on performing "America Undefined" (*From This Place*), 130; reflections on Metheny as soloist, 128; *The Way Up*, 98

sequencing: drum machines on *As Falls Wichita, So Falls Wichita Falls*, 87; New England Digital Synclavier and performing on "Are You Going with Me?" with live sequences, 87

Shorter, Wayne: influence of harmonic conception on Metheny, 39; "Nefertiti" as composition with continuously repeating melody, 128; route to band co-leading, 74; use of pedal tones and slash chords in Shorter's "Paraphernalia," performed by the Miles Davis Quartet in 1967, 38, 40; use of slash chords, 39; Weather Report, 6, 38

Simcock, Gwilyn, piano solo on "America Undefined" (*From This Place*), 127

Sivils, Gary, 8; "telling a story" as metaphor, 18

slash chords, 39–40; within "April Joy," 39, 159n45, 159n47, 160n50

Stern, Mike, as Metheny guitar student at the Berklee School of Music, 36

straight eighth notes, 10

Swallow, Steve: Gary Burton Quartet, 35–36, 158nn27–29; with Getz, 33–34; influence of Beatles on compositional ideas of, 33; influence of Evans on, 42; new ideas about musical form, 34–36; stepwise bass lines

juxtaposed with triads in "Falling Grace," 42, 160n53, 160n55

Taylor, Cecil, 33–34

Terry, Clark, 9

Vasconcelos, Naná, 100; on *As Falls Wichita, So Falls Wichita Falls*, 101; in first PMG, 83; with PMG on *Offramp* and *Travels*, 101; wordless vocals performances with PMG on "Goodbye," 109, 169n19, 170n34

Weather Report, 6, 38; Shorter's route to band co-leading, 74; as small electric band projecting breadth of color and texture, 73; use of electric and electronic keyboards, 80

Weber, Eberhard: in Gary Burton's band, 158n27, 158n29; on *Watercolors*, 10

Wertico, Paul: approach to drumming and adaptation to PMG, 94–95; drumming on "Imaginary Day," 23; drumming on *Letter from Home* and *Imaginary Day*, 95–96; joining PMG at same time as and bonding with Aznar, 95; and Pat Metheny Group, 94–96; use of flat ride cymbals, 78–79, 93

Williams, Tony, 9–10, 38; Tony Williams Lifetime, 6, 34

Zawinul, Josef (Joe): route to band co-leading, 74; use of electric and electronic keyboards, 80, 166nn17–20; Weather Report, 6, 38, 73

Zoller, Attila, 7